Shelter and Subsidies

Studies in Social Economics
TITLES PUBLISHED

STUDIES IN SOCIAL ECONOMICS

Henry J. Aaron

Shelter and Subsidies

*Who Benefits
from Federal Housing Policies?*

THE BROOKINGS INSTITUTION
Washington, D.C.

Library of Congress Cataloging in Publication Data:
Aaron, Henry J
  Shelter and subsidies.
  (Studies in social economics)
  Includes bibliographical references.
  1. Housing—United States.   2. Public housing—
United States.   3. Housing—United States—Finance.
I. Title.   II. Series.
HD7293.A613   301.5′4′0973   72-306
ISBN 0–8157–0018–0
ISBN 0–8157–0017–2 (pbk.)

9 8 7 6 5 4 3 2

THE BROOKINGS INSTITUTION is an independent organization devoted to nonpartisan research, education, and publication in economics, government, foreign policy, and the social sciences generally. Its principal purposes are to aid in the development of sound public policies and to promote public understanding of issues of national importance.

The Institution was founded on December 8, 1927, to merge the activities of the Institute for Government Research, founded in 1916, the Institute of Economics, founded in 1922, and the Robert Brookings Graduate School of Economics and Government, founded in 1924.

The general administration of the Institution is the responsibility of a Board of Trustees charged with maintaining the independence of the staff and fostering the most favorable conditions for creative research and education. The immediate direction of the policies, program, and staff of the Institution is vested in the President, assisted by an advisory committee of the officers and staff.

In publishing a study, the Institution presents it as a competent treatment of a subject worthy of public consideration. The interpretations and conclusions in such publications are those of the author or authors and do not necessarily reflect the views of the other staff members, officers, or trustees of the Brookings Institution.

Foreword

For more than three decades the federal government has sought to spur the production of more and better housing in the United States. In support of these goals, legislators and other public officials have advanced numerous and sometimes inconsistent lines of argument, often reflecting incomplete understanding of the issues. As a consequence, the Congress has enacted federal housing programs without clear understanding of their probable effects and without clearly defined standards governing the quality of housing and related residential services to be provided.

Public concern about inadequate housing and deteriorating neighborhoods grew during the 1960s and found expression in the Housing and Urban Development Act of 1968, which pledged federal assistance in building or rehabilitating 26 million housing units in the following decade. In the same act the Congress added new kinds of housing subsidies and obligated itself to enlarge the old ones. Although the commitment was massive, the underlying principles remained vague. Supporters could point to various and sometimes conflicting objectives, and the distribution of benefits under existing programs remained uncertain.

To contribute to a clarification of the rationale for governmental intervention in housing markets, this study examines the distribution of benefits associated with six major categories of federal housing programs: implicit tax subsidies to homeowners, mortgage insurance and loan guarantees, measures to improve the flexibility of mortgage operations by lending institutions, subsidies to low income renters through low rent public housing, other subsidies to low and middle income renters and homeowners, and subsidized loans to rural homeowners. The federal government, he concludes, should distribute the benefits of housing subsidies to low and moderate income families through allowances determined by personal income, net worth, and local housing costs. He warns that continued overemphasis on building or renovating structures relative to the improvement of other aspects of the residential environment will perpetuate discontent over inadequate housing.

Henry J. Aaron is a senior fellow in the Economic Studies Program at the Brookings Institution and an associate professor of economics at the University of Maryland. He wishes to thank Frank de Leeuw for valuable comments on the entire book and Philip S. Brown, Anthony Downs, Robert M. Fisher, Robert W. Hartman, John F. Kain, Ronald N. Landis, Charles E. McLure, Jr., Peter Mieszkowski, Dick Netzer, Roger G. Noll, Joseph A. Pechman, Walter S. Salant, P. Royal Shipp, Gilbert Y. Steiner, James L. Sundquist, and Stanley S. Surrey for commenting on various chapters. He is grateful for information and technical assistance from Eva K. Rapke, Abner Silverman, and Helmuth R. Wiemann of the Department of Housing and Urban Development; Frank Keefe, Boyd Marshall, and Agnes Marshall of the Federal Housing Administration; L. D. Elwell, M. Harriet Kelly, and Vernon Nafus of the Farmers Home Administration; Richard C. Pickering of the Federal Home Loan Bank Board; and John Burke and C. M. Grenn of the Government National Mortgage Association. Elizabeth Morley Knoll provided research assistance throughout the project; she and Evelyn P. Fisher are primarily responsible for Appendix A. Joan W. Keesey, John A. Gardecki, and Stephen W. Kidd provided programming assistance. Susan Dvoskin and Harriet Tamen typed the manuscript, Mrs. Fisher checked it for statistical accuracy, and Alice M. Carroll edited it. The index was prepared by Joan C. Culver.

This volume is the ninth of the Brookings Studies in Social Economics, a program of research and education on selected problems in the fields of health, education, social security, and welfare.

The views expressed in this study are the author's and should not be attributed to the trustees, officers, or other staff members of the Brookings Institution.

KERMIT GORDON
President

March 1972
Washington, D.C.

Contents

xi

Appendix Tables

Text Figures

xiii

Appendix Figure

Shelter and Subsidies

chapter one **Rationale**
for a
Housing
Policy

Nearly all countries—rich and poor—have a housing problem. And nearly all—whether centrally planned or free market economies—have a housing policy. The production and distribution of housing are circumscribed, controlled, regulated, subsidized, and taxed in numerous ways in the United States, as in most other countries.

U.S. Housing Goal

Among the Johnson administration's bequests to President Nixon was a national housing goal, a legislated promise to build or to rehabilitate 26 million housing units in the decade 1969–78. The proclaimed objective was to solve the housing problem in the United States. Although 4 million mobile homes have since been redefined as housing units, housing output has failed to keep up with original projections and the likelihood that the goal will be achieved is shrinking steadily. The success or failure of the United States in achieving the housing goal has become for many a symbol of American willingness to reorient priorities.

The Housing and Urban Development Act of 1968 was passed in response to two housing problems. A huge increase in the number of families was imminent, as children born during the post-World War II baby boom matured, left home, and formed households of their own. Clearly, these new families would create a housing shortage unless residential construction increased rapidly. America had experienced an even worse shortage after World War II when returning veterans and other newly formed households swelled housing demand. The crush of the 1970s promised to be serious; but the earlier experience indicated that with federal assistance, private industry could solve a "too little housing" problem.

The United States had, moreover, conspicuously and embarrassingly failed to fulfill the much quoted pledge of the Housing Act of 1949 to provide a decent home and a suitable living environment to all Americans. Millions continued to live in housing units officially classified as dilapidated, deteriorating, or overcrowded; many others were adequately housed only because they spent a burdensome proportion of family income on shelter. In short, America continued to suffer from a "bad housing" problem.

To deal with the "bad housing" problem, the national housing goal called for construction or rehabilitation of 6 million housing units with federal assistance, a massive increase over the prevailing levels of federal assistance. Nearly all of the direct assistance has since been channeled through five programs—low rent public housing and rent supplements directed toward low income families, and mortgage assistance, rental assistance, and subsidized loans for rural and small town borrowers dit rected toward lower middle income families.

To deal with the "too little housing" problem, the housing goal called for the construction or rehabilitation of 20 million housing units *without* federal assistance. For this, the numerically dominant part of the overall housing output, the lumber and other materials, manpower, and land necessary to construction reportedly were available. Mortgage credit might be scarce, and here the federal government had a role; it should somehow assure an adequate flow of credit.

The political tactic of tying the two housing problems together succeeded. Congress enacted the goal and passed laws creating new forms of federal assistance, largely as requested by the Johnson administration. Whether the housing strategy expressed in the national housing goal will succeed is one of the issues this study deals with.

Evaluation of U.S. Policy

In evaluating federal housing policies, three questions arise: what services do the programs provide, who benefits from them, and how efficiently are they provided? This study is concerned primarily with identifying the beneficiaries of programs, their income and other characteristics, and the size of the benefits. It first investigates the reasons why public intervention in the housing market may be necessary and then reviews evidence on the amount and quality of housing in the United States. After exploring the theoretical problems of measuring the benefits from public expenditures, the study focuses on federal housing policies. It does not attempt to encompass programs undertaken by state and local governments or activities not principally concerned with housing (such as urban renewal or defense or college student housing). Neither does it cover the dozens of federal programs that might be discussed (Appendix A gives brief descriptions of many of the programs).

The most conspicuous and questionable omission is income maintenance programs. Welfare agencies divide payments into allowances for housing, food, clothing, and other commodities; in 1969 they allocated nearly $1.4 billion for housing allowances for the poor. A substantial part of old-age, survivor's, and disability benefits, veterans' benefits and pensions, and other federal transfer payments is also spent on housing. Income maintenance programs, however, provide general economic aid, not specific support for housing.

Each of the six groups of policies that generate the bulk of all benefits from federal housing policies is evaluated separately. The most important, in its impact on income distribution, is contained in the internal revenue code. Other significant policies are reflected in programs of federal mortgage insurance and loan guarantees, federally sponsored financing instruments, public housing, special assistance through mortgage markets, and aid to residents of rural areas. The net result of the evaluations is to make apparent the need for change; an alternative plan for future federal housing aid is suggested at the end of the study.

Housing and Housing Services

Housing can denote the stock of structures in which people reside: living units, occupied or vacant, differentiated by location, by size and type (for example, single-family detached, highrise apartment, garden apartment, mobile home), and in numerous other ways. The housing stock can be increased by new construction or conversions of other property to residential use and diminished by destruction or depreciation or conversion to nonresidential use.

Housing also can denote "housing services"—the commodity produced by the housing stock in combination with maintenance and repair labor; such intermediate goods as electricity, gas, and water; and another capital good, land.[1] The present worth of housing services, after the costs of maintaining the stock are deducted, represents the value of the housing stock.

"Housing policy" is a similarly ambiguous term. Housing policy can influence the number and kind of new structures built and the maintenance, conversion, and removal of old structures. In a larger sense it can influence housing services—the quality of the housing stock and of the individual units and the cost of housing services.

Unfortunately, the boundaries between public policies are not clearly drawn; all public or private actions have some effect, possibly infinitesimal, on most economic units. For practical purposes, housing policy can be defined as encompassing government expenditures, loans, and loan guarantees for investment in structures; zoning regulations and building and housing codes; and legal provisions concerning property rights and tax treatment of residential real property or of income from it.[2] Among the public actions not directly concerned with housing that may affect it greatly is the provision of locationally fixed services such as schools, police and fire protection, and public transportation.

Residential Services

When a homeowner or renter chooses a house or apartment, he purchases not only housing services, but also a wide range of goods and services—public schools, stores, parks, public transportation, neighbors, and other amenities. Though they cost him nothing beyond the price of housing and attendant property taxes, his satisfaction—indeed, his welfare—depends on these commodities as much as on his housing. He does not express in the marketplace his demand for housing but for the entire package. Statistics on housing expenditures therefore really measure the value placed by residents on housing and residential services.

1. See Richard F. Muth, *Cities and Housing: The Spatial Pattern of Urban Residential Land Use* (University of Chicago Press, 1969), p. 18; Edgar O. Olsen, "A Competitive Theory of the Housing Market," *American Economic Review*, Vol. 59 (September 1969), pp. 612–13.

2. For example, in any period the combined investment in housing, business capital, and net foreign trade is limited by the amount of public and private saving. Programs like investment tax credits, designed to spur business investment, succeed in part if they indirectly discourage residential construction.

Improvement in the quality of neighborhood schools, for example, usually increases the amount tenants will pay for housing (exclusive of property taxes).[3] The transportation network—mass transit and the road system—affects the value placed on housing because transportation costs both money and time. The importance of transportation is readily apparent in the Watts neighborhood of Los Angeles, which has been described as "clearly . . . superior to most low-income neighborhoods. Many of the major and expanding employment centers of the Los Angeles metropolitan area, however, are practically inaccessible to Watts residents except by private motor cars, which many of them do not own. Bus connections are long, complicated and expensive. . . . Housing in Watts, therefore, is poor housing for many low-income residents and they know it and resent its crippling effects on their efforts to better their economic position."[4]

Housing segregation has been accused of cutting employment opportunities for Negroes in Chicago and Detroit by reducing access to jobs.[5] But the problem of access is a general one—the value of any residence depends partly on its distance from jobs, stores, and recreation and on the quality and price of the transportation network connecting them.

Another commodity the occupant of a residence purchases is neighbors. Their behavior and appearance affect the price prospective occupants are willing to pay for housing. To some extent, personal tastes—aversion to living among people of different races (particularly if they form a majority), dislike for crowds or for empty space—dictate choices.

The intelligence, honesty, or other attributes of his neighbors directly affect a homeowner's welfare and influence the value of his housing. For example, academic achievement depends significantly on the socioeconomic status of fellow students.[6] Scores on standardized tests—used to

3. Wallace E. Oates in "The Effects of Property Taxes and Local Public Spending on Property Values: An Empirical Study of Tax Capitalization and the Tiebout Hypothesis," *Journal of Political Economy*, Vol. 77 (November–December 1969), pp. 957–71, shows that an increase in annual public school expenditures by $100 per student raises home values by about $1,200 in New Jersey.

4. *Building the American City*, Report of the National Commission on Urban Problems to the Congress and to the President of the United States, H. Doc. 34, 91 Cong. 1 sess. (1969), p. 56.

5. John F. Kain, "Housing Segregation, Negro Employment, and Metropolitan Decentralization," *Quarterly Journal of Economics*, Vol. 82 (May 1968), pp. 175–97. For a contrary view, see Paul Offner and Daniel H. Saks, "A Note on John Kain's 'Housing Segregation, Negro Employment and Metropolitan Decentralization,'" *Quarterly Journal of Economics*, Vol. 85 (February 1971), pp. 147–60.

6. James S. Coleman and others, *Equality of Educational Opportunity*, U.S. Department of Health, Education, and Welfare, Office of Education (1966).

determine admission to many colleges, to process draftees, to select among job applicants—rise as the socioeconomic status of neighborhoods rises, unless differences in public expenditures somehow offset the influence of peers on academic achievement. Performance by students on reading tests and pupil-teacher ratios are closely linked to home values.[7] The principal means of expressing the educational value of neighborhoods is through the price offered for housing.

The residents of poor neighborhoods are victims of high prices, inferior merchandise, high interest rates, and aggressive and deceptive sales practices.[8] They pay for the costs of doing business where pilferage and default risks are above average.[9] Costs are averaged over all customers, so that reliable households suffer from living where high-cost customers are particularly numerous. Such extra costs of living are among the costs of residential services that affect the price people will pay for housing services. Another social cost that varies by neighborhood is the probability of crime. The major market response the individual can make to differences in crime rates is to alter the price he is willing to pay for housing.[10]

Housing Markets

For households the borders of the housing market are determined by where the household members work and shop. Workers must live within commuting distance of their jobs. They normally choose neighbors with roughly similar incomes. Their spending habits are seldom affected by the

7. D. M. Grether and Peter Mieszkowski in "Determinants of Real Estate Values" (California Institute of Technology and Queen's University, 1971; processed) report that if a standard New Haven house were moved from a school district that ranks in the 50th percentile to one in the 90th percentile, the value of the home would rise by $1,500 to $2,400; a decrease in the pupil-teacher ratio from 30 to 25 would add $350 to $1,400.

8. See Eric Schnapper, "Consumer Legislation and the Poor," *Yale Law Journal*, Vol. 76 (March 1967), pp. 745–92; *Annual Report of the Council of Economic Advisers*, January 1969, pp. 174–75; and *Report of the National Advisory Commission on Civil Disorders* (1968), pp. 139–41.

9. One study found that profits of furniture and appliance dealers in a black ghetto were below average (U.S. Federal Trade Commission, *Economic Report on the Structure and Competitive Behavior of Food Retailing*, Staff Report [1966]).

10. Efforts to measure the impact of crime rates on property values have not been successful. See John F. Kain and John M. Quigley, "Measuring the Value of Housing Quality," *Journal of the American Statistical Association*, Vol. 65 (June 1970), pp. 532–48; Ronald G. Ridker and John A. Henning, "The Determinants of Residential Property Values with Special Reference to Air Pollution," *Review of Economics and Statistics*, Vol. 49 (May 1967), pp. 246–57.

price of housing or vacancy rates in other cities, metropolitan areas, states, or even areas only a few blocks away. The penthouse resident on New York City's Central Park West or Chicago's Lake Shore Drive is less likely to change his spending patterns because the prices of Beverly Hills mansions or farmhouses in Idaho change or because four-story walk-ups one mile away deteriorate into slums than because the prices of luxury automobiles or transoceanic air fares change. Households are far more likely to respond to variations in the price or quantity of some complement of or substitute for housing or residential services than to developments in other housing markets.

Each household, therefore, is interested in only a small part of the total housing stock—roughly, that part in which its socioeconomic peers reside and from which members of the household can conveniently commute to work. The housing markets of all households are linked, however, by a process called "filtering."[11] The homes of the rich often become homes for the middle class or for the poor as incomes change and job patterns shift. Housing also shifts among submarkets as a result of new construction or conversion of nonresidential property to residential use. Through this process, changes in the supply of one kind of housing affect other housing markets as well. For these reasons, all housing submarkets are connected, if only tenuously.

For builders and developers, housing markets are determined by licensing or bonding requirements, by preferences for union or nonunion labor, or by building codes and zoning regulations. The skills and materials employed in most single-family and much multifamily residential construction are essentially the same, so that differences in price classes and building types are not important.

Financial intermediaries are concerned with the ability of lenders to meet repayment schedules and with the value of collateral in the event of foreclosure. Thus many lenders refuse to provide funds to borrowers whose income is low or irregular or whose collateral is a very old structure or in a poor neighborhood; such borrowers must deal with lenders who specialize in high risk lending, or they must obtain federal mortgage guarantees. Financial intermediaries help set architectural styles by agreeing or

11. The term "filtering" has been applied to different phenomena, including changes in rents or prices, measured in current or constant dollars, change in the position of a dwelling unit on the value scale, or change in the absolute or relative socioeconomic status of occupants. For a discussion of filtering, see William G. Grigsby, *Housing Markets and Public Policy* (University of Pennsylvania Press, 1963), pp. 84–130.

Table 1-1. Major Participants and Influences in the Housing Market

Market phase	Participants	Influences
Preparation: land acquisition, planning, and zoning amendments	Developer Landowner Lawyers Real estate brokers Title companies Architects and engineers Surveyor Planners and consultants Zoning and planning officials	Real estate law Recording regulations and fees Banking laws Zoning Subdivision regulations Private deed restrictions Public master plans
Production: site preparation, construction, and financing	Developer Lending institutions (interim and permanent) FHA, VA, or private mortgage insurance company Contractors Subcontractors Craftsmen and their unions Material manufacturers and distributors Building code officials Insurance companies Architects and engineers	Banking laws Building and mechanical codes Subdivision regulations Utility regulations Union rules Rules of trade and professional associations Insurance laws Laws controlling transportation of materials
Distribution: sale (and subsequent resale or refinancing)	Developer Real estate brokers Lawyers Lending institutions Title companies FHA, VA, or private mortgage insurance company	Recording regulations and fees Real estate law Transfer taxes Banking laws Rules of professional associations
Service: maintenance and management, repairs, and improvements and additions	Owner Maintenance firms and employees Property management firms Insurance companies Utility companies Tax assessors Repairmen, craftsmen, and their unions . Lending institutions Architects and engineers Contractors Subcontractors Material manufacturers and distributors Local zoning officials Local building officials	Property taxes Income taxes Housing and health codes Insurance laws Utility regulations Banking laws Union rules Rules of trade and professional associations Zoning Building and mechanical codes Laws controlling transportation of materials

Source: *A Decent Home*, Report of the President's Committee on Urban Housing (Government Printing Office, 1969), p. 115.

refusing to accept certain designs or structures. They also influence the racial composition of neighborhoods; in the past, public agencies such as the Federal Housing Administration were as guilty of discrimination as were private institutions. State and federal banking laws restrict all commercial banks, mutual savings banks, and savings and loan associations to operations within individual states; a number of states prohibit branch banking altogether or restrict branches to the municipality housing the home office. Other laws restrict mortgage lending to areas within a stipulated radius of the lending institution.

Governmental attitudes toward the shape of housing markets may conflict with those held in the private sector. Federal policies differentiate housing by eligibility for explicit subsidies, mortgage insurance or guarantees, or direct loans. Government actions—such as establishment of attendance boundaries for public schools—and development activities—such as construction of highways or preservation of open space—frequently alter housing markets by creating or destroying neighborhood ties.

Clearly, the housing market, like the fabled elephant, is different things to different people. One of the most striking features of the production and distribution of housing services is the number of parties involved in the preparation, production, distribution, or servicing of housing and the variety of laws, regulations, controls, or subsidies to which they are subject (see Table 1-1). While other industries would utilize a comparable array of professional skills and businesses, few of them are subject to so many different regulations as the housing industry.

Income Distribution

One of the reasons for governmental adoption of a housing policy is to alter the distribution of income. Graduated income taxes and cash transfers are the most obvious and most common methods of redistributing income. Such policies reflect a collective judgment that general welfare will rise if some groups have more goods and services even at the expense of others. Governments may supply those goods and services directly instead of redistributing money. Such "transfers in kind"—housing, medical care, and food—increase the quantity of goods and services available to recipients.

Economists have long held that public provision of commodities below cost to households is less efficient in improving family welfare than unrestricted transfers of income. If the government were to give a family the cash equivalent of its housing subsidy, the family could purchase unsubsidized housing equivalent to that provided by the government. Normally, a family prefers to spend only part of an unrestricted transfer on any one commodity. From the family's standpoint a cash transfer would leave them at least as well off as would subsidized housing, and usually better off.

While unrestricted transfers may be best from the standpoint of recipients, the taxpayers who finance the assistance may have aims better served by subsidies. The argument for cash transfers presupposes that the provider cares enough about the recipient to offer cash, but not so much as to be interested in how he spends it. An efficient transfer mechanism that includes subsidies to particular commodities may better reflect the collective will in the redistribution of income. Moreover, even in an essentially market-oriented economy, citizens may decide collectively that some tastes are changeable or should be ignored. The majority might decide, for example, that those who have always been poor do not realize how much they would benefit from improved housing, but that after receiving it they will want it. This paternalistic motive for redistributing income with strings attached has been acidly attacked by Edward C. Banfield:

The doing of good is not so much for the benefit of those to whom the good is done as it is for that of the *doer's*, whose moral faculties are activated and invigorated by the doing of it, and for that of the community, the shared values of which are ritually asserted and vindicated by the doing of it. . . . One recalls Macaulay's remark about the attitude of the English Puritans toward bearbaiting: that they opposed it not for the suffering that it caused the bear but for the pleasure that it gave the spectators. Perhaps it is not far-fetched to say that the present-day outlook is similar: the reformer wants to improve the situation of the poor, the black, the slum dweller, and so on, not so much to make them better off materially as to make himself and the whole society better off morally.[12]

A more practical political argument for redistributing income through commodity subsidies is that, even if they are economically inefficient, they may be more acceptable politically than cash transfers. Provision of direct housing subsidies along with cash, for example, might increase support for income redistribution. If income redistribution were government's sole objective and if beneficiaries' preferences were paramount, no housing policy would be needed. If government should choose, however, to aid households too poor to buy adequate housing, housing subsidies might assume many forms. Government might pay a part or all of rent or home-

12. *The Unheavenly City* (Little, Brown, 1968), pp. 250–51.

ownership carrying costs for families with incomes below stipulated levels or provide housing to them below cost. It would be wasteful to reduce housing costs for families with incomes above the stipulated levels. Thus it would be wasteful to subsidize construction, borrowing, or other elements of housing costs whose benefits did not accrue principally to families with inadequate incomes.

Most federal housing policies are not so limited. They directly assist groups whose incomes and housing are adequate by most standards. Many federal programs subsidize costs of construction, in general, instead of low income or badly housed families. If such programs are to be justified, the desire to redistribute income cannot be the central motivation.

Inefficiencies of the Free Market

Even if no one cared about his neighbors' opulence or squalor, each person would probably feel the effect of others' investment in and consumption of housing services. Pride or shame about the general appearance of a neighborhood or town may induce such public actions as zoning regulations to compel each family to take into account the effects on others of its outlays on housing. The justification for zoning regulations might apply equally well to subsidies designed to promote better housing or to taxes designed to promote or discourage expenditures on housing. The conviction, in rich countries and poor, that housing is a problem to be settled publicly must somehow reflect the impact of each family's housing on others. It is hard to escape the conclusion that the reaction against particularly odious housing—"No one should have to live that way"—or the political commitment of the United States to "a decent home and a suitable living environment"[13] for all is founded as much on personal distaste as on sympathetic concern.

The very vagueness of the justification for a public housing policy makes it difficult to decide what public action should be taken. Codes establishing minimum housing standards and subsidies ensuring that all households can meet the standards might be the solution. Conversely, limits on consumption of housing and taxes to enforce those limits might express the public will. In any case, the rhetoric of politicians and of others suggests that housing is regarded as a special kind of commodity in that many families care far more about how others are housed than about how they are

13. Housing Act of 1949 (63 Stat. 413).

clothed, entertained, or otherwise provided for. Whether altruism, selfishness, the visibility of squalid housing,[14] or some other reason stirs this concern is far from clear.

Bad housing has long been alleged to cause poor health, low levels of educational achievement, and high crime rates.[15] That these social ills do coincide is beyond dispute, but that the one is cause and the others consequence has never been proved. Conclusive results are hard to come by because adversity is usually hydra-headed. The allegedly adverse effects of housing have nevertheless been used to considerable political effect in support of various housing programs.

For a strong believer in the marketplace as the arbiter of economic decisions the adverse effects would not necessarily justify a public policy on housing. If bad housing harmed only the tenant, then he might be presumed to calculate that harm in deciding how much to spend on housing; and if he were so poor that he had to live in a self-damaging environment, this fact would argue for cash transfers which he could spend as he thought best. But if the consequences of bad housing were visited on his neighbors or his neighborhood, even the strongest advocate of market allocation would concede that a case for public action exists. Recognition of these consequences would not enable him, however, to decide whether housing codes, taxes on bad housing, or subsidies for the improvement of housing would best force owners and tenants to assess the costs imposed on other parties.

Housing Maintenance

One of the most serious consequences of an unregulated housing market is the failure of households to coordinate their actions. The property owner is caught in a predicament like the prisoners' dilemma: Each suspect in a criminal investigation must choose, in response to police offers, whether to confess and receive a light sentence or remain quiet and risk being exposed

14. This point was expressed forcefully two decades ago by Paul A. Samuelson on returning from England. "It is easy for an observer to see the inadequacies of the London slums. It is much harder to see the vitamins that the pre-war Cockney occupants were not getting. I wonder if the alleged especial inadequacy of housing is not an optical illusion." Quoted by Leland S. Burns in "Housing as Social Overhead Capital," *Essays in Urban Land Economics: In Honor of the Sixty-fifth Birthday of Leo Grebler* (University of California, Los Angeles, Real Estate Research Program, 1966), p. 16.

15. See Alvin L. Schorr, *Slums and Social Insecurity*, U.S. Department of Health, Education, and Welfare, Social Security Administration (1963); and Jerome Rothenberg, *Economic Evaluation of Urban Renewal: Conceptual Foundation of Benefit-Cost Analysis* (Brookings Institution, 1967), bibliography, pp. 58–60.

by his confederates and punished more severely. If each suspect confesses so as to minimize the risk to himself, all will suffer more than if none confessed.

In real estate, if net profitability declines when improvements are made on a single piece of property, no owner is likely to invest in improvements because they yield less to him than they cost. Although the sum of the benefits from investments by all owners in the neighborhood might far exceed costs, no owner acting independently can capture these benefits. Hence, the dilemma—acting in their individual self-interest, all are injured, but no market mechanism exists to induce the coordinated action that would benefit all. Each person pursues the selfish, beneficial short-run strategy to the long-run detriment of all.

Actually the problem is more complex. Investments on one property can alter the value or the rate of return on investments in neighboring properties. For instance, installation of modern plumbing in one building may trigger similar investments in competing structures. The dynamic consequences are probably more important than the static problems arising from the prisoners' dilemma.

Medium or high quality housing may be as much affected by the prisoners' dilemma as is slum and other dilapidated property. Indeed, such visible improvements as elaborate apartment lobbies or expensive landscaping seem likely to affect neighboring property values at least as much as does replacement of a broken toilet or repair of rotted flooring. As an explanation of slums, the argument of the prisoners' dilemma proves too much. It is an overly elaborate analogy from the homely fact that how well each man tends his garden affects his neighbors' too, and that if he disregards his neighbors' interests he may tend it less well than he should. It argues not only that slums may be self-perpetuating, but also that investment in real property in general may be too low. It could be used to justify slum clearance, wholesale or selective renewal, widespread subsidies to real property, strictly enforced housing codes, or investment in public facilities to encourage private investments. Collective action may sometimes improve private investment decisions. Unfortunately, the interdependencies are not well understood; neither are the remedies.

Housing Information

If markets are to operate efficiently, buyers and sellers must be capable of judging the price and quality of commodities. Moreover, markets for all goods and services must exist. Some parts of the housing market are highly competitive; others are virtual monopolies; in many parts information is scarce and dear; for certain goods and services, markets do not exist. In a number of instances, public action may have caused market imperfections or prevented the existence of certain markets.

Each step taken to protect inexpert buyers and sellers in the exchange of housing and of housing services has imposed some costs. Purchasers of housing, like those of many modern products, are protected only by laws covering contracts, negligence, and fraud. Consumers and investors ignorant of the structural and material attributes that affect the durability of a house are free to purchase expert advice; they are presumed to have made well-informed decisions when they fail to secure advice. Since World War II, restrictions on the construction and sale of housing have become common and have significantly decreased low quality construction.

Housing differs from most commodities because it is so costly; the financial consequences of a bad blunder can be catastrophic. Until recently, housing was usually produced not by large corporations, but by smaller firms whose life expectancy was relatively short or uncertain. The long and often sweeping warranties or guarantees that are issued on such complex consumer goods as refrigerators, automobiles, or air conditioners by corporations that will later be interested in replacement sales[16] barely exist in housing. The courts in recent years have, however, broadened the responsibility of corporations for defective products, including housing, by extending the concept of negligence.[17]

In principle, a variety of techniques could be employed to protect investors in housing. Sellers might be required to provide information to buyers, to post bonds, or otherwise to secure buyers against loss or injury due to misrepresentation or faulty construction. Transfers of real property might be made legally binding only after appraisal or inspection by licensed experts beholden neither to buyer nor to seller. In most urban areas of the United States, state and local governments have enacted building codes that stipulate acceptable types of construction and materials and housing

16. Federal regulation of warranties and guarantees seems inevitable. In 1970 and 1971 the Senate passed a bill providing minimum standards for guarantees and warranties on consumer products valued at $5 or more; the bill did not pass the House.

17. See Gustav Rinesch, "Warranties for the Protection of the Consumer," *Business Lawyer*, Vol. 24 (April 1969), pp. 857–66; Joseph A. Valore, "Product Liability for a Defective House," *Insurance Law Journal*, No. 558 (July 1969), pp. 395–405; and Clyde R. White, "A 'New' Tort in Texas—Implied Warranty in the Sale of a New House," *Southwestern Law Journal*, Vol. 23 (October 1969), pp. 750–56.

codes that set standards for all units available for occupancy. Such codes frequently are designed to do more than protect buyers or renters of housing. Many have been adopted to meet the terms of eligibility for federal programs.[18] Often they require obsolete building practices that protect certain labor skills or assure demand for locally produced materials.[19] In most cases, codes define acceptable inputs but not the performance of the structure. States also offer a limited protection by licensing real estate brokers and salesmen. That no state requires all sales of real property to take place through a broker suggests that licensing is intended to protect buyers and sellers from unscrupulous brokers rather than from each other. States also license plumbers, electricians, and other building trades and require such protection at time of sale as title insurance.[20]

Far more subtle and more serious than the problem of inexpertness among consumers is the inexpertness among lenders. Because housing is highly durable, its total cost is large in comparison to its current cost and to the annual income of most families. Credit plays a major role at every step in housing markets—builders use construction loans, ultimate owners typically borrow to finance purchases. The interest rate on loans depends in part on the probability of default as perceived by the borrower, a prediction that even lenders are inadequately informed to make. The rules of thumb that govern the award of mortgages testify to the lack of adequate information on which to measure risk. As with all actuarial risks, probabilities of loss can be calculated only from a large body of experience. Analysis of the numerous factors and complex relationships inherent in losses due to defaults demands far more experience than even the largest lenders have. Public action to underwrite losses is probably justified while the needed information accumulates. There is some indication, for example, that federal loss protection has encouraged private lending for longer terms and

18. Some communities, by remaining without codes or other elements of a "workable program for community improvement" as defined by the Department of Housing and Urban Development, were until 1969 able to remain ineligible for public housing, rent supplements, or other federal programs intended for low and middle income residents. Some members of Congress supported the workable program to enable localities to keep out distasteful programs; others felt that a workable program would contribute to orderly growth.

19. See *Building the American City*, Report of the National Commission on Urban Problems, pp. 254–72.

20. Many economists argue that licensing in any field of activity restricts entry to the field and enables members of the profession to charge high prices. Members typically award licenses, and their interest in earning high incomes may conflict with their devotion to excluding only the unqualified.

secured by smaller down payments than would otherwise have been acceptable.[21] Default rates also vary with unemployment, inflation, and other economic circumstances not amenable to actuarial analysis; since public policy alters those conditions, it ought also to protect private households and businesses against their side effects.

Property Rights

Property owners often frustrate efforts to bring about economically desirable consolidation of properties. A single owner bargaining for a disproportionate share of the profits can block a project. And a group of owners agreeing to force a developer's hand may make consolidation impossible. Fear of failure may even keep a developer from trying to consolidate properties.

In putting together the acreage for Columbia, Maryland, James Rouse had to make 169 separate purchases.[22] To avoid driving up prices, the Rouse Company operated with cloak-and-dagger secrecy, using dummy corporations with such names as Cedar Farms, Potomac Estates, and Serenity Acres. Altogether, Rouse accumulated 15,600 acres at a total cost of $23 million;[23] one of the properties—a gasoline station that was to be demolished—cost $75,800. Rouse's experience is repeated countless times on a smaller scale and often with less success by developers seeking to amass land held by separate owners.

Governments encounter the same problems in trying to consolidate the holdings of several owners. Under the law of eminent domain, private owners may be compelled to sell holdings at a "fair" price for "public" purposes. The price is determined by negotiation or by judicial or administrative action. The comprehensiveness of the term "public purpose" is far from clear; it does not, however, include the transactions of private developers, even though their projects may be socially beneficial. Those transactions may sometimes be impossible in free markets. This form of market failure may be both extensive and costly.

21. See George F. Break, "Federal Loan Insurance for Housing," in Break and others, *Federal Credit Agencies,* Prepared for the Commission on Money and Credit (Prentice-Hall, 1963), p. 19.

22. *Redoing America: A Nationwide Report on How to Make Our Cities and Suburbs Livable* (Harper & Row, 1968), p. 171.

23. James W. Rouse, "The City of Columbia, Maryland," in H. Wentworth Eldredge (ed.), *Taming Megalopolis* (Doubleday, 1967), Vol. 2, p. 842.

Monopoly and Discrimination

Monopolistic control and market power are harmful elements of a free market. By controlling the supply of workers to the construction industry, certain building trades allegedly inflate wages artificially, establish arbitrary work rules, and restrict the introduction of cost-reducing technology and materials, thereby keeping building costs high. It is alleged that contractor associations have united to resist the introduction of industrialized housing, and that building trades discriminate against blacks, Mexican-Americans, Puerto Ricans, and others in their apprenticeship programs.[24] To the extent that they exist, such monopolistic practices justify public action in the names of efficiency and equity.

Public action ought also to be used to prevent discrimination against minorities in the sale and rental of housing. Legal prohibitions against discrimination, even if enforced, may not prevent segregation, however. Thomas Schelling has shown that segregation can occur without discrimination. Nearly complete residential segregation would result even if most people were averse to it so long as most people refuse to live in a neighborhood dominated by members of other groups. Normal movement of people is sufficient to cause this result.[25]

Whatever economic losses or gains discrimination in housing or its abolition might cause, it is clear that concern about the moral reprehensibleness and social divisiveness of discrimination, rather than calculation of economic costs, has motivated efforts to end it.

Collective Protection

Collective action has been criticized for creating worse problems than it solves. For example, inspection of new houses for compliance with housing codes may prevent the relatively few unscrupulous contractors from duping unwary buyers, but all builders must bear the slight delays and attendant

24. See *Building the American City*, Report of the National Commission on Urban Problems; J. T. Dunlop and D. Q. Mills, "Manpower in Construction: A Profile of the Industry and Projections to 1975," in *The Report of the President's Committee on Urban Housing*, Vol. 2, *Technical Studies* (1968), p. 273; F. Ray Marshall and Vernon M. Biggs, Jr., *The Negro and Apprenticeship* (Johns Hopkins Press, 1967); and "Philadelphia Plan," *Congressional Record*, daily ed., July 30, 1969, pp. S8837–39.

25. "On the Ecology of Micromotives," Discussion Paper No. 2, Public Policy Program, Kennedy School of Government, Harvard University (Harvard University Program on Technology and Society, October 1970; processed).

costs of inspections, and taxpayers must pay the inspectors' salaries. The unsettled issue is whether the benefits of preventing large losses for some buyers are worth the costs of building inspections, small for each builder and taxpayer, but perhaps quite large in the aggregate.

The same question arises with respect to every form of inspection, licensing, bonding, and other consumer or investor protection device. Government agencies and private businesses must decide whether fraud by employees or clients, shoplifting by employees or customers, and other illicit acts cost more than efforts to prevent them. Often the cheapest policy is to let the illicit act continue at a controlled though high level. Unfortunately, the benefits from collective action often are not measurable, or are subject to special value standards.[26] For this reason, those who doubt the efficacy of collective action to protect the few from large losses at the cost of small burdens for the many face little risk of refutation or hope of vindication, except in the most clear-cut (and therefore uncontroversial) cases.

Adjustment Lags and Cyclical Problems

Each year new residential construction amounts to less than 3 percent of the housing stock. Each year only one-fifth of households change their residence. Thus the character of the housing stock and residential patterns evolve gradually. Several years are required for ordinary market forces to correct housing shortages or deficiencies. These forces include new construction, improvement or deterioration of existing units, conversions of real property to or from residential use, splitting or consolidating existing housing units, and filtering.

If market forces work quickly and efficiently, housing problems due to population movements or income shifts do not persist. Tenants move, owners alter units and change rents, and maladjustments quickly vanish. On the other hand, if the forces work slowly and inefficiently and problems persist, public action might be justified to speed adjustments. Such action might range from efforts to increase the housing stock, in order to raise vacancy rates and thereby facilitate changes of residence, to moving allowances or small loans for property improvement.

26. See Thomas C. Schelling, "The Life You Save May Be Your Own," in Samuel B. Chase, Jr. (ed.), *Problems in Public Expenditure Analysis* (Brookings Institution, 1968), pp. 127–62.

Little solid information exists on the speed with which the housing market adjusts to changes in housing demand. One recent study reports evidence that rents respond fairly slowly to changes in income of tenants and capital costs; only three-fifths of the long-run effects are realized after three years.[27] The kind of public action, if any, that is necessary to deal with large changes in demand is thus difficult to choose.

Credit Fluctuations

Because credit is prominent in the construction and purchase of new housing and in the transfer of existing units, changes in interest rates and in the availability of credit affect the price of housing services more than the price of most other capital and consumer goods. For example, an increase in interest rates from 6 percent to 9 percent raises the cost of amortizing a thirty-year loan by 34 percent. Such increases may be partly offset by declines (or smaller increases than would otherwise occur) in the price of housing units or in other costs that enter into the total cost.

Interest rates fluctuate widely around long-run trends, rising when demand for credit is high or the supply of credit is low. These short-run fluctuations may cause large inverse swings in the rate of housing construction; rises in the price of housing services lower the amounts demanded, as a result of which demand for *additions* to the housing stock is greatly reduced. Credit rationing or other imperfections in capital markets may reduce the mobility of households. Normal population movements can cause housing shortages in particular areas during periods of credit stringency. Without new construction, such shortages might persist, unless large and inequitable price increases occur to reduce the amount demanded. Large variations in the amount of housing constructed or in demand that impose excessive or inequitable costs would create strong pressures for public action. Such action might include measures to assure a steady flow of credit to housing.

Family Formation

In the United States, individual households occupy most housing units, and few demand more than one unit. Demand for additions to the housing stock thus depends on the rate of household formation. Because birthrates

27. Frank de Leeuw, assisted by Nkanta F. Ekanem, "Time Lags in the Rental Housing Market," Working Paper 112-19 (Urban Institute, June 3, 1970; processed), p. 39.

were low in the 1930s and high in the late 1940s and 1950s, household formation will rise from an annual rate of 890,000 during the early 1960s to 1,340,000 during the early 1970s. This demographic factor alone will require a big jump in housing investment during the 1970s. The promise to eradicate substandard housing, to increase vacancies, and otherwise to expand the housing stock contained in the Housing and Urban Development Act of 1968 will further expand housing demand. The housing act's goal of construction or rehabilitation of 26 million housing units during the decade 1969–78 will require investment of perhaps 4.3 percent of the gross national product in housing in 1975 as opposed to 3.5 percent in 1969.[28] While neither the level nor the increase is extraordinary—nonfarm residential construction absorbed 4.9 percent of GNP in 1950, up from 3.8 percent in 1949—it will depend on a reduction in some other major component of GNP.

Had public decision makers decided to do nothing about the unusually large housing demand during the 1970s, no housing goal would have been set. Fiscal and monetary policies, based on a broad range of considerations, would only by coincidence have made possible fulfillment of the housing goal. In all likelihood, fewer units would have been built in the 1969–78 decade and more units in succeeding years.

The choice between the high goal of the housing act and no official action to meet the bulge in housing demand affects income distribution. Construction costs are likely to rise less if the residential construction rate is low than if it is high. On the other hand, if relatively few units are built, substandard housing units are unlikely to be eradicated and price increases in areas of acute shortage are likely to be severe. Households that spend a relatively large fraction of their income on housing or derive a relatively small proportion of income from investments in housing will be hardest hit by increases in housing prices. A complex system of taxes or transfers could shield personal incomes from the consequences of an uncontrolled housing market. However, income redistribution is a divisive political act. Those who are concerned about income distribution may therefore advocate policies to keep down housing costs, even though such policies might disrupt the workings of a perfectly functioning market.

This concern may explain why many governments adopt rent controls, particularly in wartime when construction must be curtailed. Wartime

28. Computed from estimates in *Second Annual Report on National Housing Goals*, *Message from the President of the United States*, H. Doc. 91-292, 91 Cong. 2 sess. (1970), pp. 69, 107.

shortages are apt to increase the price of housing more than that of other goods; real incomes of tenants fall while those of landlords rise. New construction becomes highly profitable and builders will increase their activity if rent control does not apply effectively to new buildings and if wartime priorities do not preclude construction. The application of controls to new units may reduce or stop new construction. Controls on existing units are a kind of tax on owners with proceeds given to tenants. Controls thereby discourage maintenance, repairs, and improvements, even though tenants would willingly pay increased rents to finance improvements. Furthermore, as tenants move, rent control becomes less efficient. It is a plausible instrument, however, if immediate shifts in income distribution are a more important cause for concern than deferred damage to the housing stock and if less costly instruments are not available.

The facts that housing is highly capital intensive and durable and that most families devote a large part of their budgets to housing explain why free market adjustments to shifts in demand may be unacceptable. Housing is sufficiently different from other investments and housing services from other consumer goods to require special public attention.

Summary

A nation committed to market allocation of most resources might intervene in the housing market in order to alter income distribution. It might act to restrict the benefits or costs of housing transactions passed on to persons not directly involved, or to correct imperfections in the functioning of housing markets. It might also wish to offset the consequences of fiscal and monetary policies on the housing sector.

These justifications for interfering in the housing market are extremely vague. Because evidence about the causes for public concern is scarce or nonexistent, it is hard to know which policies most effectively remove causes of concern or whether actual policies achieve their stated goals. Housing codes, for example, may attempt to control the effect of one family's housing on another's welfare or to limit the dangers of consumer ignorance, but their success in doing so is unknown. Therefore it is impossible to know whether they bring about better housing—for the poor, the middle class, or the rich—or even improve methods of production. It has been argued that housing codes—designed to ensure decent housing for the poor—may in fact deny the poor the opportunity to occupy cheap housing below code standards and to use the money saved on housing for such other things as better or more food.

Public policies themselves create hindrances to efficiency. Compliance costs, delays in inspections, added uncertainties, all may result from public action designed to solve particular problems. Once again, the magnitude of these costs is unknown.

Unfortunately, the numerous but vague reasons why public action might improve the functioning of the housing market offer little guidance in selecting among alternative policies. Moreover, the cost of interfering in the operation of the housing market is vague. The problems may well be extremely serious, and collective action may be the only solution. Political leaders may be excused if they act on less than complete information.

They cannot be excused so readily, however, for confusing the inadequacies of housing with the inadequacies of concomitant residential services. Governments tend to treat the problems of decaying neighborhoods —the dilapidated structures, poor schools, inadequate transportation, high crime rates—with programs aimed principally at physical renewal or reconstruction. That tendency may reflect a recognition that it is easier to renew structures than to deal with other problems; it may also reflect the confusion of the physical, social, and economic problems of decaying neighborhoods with the "housing problem."

chapter two **Housing
Numbers
and Housing
Information**

The national housing goal established during the Johnson administration reflects concern over an anticipated shortage of housing and a desire to provide adequate housing for all. That goal, like other social or economic goals, is based on perceptions of need shaped by various statistical series. Housing conditions, costs and expenditures, crowding and other measurable characteristics, projections of family formation, growth of seasonal homes, all help define the public view of the housing problem. Public and private perceptions of the housing problem, of whether it is growing more or less serious, and of what the future holds all depend in large part on the story that numbers tell.

Unfortunately, the numbers tell a confusing story. To illustrate: in 1960, 13.2 million occupied housing units were classified as dilapidated, deteriorating, or sound but lacking some basic plumbing facilities;[1] the same number of households—13.2 million—was officially counted as poor. By 1966 the number of poor had dropped to 10.5 million,[2] and the number of deficient housing units to 10.8 million. But pairing of poverty and deficient housing is deceptive: in 1966 only 34 percent of the poor households lived in dilapidated or deteriorating housing. How did several million poor households afford sound housing?

More facts only increase the confusion: 4.7 million nonpoor households lived in dilapidated or deteriorating housing—which means that less than

1. U.S. Bureau of the Census, *U.S. Census of Housing: 1960*, Vol. 1, *States and Small Areas, United States Summary*, Final Report HC(1)-1 (1963), p. 1–4.
2. Bureau of the Census, *Current Population Reports*, Series P-60, No. 71, "Poverty Continues to Decline in 1969" (1970), p. 3.

23

41 percent of the inadequate housing was inhabited by the poor. In fact, some households with incomes in excess of $15,000 a year lived in housing classified as dilapidated or deteriorating. Why are so many who are not poor so badly housed? The statistics on housing conditions reflect the complexities of housing and environmental characteristics.

Housing statistics are compiled for many purposes. The statistics devoted to measuring the conditions under which families are housed and how much of their income goes into housing have many shortcomings. Many writers have protested these essentially inadequate measures. The National Commission on Urban Problems in 1968 remarked on

the ridiculously inadequate data now at hand. Nearly everyone concerned with the subject has known and said this since the first census of housing was published in 1940, more than a quarter of a century ago. Yet these same critics of the data have gone ahead to use, revise, and manipulate these statistics (and often others that are worse) to produce elaborate and rickety structures of partial or misleading facts. Personal guesses and farfetched assumptions with little relation to the actual world around us clutter the housing and urban problems field.[3]

The statistics can sustain inferences about the adequacy of the housing stock and trends in housing quality in the nation, but not in small areas; they tell little about the quality of residential services anywhere.

Housing Condition

Each decennial census since 1940 has reported on physical characteristics of housing. Until 1970 each census contained evaluations of housing condition.[4] Special surveys have supplied data on the quantity, physical characteristics, and condition of housing.

The census is designed to obtain data on households and to a limited extent on the structures in which they reside. Since answers to all questions are mandatory, the questionnaire must not be so long as to be burdensome. For budgetary reasons, questions cannot be designed to meet the special characteristics of different population groups, regions, or communities.[5]

3. *Building the American City*, Report of the National Commission on Urban Problems to the Congress and to the President of the United States, H. Doc. 91-34, 91 Cong. 1 sess. (1969), p. 68.

4. See Bureau of the Census, *1960 Censuses of Population and Housing: Procedural History* (1966), pp. 232–34.

5. Arthur F. Young and Joseph M. Selove, "Methods of Measuring Housing Quality," American Statistical Association, *Proceedings of the Social Statistics Section, 1968*, pp. 49–51.

As a result, the census is largely limited to questions of observable fact, requiring little estimation or judgment by either respondent or census taker. The major exception to this rule was the effort (until 1970) to evaluate housing condition—to determine what fraction of all housing units did not provide adequate shelter. In other words, the goal was to determine the flow of housing services rather than of residential services. Census enumerators received explicit instructions not to allow the poverty or wealth of a neighborhood, the race of tenants or of their neighbors, or anything other than physical characteristics of housing to affect their evaluation of the structure's condition; the Census Bureau suspects that these warnings were ineffective in many cases.[6]

Defects in Statistics

Housing units in 1960 were classified as dilapidated, deteriorating, or sound, and defects as slight, intermediate, or critical.[7] "Sound" denoted no defects or "some *slight* defects"; if there were "*a large number of slight* defects" the enumerator was to be "sure there are no more *serious* defects." "Deteriorating" indicated at least one *intermediate* defect, or "flaws . . . [that] indicate a lack of *proper* upkeep," or "repairs needed . . . to provide *adequate* shelter or protection against the elements." "Dilapidated" signified "one or more *critical* defects" or at least two, but perhaps five or six, *intermediate* defects that made the unit "no longer . . . *safe* and *adequate* shelter."[8]

Clearly, the enumerators had to apply considerable judgment. The criteria for evaluating housing condition were vague and in some cases useless. Moreover, the typical enumerator had no particular expertise in real estate, received only thirty minutes of training, and was paid on a piece-rate basis that led him to spend probably less than one minute per unit in evaluating condition.[9] It may not be surprising, therefore, that of all housing units classified as dilapidated in an evaluation program subsequent to the 1960 census, 23 percent had been classified in the 1960 census as sound, 39 per-

6. Bureau of the Census, *Measuring the Quality of Housing, An Appraisal of Census Statistics and Methods*, Working Paper 25 (1967), pp. 24, 57.
7. Bureau of the Census, *1960 Censuses of Population and Housing*, pp. 232–34. In the 1950 census and the 1956 national housing inventory, housing units were classified as dilapidated (corresponding to dilapidated in 1960) or not dilapidated (corresponding to deteriorating and sound in 1960).
8. Bureau of the Census, *Measuring the Quality of Housing*, p. 56. Emphasis added.
9. Ibid., p. 23.

cent as deteriorating, and only 38 percent as dilapidated. Of units classified as deteriorating in the evaluation program, 58 percent had been classified in the census as sound, 9 percent as dilapidated, and only 33 percent as deteriorating.[10] The Census Bureau concluded that statistics on dilapidated or deteriorating units reported in the 1960 census were unreliable and inaccurate and that "there does not appear to be any feasible method of improving the quality of enumerator ratings in a decennial census."[11]

The Department of Housing and Urban Development uses a different set of classifications, listing housing units as standard or substandard. "Substandard" units include all dilapidated units, plus all deteriorating and sound units that lack hot running water, a private flush toilet, or a private bathtub or shower. These statistics could be described more accurately as plumbing statistics, since only 11.7 percent of substandard units had all plumbing facilities in 1966.[12] Use of a measurable characteristic makes statistics on substandard housing more accurate than those on dilapidated or deteriorating housing.

Many important housing characteristics are irrelevant to the determination of whether a unit is substandard, dilapidated, or deteriorating. Among the neglected characteristics are rodent or insect infestation, inadequate electrical wiring, dampness, and plumbing connected to unapproved water supply or sewer systems.[13]

Because of the gross shortcomings in statistics on dilapidated housing, the Census Bureau decided not to measure housing quality in the 1970 census. However, the bureau acceded to "urgent requests"—presumably from HUD, other federal agencies, and private groups—that it compile estimates of substandard housing.[14] It also agreed to make a sample survey of the housing stock to determine how the components measured in 1960 had changed.

10. Ibid., Table III-5, p. 21. Somewhat more surprising was the low correlation in successive evaluations of condition in housing surveys by experts; see ibid., pp. 31–34.

11. Ibid., pp. 5–6. The census sought to measure housing quality in the aggregate. Criticisms are related to the use of census data on units, blocks, or communities, despite Census Bureau protestations that the data were unreliable.

12. In 1950, 74 percent, in 1960, 73 percent, and in 1966, 69 percent of all substandard housing units were so classified *only* because they lacked certain plumbing facilities.

13. See Oscar Sutermeister, "Inadequacies and Inconsistencies in the Definition of Substandard Housing," in *Housing Code Standards: Three Critical Studies*, Prepared for the Consideration of the National Commission on Urban Problems, Research Report 19 (Government Printing Office, 1969), pp. 78–108.

14. The bureau's methods for estimating 1970 data are described in Appendix B.

Uses of Statistics

Statistics on housing condition can be used to discover changes over time in housing quality or to compare quality among geographical areas or groups of people. Over time, general housing conditions have improved (see Table 2-1). The number of dilapidated units fell by nearly half between 1950 and 1966. The proportion of all housing classified as dilapidated fell even more sharply because the housing stock grew rapidly during this period.

Unfortunately, evaluation studies conducted after the 1960 census showed that the decline in dilapidated housing was only 0.2 percent rather than the 41.9 percent reported in the census.[15] Some units classified as dilapidated in 1950 may have been placed in the new intermediate category, deteriorating, in 1960.

Table 2-1. Condition of Occupied Housing Units in the United States, 1950, 1960, and 1966

	1950		1960		1966	
Condition	Millions of units	Percent of total	Millions of units	Percent of total	Millions of units	Percent of total
Census Bureau classification						
Sound or deteriorating	39.1	90.9	50.7	95.7	58.5	96.4
Sound	39.1ᵃ	90.9ᵃ	43.8	82.6	52.2	86.1
With all plumbing facilities	27.7	64.5	40.4	76.2	n.a.	n.a.
Lacking one or more plumbing facilities	11.4	26.4	3.4	6.4	n.a.	n.a.
Deteriorating	n.a.	n.a.	6.9	13.1	6.3	10.3
Dilapidated	3.9	9.1	2.3	4.3	2.2	3.6
Total	43.0	100.0	53.0	100.0	60.6	100.0
HUD classification						
Standardᵇ	27.7	64.5	44.5	84.0	n.a.	n.a.
Substandardᶜ	15.3	35.5	8.5	16.0	n.a.	n.a.

Sources: For 1950, U.S. Bureau of the Census, *Measuring the Quality of Housing: An Appraisal of Census Statistics and Methods,* Working Paper 25 (1967), p. 16; for 1960, U.S. Department of Housing and Urban Development (HUD), *1969 HUD Statistical Yearbook* (1970), p. 354; for 1966, Bureau of the Census, Survey of Economic Opportunity, spring 1967, unpublished tabulations. Figures are rounded and may not add to totals.
n.a. Not available.
a. Includes deteriorating units.
b. Includes nondilapidated units with hot water and other plumbing facilities.
c. Includes all dilapidated units and nondilapidated units without hot water or other plumbing facilities.

15. Bureau of the Census, *Measuring the Quality of Housing,* p. 20.

The number and proportion of housing units classified as substandard fell faster than the number and proportion of dilapidated units, as modern plumbing was installed in sound or deteriorating units previously without it. Trends in the objectively measured substandard units are more reliable than trends in dilapidated housing.

Purely objective measures of housing condition also indicate that housing conditions have improved (see Table 2-2). In the last generation housing has become less crowded and the proportion of families without access to such modern plumbing facilities as a private toilet, hot and cold running water, and a private bath or shower has plummeted. Reliable information on such physical characteristics depends only on the technical matters of sample and questionnaire design.

The improvement in aggregate housing quality is best summarized by comparing real per capita consumption of housing with other broad categories of consumption goods (Figure 2-1). From 1950 to 1970 real per capita consumption of housing services more than doubled, a rate of growth unmatched by other broad expenditure categories such as durable goods, nondurable goods, and transportation services.

Table 2-2. Occupants per Room and Plumbing Shortages in U.S. Housing, 1940, 1950, 1960, and 1970

In percent

Measure	1940	1950	1960 Total	White	Non-white	1970 Total	Negro
Occupants per room in housing unit							
0.75 or less	54.9	60.1	65.3	67.0	49.4	72.4	58.9
0.76–1.00	24.9	24.1	23.1	23.2	22.3	19.4	21.1
1.01–1.50	11.3	9.6	7.9	7.3	14.3	6.0	12.4
1.51 or more	9.0	6.2	3.6	2.5	14.1	2.2	7.5
Units without private toilet	40.3	28.6	13.2	11.6	30.6[a]	5.0	12.2
Units without running water or hot running water	n.a.	29.9	12.8	10.6	34.8[a]	4.8	13.8
Units without private bath or shower	43.8	30.7	14.8	12.7	35.8[a]	5.8	14.4

Sources: For 1940, 1950, and 1960, Bureau of the Census, *U.S. Census of Housing: 1960*, Vol. 1, *States and Small Areas, United States Summary*, Final Report HC(1)-1 (1963), Tables J, O, P, 3, 6, 24, 25, pp. xxix, xxxvi, xxxviii, 1-4, 1-22, 1-213, 1-217; for 1970, Bureau of the Census, *U.S. Census of Housing: 1970, General Housing Characteristics*, Final Report HC(1)-A1, *United States Summary* (1971), Tables 3, 4, 8, 9, pp. 1-16, 1-22, 1-41, 1-47. Percentages are rounded and may not add to 100.

n.a. Not available.

a. Data based on occupied units only.

Figure 2-1. Real per Capita Consumption of Housing, Durable and Nondurable Goods, and Transportation Services, 1929–70[a]

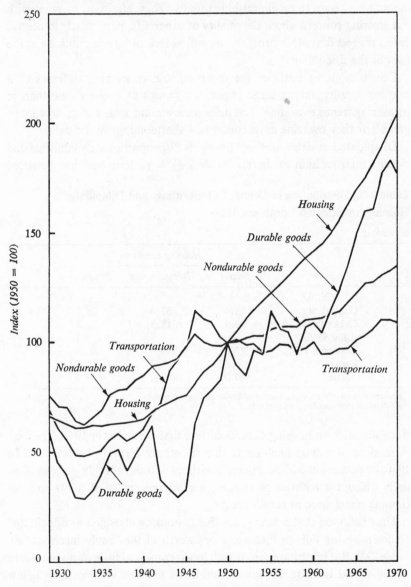

Sources: Population data from U.S. Bureau of the Census, *Current Population Reports*, "Estimates of the Population of the United States and Components of Change: 1940 to 1970," Series P-25, No. 442 (1970), p. 13; other data from U.S. Department of Commerce, Office of Business Economics, *The National Income and Product Accounts of the United States, 1929–1965: Statistical Tables* (1966), Table 2.6, and *Survey of Current Business*, Vol. 49 (July 1969), Table 2.6, and Vol. 51 (July 1971), Table 2.6.

a. Housing includes space-rental value of owner-occupied nonfarm dwellings; space rent of tenant-occupied nonfarm dwellings (including lodging houses); and the rental value of farmhouses.

The picture that emerges from these statistics is one of progressive and rapid improvement in overall housing quality. Bad structures persist, but the number seems to be diminishing rapidly. These statistics, together with the growing concern about the quality of urban life, particularly in central cities, suggest that other problems as well as lack of housing must lie at the root of the discontent.

Census housing statistics are more reliable concerning differences in housing quality among large regions or groups at a given time than in measuring trends over time. The differences among areas and groups are so great that they override most conceptual shortcomings in the data.

Dilapidated or deteriorating housing is disproportionately concentrated outside metropolitan areas (see Table 2-3), a pattern that has persisted

Table 2-3. Distribution of Sound, Deteriorating, and Dilapidated Housing, in Selected Locations, 1966

In percent

	Housing condition		
Location	Sound	Deteriorating	Dilapidated
Inside SMSA[a]			
Central city	33.4	32.4	26.1
Urban fringe	34.9	18.3	16.9
Outside SMSA[a]			
Nonfarm	27.5	40.9	43.5
Farm	4.2	8.4	13.5
Total	100.0	100.0	100.0

Source: Bureau of the Census, Survey of Economic Opportunity.
a. Standard metropolitan statistical area.

since statistics on housing condition were first compiled in 1940. The lack of modern plumbing facilities is almost entirely a rural phenomenon. In 1970, 89 percent of all housing units without a flush toilet, 79 percent of all units without a bathtub or shower, and 92 percent of all units without running water were in rural areas.[16]

The likelihood that a family will live in housing classified as dilapidated or deteriorating falls as income or net worth of the family increases (see Table 2-4). But most households with low income and little or no net worth live in sound housing. About two-thirds of families with incomes below $1,000 a year and with zero or negative net worth live in sound housing. At the other end of the scale, a few households in relatively high income

16. Bureau of the Census, *U.S. Census of Housing: 1970, General Housing Characteristics*, Final Report HC(1)-A1 (1971), Table 10, p. 1-53.

Table 2-4. Housing Condition by Annual Income and Net Worth
of Occupants, 1966

In percent

Dollar bracket	Portion of all households in bracket	Housing condition		
		Sound	Deteriorating	Dilapidated
Annual income				
Under 1,000	5.9	67.4	19.9	12.7
1,001-2,000	9.4	70.5	20.3	9.2
2,001-3,000	8.5	76.2	16.4	7.4
3,001-4,000	7.9	79.9	14.3	5.9
4,001-5,000	7.8	82.8	13.5	3.7
5,001-6,000	8.9	86.0	10.9	3.1
6,001-7,500	13.5	90.1	8.5	1.4
7,501-10,000	16.3	93.5	5.9	0.6
10,001-15,000	15.3	96.4	3.3	0.3
15,001-25,000	5.4	98.4	1.4	0.1
Over 25,000	1.0	100.0	0.0	0.0
Net worth				
Negative	12.4	69.2	21.2	9.6
0	6.0	62.4	23.3	14.3
1-1,000	12.2	75.2	17.9	6.9
1,001-2,000	5.8	82.1	13.3	4.6
2,001-3,000	4.5	84.5	12.0	3.4
3,001-4,000	3.9	84.0	12.7	3.2
4,001-5,000	3.5	86.7	11.4	1.9
5,001-7,500	7.8	89.6	8.4	2.0
7,501-10,000	6.3	91.7	7.0	1.3
10,001-15,000	10.0	92.7	6.2	1.1
15,001-25,000	11.8	95.7	4.0	0.4
25,001-50,000	9.4	95.7	3.9	0.4
50,001-100,000	4.0	98.8	1.2	0.1
Over 100,000	2.3	98.0	1.8	0.3

Source: Bureau of the Census, Survey of Economic Opportunity. Percentages are rounded and may not add to 100.

brackets and some in even the highest net worth categories inhabit housing classified as dilapidated or deteriorating, a fact that reinforces doubt on the reliability of statistics on housing condition.

The proportion of households in bad housing seems also to vary by race, even after allowances for differences in economic circumstances. Three-fourths of all whites classified as poor, but only two-fifths of poor non-whites[17] live in housing classified as sound (see Table 2-5). The most strik-

17. Families and unrelated individuals are considered poor in government statistics if their annual incomes are below specified thresholds estimated separately on the basis of farm or nonfarm residence, age and sex of head of household, and family size.

Table 2-5. Housing Condition of the Poor, by Race and Region, 1966

In percent

	Housing condition		
Race and region	Sound	Deteriorating	Dilapidated
White, all regions	73.4	18.5	8.1
Northeast	79.6	13.8	6.5
North Central	77.7	16.6	5.7
South	66.3	23.2	10.5
West	73.6	17.6	8.8
Nonwhite, all regions	43.0	33.4	23.6
Northeast	55.5	26.0	18.6
North Central	45.7	41.7	12.6
South	36.7	35.3	28.0
West	59.6	19.7	20.6
Total, all regions	65.6	22.3	12.0
Northeast	75.2	16.0	8.7
North Central	72.6	20.6	6.8
South	55.3	27.7	17.0
West	71.1	18.0	11.0

Source: Bureau of the Census, Survey of Economic Opportunity. Percentages are rounded and may not add to 100.

ing fact contained in Table 2-5 is that nearly two-thirds of the poor live in sound housing and only about one-eighth in dilapidated housing.

Housing costs and housing condition are not closely related, for renters and home buyers purchase residential services, not just housing services. The imprecision of indexes of housing condition further weakens the connection. Although the proportion of housing classified as dilapidated or deteriorating is generally higher for relatively cheap housing than for more expensive, most housing for whites in all but the very lowest rental categories is classified as sound (Table 2-6). For nonwhites the proportion of dilapidated or deteriorated housing in most rental categories is higher than for whites. Much the same is true of owner occupied homes; the overwhelming majority of houses owned by whites are classified as sound. Most owned by nonwhites, except in the lowest value bracket, are also classified as sound, but in each value bracket the proportion is below that for whites.

Racial Discrimination

Plausible explanations for the apparently better housing conditions of whites than of nonwhites are easier to advance than to prove. Racial discrimination in housing markets might explain why nonwhites are more

Table 2-6. Condition of Rental and Owner Occupied Housing of Nonfarm Families, by Race, 1966

In percent

Dollar bracket	White households				Nonwhite households			
	Portion in bracket	Housing condition			Portion in bracket	Housing condition		
		Sound	Deteriorating	Dilapidated		Sound	Deteriorating	Dilapidated
Monthly rent								
0–10	2.2	74.8	19.7	5.6	3.6	51.2	23.0	25.8
11–20	1.3	33.2	34.9	31.9	4.9	22.1	33.8	44.2
21–30	4.7	55.9	32.6	11.5	8.8	36.1	30.4	33.5
31–40	8.1	72.9	19.7	7.4	11.0	40.7	40.2	19.1
41–50	10.7	76.7	18.8	4.4	13.1	43.8	35.3	20.9
51–60	12.5	78.4	17.5	4.1	13.8	58.1	31.9	10.0
61–75	17.9	86.0	11.6	2.3	17.9	65.3	27.2	7.6
76–90	15.6	90.1	8.4	1.5	12.8	67.3	26.3	6.4
91–100	6.7	91.8	4.1	4.0	4.5	78.1	15.0	6.8
101–125	10.7	97.2	2.6	0.2	6.0	82.9	14.0	3.1
Over 125	9.8	98.1	1.6	0.2	3.6	89.0	9.7	1.3
Home value								
0–2,500	5.7	65.0	21.9	13.1	15.0	30.9	33.1	36.0
2,501–5,000	4.7	70.9	25.0	4.1	9.4	45.0	39.0	16.0
5,001–7,500	8.1	83.6	15.1	1.3	17.4	68.9	25.2	5.9
7,501–10,000	9.2	92.4	7.0	0.5	12.8	80.4	17.3	2.3
10,001–12,500	14.5	95.9	3.8	0.2	13.4	88.7	10.0	1.3
12,501–15,000	8.2	98.6	1.4	0.0	6.0	89.4	10.6	0.0
15,001–17,500	14.5	98.6	1.3	0.1	7.3	90.8	9.2	0.0
17,501–20,000	7.7	99.0	0.9	0.1	3.2	90.9	8.4	0.7
20,001–25,000	12.1	98.5	1.3	0.2	5.7	94.8	4.5	0.7
Over 25,000	15.6	98.3	1.5	0.2	9.7	96.5	3.0	0.5

Source: Bureau of the Census, Survey of Economic Opportunity. Percentages are rounded and may not add to 100.

poorly housed than whites at any rent level or home value. Bias in enumerator attitudes might influence their evaluation procedures. Enumerators might be influenced by the quality of urban services, such as streets, or by such neighborhood characteristics as the quality of surrounding buildings or of street litter.

One study found that renters paid about 8 percent less and homeowners paid 5 percent less in all-white areas than in all-black areas, even after the influences of a large number of structural, neighborhood, and public services had been considered.[18] Another found that Negroes pay 2–5 percent more than whites for housing of any given quality,[19] and a third that the median price of owner occupied houses was $2,555 higher in all-black than in all-white neighborhoods in St. Louis (after adjusting for other property and neighborhood characteristics).[20] In New Haven black males pay about 7 percent more than white, and black females 17–18 percent more than white, for otherwise similar rental housing.[21] Both blacks and whites tend to pay more for housing in predominantly white neighborhoods than they do in predominantly black neighborhoods. The full costs to blacks of racial segregation may be even greater if they are compelled to purchase only slightly overpriced, low quality housing in areas with poor residential services, rather than higher quality housing in better neighborhoods that they would prefer.

The apparently better housing conditions of whites may be a result of census enumerators' bias or of neighborhood factors that influence their evaluation of housing quality. According to the Census Bureau:

The 1960 instructions are explicit in exhorting the enumerators not to be influenced by the characteristics of the neighborhood in making their ratings. The question is how effective this exhortation was. On this question there is no evidence, but we have a plausible opinion that exhortation cannot be effective. This opinion stems from well-established psychological research concerning the basic "perceptual-contrast phenomenon," which is known to operate in all types of elementary perceptions—sight, sound, touch, etc.[22]

18. John F. Kain and John M. Quigley, "Measuring the Value of Housing Quality," *Journal of the American Statistical Association*, Vol. 65 (June 1970), p. 540.

19. Richard F. Muth, *Cities and Housing: The Spatial Problem of Urban Residential Land Use* (University of Chicago Press, 1969), pp. 238–39.

20. Ronald G. Ridker and John A. Henning, "The Determinants of Residential Property Values with Special Reference to Air Pollution," *Review of Economics and Statistics*, Vol. 49 (May 1967), p. 256.

21. Thomas King and Peter Mieszkowski, "An Estimate of Racial Discrimination in Rental Housing," Discussion Paper 307 (Cowles Foundation, 1971; processed).

22. *Measuring the Quality of Housing*, p. 24.

Whether failure to follow instructions would lead census enumerators to overestimate or underestimate the amount of deficient housing in "bad" neighborhoods is unclear. Middle class white enumerators might find conditions in black neighborhoods alien and frightening and react by putting housing units in lower categories than they deserve; alternatively, they might adjust their standards downward. Or they might be just as inaccurate in black as in white neighborhoods.

The effect of changing racial composition on housing costs has been studied more, perhaps, than any other environmental factor. While some studies seem to refute the widely held view that an infusion of blacks into a neighborhood reduces property values,[23] one suggests that prices, of owner occupied homes at least, drop when blacks move into a previously all white area due to panic reactions of whites. When a stable equilibrium in racial composition is achieved, however, prices return to levels and trends set by the larger community.[24] An earlier study had found that an influx of blacks caused no drop in property values except in relatively high price areas where the scarcity of high income blacks might not offset the drop in demand by more numerous high income whites.[25]

Expenditures on Housing

Statistics on housing expenditures as a fraction of household income are compiled to reveal whether some households spend excessive parts of income to obtain "adequate" housing. These statistics suffer from three major conceptual flaws. First, variations in tastes at any given income might cause substantial differences in expenditures for residential services. Second, residential services are a package of goods, including both housing services and other amenities. For a given outlay, some families will prefer relatively good housing and poor amenities; others will choose the reverse. Third, housing expenditures are only loosely related to current family incomes. Incomes vary from year to year, but housing expenditures are fairly stable; as a result, the fraction of current income spent on residential

23. Muth, *Cities and Housing;* Kain and Quigley, "Measuring the Value of Housing Quality."

24. Jack M. Guttentag, "Racial Integration and Home Prices: The Case of West Mt. Airy," *Wharton Quarterly*, Vol. 10 (Spring 1970), pp. 21–23, 31.

25. Luigi Laurenti, *Property Values and Race: Studies in 7 Cities* (University of California Press, 1960); also see Anthony Downs, "An Economic Analysis of *Property Values and Race* (Laurenti)," *Land Economics*, Vol. 36 (May 1960), pp. 181–88.

services will vary.[26] Thus statistics on the fraction of income spent on housing should be interpreted with caution.

These conceptual problems are compounded by the difficulty of constructing questions that elicit accurate information. Decennial censuses since 1940, for example, have included estimated market values of properties and gross rent, including the cost of electricity, gas, and water. Owners can estimate with some accuracy the value of properties sold through arm's-length transactions shortly before the census, *if* they answer the question honestly. But fewer than 20 percent of all owner occupied houses are sold each year,[27] so that the typical owner must rely on his knowledge, if any, of the recent selling prices of nearby, similar structures; on appraisals made for such special purposes as to obtain financing for major improvements; or on pure guesswork. Some homeowners may be influenced by values assessed for property taxation. Not only are homeowner estimates likely to be inaccurate, but errors are unlikely to be random, since the average period elapsed since sale varies systematically by neighborhood and the ratio of assessed value for property tax to actual sales prices varies widely within and among jurisdictions.

Reports by tenants on gross rents are believed to be reasonably accurate measures of what they actually pay.[28] The problem is what they get; some rents include, others exclude, appliances such as refrigerators or washers and dryers (for joint or private use), garages, wall-to-wall carpeting, draperies, or other furnishings. Once again, the provision of such commodities is not geographically random so that systematic biases of uncertain magnitude are present in value and rent statistics.

Low income Americans spend a larger part of their income on housing than do high income Americans. Households with incomes under $1,000 per year spend 85 percent of income on housing, those with $15,000 or more spend 15 percent (see Table 2-7). At first glance these statistics are shocking, at second glance misleading, and on close examination largely

26. See Richard F. Muth, "The Demand for Non-Farm Housing," in Arnold C. Harberger (ed.), *The Demand for Durable Goods* (University of Chicago Press, 1960), pp. 29–96; Milton Friedman, *A Theory of the Consumption Function* (Princeton University Press for the National Bureau of Economic Research, 1957); and Margaret G. Reid, *Housing and Income* (University of Chicago Press, 1962).

27. Twenty percent of all households change residence at least once each year (Bureau of the Census, *Current Population Reports*, Series P-20, No. 188, "Mobility of the Population of the United States: March 1967 to March 1968" [1969], Table 1), but presumably residents of owner occupied houses move less often than do renters.

28. Bureau of the Census, *1960 Censuses of Population and Housing, Procedural History*, pp. 242–47.

Table 2-7. Income and Housing Expenditures of U.S. Households, 1961

Income after taxes (dollars)	Average income before taxes (dollars)	Average total expenditures (dollars)	Average housing expenditures		
			Dollars	As percent of income	As percent of total expenditures
Under 1,000	578	1,345	491	84.9	36.5
1,000–1,999	1,544	1,837	624	40.4	34.0
2,000–2,999	2,621	2,816	844	32.2	30.0
3,000–3,999	3,728	3,727	1,065	28.6	28.6
4,000–4,999	4,914	4,557	1,231	25.1	27.0
5,000–5,999	6,040	5,427	1,511	25.0	27.8
6,000–7,499	7,501	6,360	1,725	23.0	27.1
7,500–9,999	9,706	7,781	2,052	21.1	26.4
10,000–14,999	13,595	10,114	2,592	19.1	25.6
15,000 and over	28,399	15,874	4,264	15.0	26.9
Total	6,293	5,315	1,459	23.2	27.5

Source: U.S. Bureau of Labor Statistics, *Survey of Consumer Expenditures, 1960–61*, BLS Report 237-93—USDA Report CES-15, "Consumer Expenditures and Income: Total United States, Urban and Rural, 1960–61" (1965), p. 16.

meaningless. Annual income may inadequately describe the long-term economic circumstances upon which housing expenditures depend. Table 2-7 reveals that low income households dissave while high income households save. As a result, expenditures on housing as a proportion of total expenditures are only modestly higher for households with incomes below $1,000 (36.5 percent) than for those with incomes of $15,000 or more per year (26.9 percent).

Even this difference is misleading, however. Housing expenditures frequently involve long-term commitments, such as mortgages, leases, or other contracts, so that households cannot and often do not want to alter housing expenditures when income changes, perhaps temporarily. When income drops, due to unemployment or illness, for example, a decision to move to a cheaper residence would be foolhardy unless income is expected to remain low. More typically, households maintain living standards by dissaving, going into debt, or reducing other expenditures.

The statistics in Table 2-7 are averages over households of all ages and all sizes. Homeowner families with older heads are more likely to have completed payments on home mortgages than are households with a younger head. Older households are also less likely than younger to buy such household belongings as furniture and appliances. Since money expenditures do not include imputed rental payments on owned assets, older households tend to spend less on housing than do younger households. On the other hand, at any income level larger families tend to spend less on housing than do smaller families. Because two (or more) can be housed nearly as cheaply as one (but not fed or clothed as cheaply as one), larger families must divert to other uses some part of the expenditures smaller families would make on housing. When average housing expenditures were related to average total household expenditures, family size, and the age of the household head, they proved to depend heavily on family size and age of head, but the fraction of income spent on housing was almost the same for all income classes.[29] Presumably, the quality of housing (residential) services that low income households can buy is a more important issue than the proportion of their income spent on housing.

The Housing Goal in Perspective

The national housing goal calling for construction or rehabilitation of 26 million units was enacted because of a confluence of two problems. Demographic trends indicated that demand for housing would grow during the 1970s as children born during the "baby boom" of the late 1940s and 1950s reached maturity, married, and created new households.

An increasingly affluent population raised demands for seasonal and vacation homes and for larger and better quality year-round housing. At the same time, vacancy rates were nearing the minimums necessary to sustain easy movement of population in response to shifting job opportunities and other causes of migration. The emerging housing shortage was accompanied by the failure of the United States to provide a decent home and a suitable living environment to all Americans, which the Housing Act of 1949 had promised. The housing of millions of citizens continued to be classified officially as dilapidated, deteriorating, or overcrowded. The country still had a "bad housing" problem.

The coexistence of these two housing problems created a unique political opportunity for the Johnson administration to link popular efforts to prevent a general housing shortage, which would inconvenience most Americans, with traditionally less popular programs to improve housing conditions of the poor. As presented to Congress, the national housing goal called for construction or rehabilitation of 6 million housing units with federal assistance—a massive increase over the levels of federal

29. The income elasticity of housing expenditures was estimated at 0.949. See Appendix C for the equation and source of data used for this estimate.

assistance prevailing before 1968—and of 20 million housing units *without* federal assistance. The estimates of the sources of demand and the kinds of housing to be supplied have changed since 1968; the most recent are shown in Table 2-8.

Table 2-8. Projected Housing Needs and Sources, National Housing Goal, 1969–78

In millions

Projected needs	Units	Projected sources	Units
For net household formation	13.5	Unsubsidized starts	
To increase vacancies	3.5	1–4 family structures	8.9
To replace demolitions, casualty, and other losses of nondilapidated units	2.0	5 or more family structures Subsidized starts	7.1
To replace all existing dilapidated units	1.8	Rental programs Homeownership programs Subsidized rehabilitations	2.6 2.4 1.0
To replace all units becoming dilapidated over the decade	3.5	Shipments of mobile homes Discrepancy	4.0 0.5
To replace mobile homes scrapped over the decade	1.2		
To rehabilitate nondilapidated substandard units	1.0		
National housing goal, total	26.5	National housing goal, total	26.5

Source: *Second Annual Report on National Housing Goals, Message from the President of the United States,* H. Doc. 91-292 (1970), pp. 23–24, 44–53.

The national housing goal is part forecast, part political commitment. Like all other forecasts of demand for housing and of residential construction (and, indeed, like all other political commitments), it is prey to vast uncertainties. First, if prices are flexible, the amount of any product demanded will always equal the amount supplied. Housing prices are reputedly sticky, reacting to shortages and especially to gluts only after some delay. In time, however, flexibility of housing prices will assure that demand equals supply. Forecasts of housing "needs" logically must, and in fact do, rest on popular norms about how much housing people should have and how much they should have to pay for it. Since these norms vary over time and among people, forecasts of needs cannot be objective. In addition, the forecast rests on much extremely shaky evidence.

Demographic Trends

The housing goal projects formation of 13.5 million households over the decade 1969–78. The adult population a decade hence can be forecast with some precision because death rates change slowly, birth rates are irrelevant, and net migration is minor in the United States. Household formations depend on the average age of marriage, the number of aged parents who live with children, and the number of unmarried adults who live with parents, with each other, or alone, and in fact on the availability and price of housing. The uncertainties of each of these factors cause estimates of household formations to vary. Domestic migration adds to housing demand, but only to the extent that livable units are left vacant in areas of declining population. Migration also influences the rate of demolitions, as do highway construction, urban renewal, and other public programs. Because of the many reasons that net household formations might vary, they are not a satisfactory index of that portion of housing demand due to demographic factors. To further complicate matters, migration itself is influenced by the availability of housing.

The housing goal calls, somewhat unrealistically, for the construction or rehabilitation of nearly two housing units for each new household. Between 1950 and 1969, nonfarm housing starts exceeded nonfarm net household formation by 35 percent.[30] If that rate were duplicated during the goals decade, 18.2 million units would be begun. Only during the quinquennium 1950–55, when the housing deficit accumulated during the Depression of the 1930s and perpetuated during the 1940s was largely worked off, were there more than five housing starts for every three households formed. During the period 1955–69, housing starts exceeded household formation by 28 percent. At that rate 17.3 million housing units would be built during the goals decade.

Increased Vacancies

Vacancies are a blessing to households that wish to move, but empty housing represents idle resources. Too few vacancies inhibit population mobility; but too many mean that resources that could have been used for other purposes are tied up in housing. The housing goal originally called for an increase in vacant units of 4.4 million over the goal decade; in 1970 the number was reduced to 3.5 million, still enough to increase vacancies from 9.2 percent in 1969 to 11.8 percent of the housing stock in 1978.[31]

30. U.S. Department of Housing and Urban Development, *1969 HUD Statistical Yearbook* (1970), Tables GS 14 and GS 81, pp. 327, 365.

31. *First Annual Report on National Housing Goals, Message from the President of the United States*, H. Doc. 91-63, 91 Cong. 1 sess. (1969), p. 15; *Second Annual Report on National Housing Goals, Message from the President of the United States*, H. Doc. 91-292, 91 Cong. 2 sess. (1970), p. 55.

The effort to raise vacancies during a decade of unprecedented housing demand seems oddly timed. If vacancies were to remain at a constant proportion of the housing stock, they would rise by only 1.3 million units; an increase in the vacancy rate to 10 percent would require only 2 million units.[32] Vacancies are most unlikely to rise sharply while basic housing demand is at record levels. Indeed, a protracted period of low vacancies, lasting perhaps into the 1980s, will probably be necessary to spur residential construction. As Frank S. Kristof observed, "There are few entrepreneurs who are willing to produce new housing to increase the vacancy supply."[33]

Quality Improvements

The housing goal of 1968 is more a statement of political objectives than a forecast of demand. As a conditional statement of what must be done if all Americans are to be decently housed in a suitable environment by 1978, it projects a need for construction or rehabilitation of 8 million housing units—nearly one-third of all new housing—to replace dilapidated or substandard housing units. To achieve this part of the goal would require that all occupants of substandard housing units have enough income or subsidies to acquire standard housing. In addition, they would have to be forced to use this purchasing power to buy standard housing. As Table 2-4 shows, some families in most income and net worth classes inhabit dilapidated (and therefore substandard) or deteriorating housing. None of the housing programs yet devised reaches only those families in substandard housing. Moreover, vacated substandard units may be reoccupied many times over a decade. To remove all substandard units would require housing assistance for many more than 8 million households if substandard units are to be kept vacant. By 1978, in all probability, substandard housing will have been reduced but not eradicated.[34]

Wholesale revisions since 1968 have undermined confidence in the housing goal. First, some of the unassisted starts scheduled for the first half of the decade were pushed back into the second half, then the number of unassisted conventional starts was reduced as the concept of housing

32. *Second Annual Report on National Housing Goals*, p. 55.

33. *Urban Housing Needs Through the 1980's: An Analysis and Projection*, Prepared for the Consideration of the National Commission on Urban Problems, Research Report 10 (Government Printing Office, 1968), p. 42.

34. Kristof estimates that the number of substandard units will drop from 11.4 million in 1959 to 6.9 million in 1969, 3.8 million in 1979, and 2.1 million in 1989 (ibid., p. 22).

unit was broadened to include 4 million mobile homes. Between 1968 and 1970 unassisted housing starts projected for 1970, 1971, and 1972 were cut by one-third. About the only constant has been the total units to be started or rehabilitated with federal assistance, which has been in the 26–26.5 million units range in all versions.

Rhetoric or Reality?

A housing goal predicated on implausible increases in the number of vacancies and on unprecedented private unassisted construction is unlikely to generate widespread confidence. Even if the goal is feasible, the question remains whether public policy makers have the will to undertake the policies necessary to meet the assisted portion of the goal or the ability to persuade the private sector to meet the unassisted portion; does the goal represent, on the one hand, the substitution of "rhetoric for reality,"[35] or a "pipedream,"[36] or, on the other hand, "the product of knowledge, experience, imagination, and conviction."[37] Thus far the pessimistic view appears to be correct. One forecast suggests that, depending on economic and monetary conditions, housing output will fall short of the goal by 1.6 to 4.0 million units.[38] Even if the goals were achieved, they would not directly affect the quality of residential services consumed with housing. The hope held out by the housing goal that both the "too little" and the "bad" housing problem can be solved is certain to be frustrated because the improvement of residential services depends on other programs that have not been undertaken.

Summary

Public awareness of the housing problem is shaped by statistics that are conceptually inadequate and empirically inaccurate. They refer to housing alone, not to the package of residential services that households buy and

35. Anthony Downs ("Moving Toward Realistic Housing Goals," in Kermit Gordon [ed.], *Agenda for the Nation* [Brookings Institution, 1968], p. 177), quoted by Robert C. Wood, in *National Housing Goals*, Hearings before the Subcommittee on Housing of the House Committee on Banking and Currency, 91 Cong. 1 sess. (1969), pp. 114–15.

36. Ada Louise Huxtable, quoted by Wood, in ibid.

37. Wood, in ibid.

38. Charles L. Schultze and others, *Setting National Priorities: The 1972 Budget* (Brookings Institution, 1971), p. 287.

on which their satisfaction or discontent depends. Their compilation demands greater judgment than census enumerators or even real estate experts can consistently apply. Other statistics—on the availability of appliances, on overcrowding, and on other objectively measurable attributes—are more accurate. Only a few local indexes of housing quality based on objective data have been compiled.

The national housing goal that is based on these figures and on projections is itself an expression more of political commitment than of realistic forecasting. Prospects for achieving the housing goal are dubious, but even if unassisted housing production falls far short of the goal, housing quality will continue to improve for most Americans. However, if federally assisted housing starts do not progress at levels projected in the goal, poor and lower middle income families will find it increasingly difficult to improve their housing circumstances as millions of new households bid for available housing. Neither success nor failure in the housing effort will affect directly the adequacy of other residential services that form a large part of the housing problem.

chapter three **Housing**
Policies
and
Income
Distribution

Housing policies affect income distribution in various ways. Even the simplest of policies—a universal housing subsidy—would have at least three distinct effects on income distribution; it would alter the net price of housing services for all recipients of the subsidy, alter incomes by changing relative wage and profit levels, and further alter the price of housing services by changing construction costs or through filtering. These effects are examined in this chapter, and a model is established for measuring the distributional effects of housing policies. Most actual housing policies are far more complex than a universal subsidy. Succeeding chapters present estimates of the income redistribution caused by major federal housing policies.

The Incidence of Subsidies

Such federal programs as public housing, rent supplements, and income tax benefits for homeowners directly reduce the price of housing. The several federal interest subsidy programs seek the same objective indirectly, through credit subsidies to builders or owners whose benefits are intended for tenants.

On Recipients

These policies result in budget costs to the federal government and sometimes to state and municipal governments. They also result in benefits to tenants. If benefits equaled costs less administrative expenses, the amount to be distributed could be easily determined, though identification of program beneficiaries might be difficult.

Unfortunately, the matter is not so simple. Suppose, for example, a friend gives you a new gold-plated cigarette lighter costing $50. Moreover, he has had your initials engraved on the lighter, so that you cannot exchange it for anything else. How much is the gift worth to you? The answer depends both on your need and on your preferences. If forced to choose between cash and the lighter, you could probably settle on some amount, say, $20, that would make you indifferent. In economic terms the cigarette lighter would have brought a benefit of $20 for you; the remaining $30 is "deadweight" loss, a cost incurred that generated no benefits for you.[1] Thus the benefit of the gift to the recipient would be $20 rather than the $50 cost incurred by the giver. The difference between cost and benefit is likely to be greater the more remote the gift is from usual purchases by the recipient; if the gift had been a shirt the deadweight loss would likely have been very small, if a dozen eggs none at all. In short, gifts that lead the recipient to consume more of a product than he would have consumed if the gift were cash provide him benefits worth less than cost; gifts that do not distort his pattern of consumption bring the recipient benefits equal to cost.

Public subsidies are undertaken for many reasons other than improving the self-perceived well-being of recipients;[2] benefits may also accrue to neighbors of the recipient or to all citizens of the city or country in which he lives. The essential point is to distinguish among benefits to the recipient, benefits to others, and costs.

Housing subsidies are not gifts. They reduce prices, but usually not to zero. The recipient normally must spend some of his own income to qualify for a subsidy. Usually he will spend less than he would have spent without the subsidy and in most cases he will occupy better housing. Subsidies may be offered either on a certain quantity of housing or on as much housing as the recipient wants. (All U.S. housing programs set a ceiling on the value of assisted units.) Figure 3-1 portrays both situations

---

1. People give products rather than cash because the giver derives certain benefits that offset deadweight loss. Gifts of "products" indicate "thoughtfulness" and may conceal actual expenditures. Public policy makers do not aim for thoughtfulness in this sense. That they wish to practice an analogous form of deception is perhaps harder to dismiss.

2. See Chapter 1, pp. 1–22.

Figure 3-1. Demand Response to a Housing Subsidy

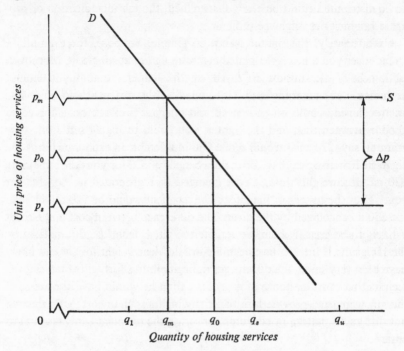

Quantity of housing services

The demand curve D shows the amount of services a typical household would demand at various prices. The supply curve S is drawn as if the supply of housing services were perfectly elastic at the market price p_m;[3] at that price, households wish to buy q_m units of housing services. At a subsidized price of p_s, households would like to buy q_s units of housing services. The public cost of the subsidy will be $\$(\Delta p \times q_s)$, where Δp is the amount of the subsidy. The cost to households will be $\$(p_s \times q_s)$; whether this amount is greater or smaller than the cost of unsubsidized housing $\$(p_m \times q_m)$ will depend on how much purchases increase in response to the subsidized price.

When the subsidy is an all-or-nothing offer, as under low rent public housing, the quantity, q_u, may be more than the recipient can afford. (By analogy, Rolls Royces may provide more automobile services than Volkswagens, but many owners would choose Volkswagens even if Rolls Royces

3. See Richard F. Muth, "The Demand for Non-Farm Housing," in Arnold C. Harberger (ed.), *The Demand for Durable Goods* (University of Chicago Press, 1960), pp. 29–96.

carried a 50 percent subsidy.) At the other extreme, the subsidy may be provided on condition that the household buy so few housing services q_1 that it would reject the subsidy. In most cases the amount of housing services the recipient must buy lies between these extremes, say at q_0.[4]

The benefit to the recipient of the subsidy typically is smaller than the public cost of the subsidy. As in the cigarette lighter example, it equals the unrestricted cash transfer that would leave the recipient as well off without the subsidy as he is with it; the exact amount of the benefit is impossible to determine.

Just as an individual may choose to give a cigarette lighter worth less to the recipient than its cash value, so may the public rationally provide housing subsidies worth less to occupants than their cost. For each dollar spent on an open-ended 50 percent housing subsidy, the benefit to the household can plausibly be estimated to equal approximately 75 cents in cash.[5] For smaller subsidies the deadweight loss is smaller; for larger subsidies it is larger. If the subsidy is not open ended, the deadweight loss may be greater or smaller than if the subsidy is open ended.[6] This difference suggests that costs of housing subsidies overstate benefits to direct recipients. Housing subsidies must produce significant social benefits if they are to be judged better than cash transfers as devices for improving consumer welfare.

On Labor and Capital

Housing programs indirectly change incomes of far more households than those they reach directly through subsidies. Assume a policy of subsidy payments to all households equal to some fraction of the cost of housing services.[7] Assume that only two goods—housing services and a composite of all other goods—exist; that each is produced with two factors

4. The reactions illustrated in Figure 3-1 may also be portrayed with indifference curves; see Appendix C.

5. See Henry J. Aaron and George M. von Furstenberg, "The Inefficiency of Transfers in Kind: The Case of Housing Assistance," *Western Economic Journal*, Vol. 9 (June 1971), pp. 184–91 (Brookings Reprint 210).

6. The deadweight loss is necessarily greater if the household is required to purchase more than q_s in housing services, since beyond q_s household welfare falls while subsidy costs increase. At one point between q_s and q_m, housing subsidies are as efficient as cash transfers in raising the welfare of the recipient.

7. Renters would be subsidized on the basis of actual costs, owners on the basis of imputed housing costs. The fair market rental of a homeowner occupant's house is his imputed cost as tenant; it is offset by his imputed income as landlord. See Chapter 4.

of production—capital and labor—under competitive conditions; and that all household income is of two kinds—wages and salaries for labor performed, or rent, interest, and profits on capital goods.[8] Capital goods include the stock of housing and machines, structures, and inventories used in producing other goods. The capital stock grows over time by the net saving of households and businesses. Assume further that the savings rate depends only on income and other socioeconomic factors, such as family size or wealth, and is unaffected by the rate of return to savers through rent, interest, and profits, and that all families have the same spending propensities. The supply of labor depends only on population growth. Both labor and capital can move freely between industries.

This approach vastly oversimplifies the economy. It fails to differentiate among goods other than housing. It presumes that competition is pure, that businessmen work always to maximize profits, and that workers always seek the highest wages. It also assumes that taxes imposed to support the housing subsidy affect all incomes proportionately. Despite these implausible assumptions, most economists feel that useful inferences can be drawn from such a model of the economy.

The impact of a universal housing subsidy on incomes—on wage rates and the yield on capital—hinges on the relative amounts of labor and capital used in the production of housing services and other goods. Production of housing services is among the most capital intensive activities in the U.S. economy. Housing services require the combination of more capital—the house or apartment—per unit of labor—maintenance and, in rental units, managerial services—than does any other major category of consumer or investment goods.[9] Production of the housing stock is not nearly so capital intensive as the production of services.

A housing subsidy will increase consumption of housing services and necessarily cause the housing stock to grow. Capital to produce more housing services must be withdrawn from the production of other goods. The labor released simultaneously from the production of other goods will

8. See Peter M. Mieszkowski, "On the Theory of Tax Incidence," *Journal of Political Economy*, Vol. 75 (June 1967), pp. 250–62, and "Tax Incidence Theory: The Effects of Taxes on the Distribution of Income," *Journal of Economic Literature*, Vol. 7 (December 1969), pp. 1103–24; and Arnold C. Harberger, "The Incidence of the Corporation Income Tax," *Journal of Political Economy*, Vol. 70 (June 1962), pp. 215–40.

9. Edward F. Denison has described the contribution of labor as "almost negligible" in *Why Growth Rates Differ: Postwar Experience in Nine Western Countries* (Brookings Institution, 1967), p. 124.

not be fully absorbed in the more capital intensive production of housing services unless production methods change. Labor can be fully employed only if producers adopt somewhat less capital intensive methods of production. Workers would then be less productive relative to a unit of capital, and wages and salaries would tend to decline relative to the yield from capital. The pressure on wages would be diffused throughout the economy because of labor's mobility.

Not only would this adjustment in wages to increased demand for a capital intensive good work slowly and unevenly, but technological advances and increased education would be constantly raising labor productivity. Real wage levels might rise continuously. However, increased demand for a good that requires more capital per unit of labor than the economywide average will tend to raise the yield on capital relative to wages. Accordingly, households whose incomes are derived largely from rent, interest, and profits will tend to gain at the expense of those with incomes principally in wages and salaries.

If the model is relaxed to include three commodities—housing structures, housing services, and a composite of all other goods—the conclusions may vary. The production of housing services is highly capital intensive; however, the production of structures is relatively labor intensive.[10] A subsidy will encourage the consumption of more housing services which in turn will cause the desired stock of structures to increase. Growth and maintenance of the stock will tend to raise wages in the labor intensive construction industry. Increased consumption of capital intensive housing services, on the other hand, will tend to raise the yield on capital. During the period when the stock of residential structures is expanding to meet increased demand for housing services, the relative impact of housing subsidies on capital and labor income is unpredictable. Once construction activity returns to normal levels, however, the increased demand for housing services would increase the yield on capital—rent, interest, and profits—relative to wages and salaries.

10. Direct labor requirements constituted 80 percent of gross product less indirect business taxes originating in contract construction in 1970, a larger fraction than in all other major private sectors of the economy except for finance and insurance (89 percent) (U.S. Department of Commerce, Office of Business Economics, *Survey of Current Business*, Vol. 51 [July 1971], Table 1.22, p. 21). The figures do not include labor embodied in products purchased by the construction industry. They do include nonresidential construction, which is probably not so labor intensive as residential construction.

On Consumers

To the extent that programs to encourage consumption of housing services increase the yield on capital, they influence the relative prices of all commodities. The prices of commodities produced with high ratios of capital to labor will rise relative to those with low ratios. Households with high expenditures for goods produced by relatively capital intensive methods (for example, gasoline or automobiles) will lose, those that concentrate on relatively labor intensive goods (for example, doctors' services or restaurant meals) will gain. Those who are not direct program beneficiaries will pay more for housing than they would if such programs did not exist.

In summary, each household is affected in three ways by housing subsidies. Those who receive the subsidy are encouraged by reduced costs to consume more housing services. The total demand for a capital intensive product rises, driving up the return on capital relative to that on labor. As a result, the price of all capital intensive goods rises relative to that of all labor intensive goods to the benefit of consumers who spend more of their incomes than average on labor intensive goods and to the detriment of those who spend less.

These effects are not uniformly applicable. For example, labor includes many skills that are not freely transferable from one industry to another. Although an increase in the consumption of housing services may raise the yield on capital relative to the general level of wages and salaries, some wages and salaries may rise sharply. Construction workers, for example, will gain if others cannot freely enter the construction industry, and workers in some relatively labor intensive occupations may gain if entry of additional labor is limited.

In addition, the relative price of various kinds of housing may shift, so that housing displaced through subsidy programs filters through to nonrecipients of the subsidy. If filtering works well, such benefits will be widespread and large. Most public policies subsidize demand by particular households for particular kinds of housing. They reduce the supply of certain kinds of housing—usually low quality housing (consumed by the poor)—and increase the supply of others—high quality housing (consumed by the nonpoor). By changing the supply of different kinds of housing, these policies change the cost of housing to various groups. Because the housing stock does not adjust instantaneously to changes in demand, policies that increase demand for certain kinds of housing may drive prices up, generating benefits not for the recipient of the subsidy but for previous property owners or for speculators. Who will lose or gain will depend on the speed and efficiency of filtering,[11] the net change in the housing stock, and the relative quality of the units added to or removed from the housing stock. At least as important as the direction of housing subsidies is their size. Whether a program to subsidize home purchases by the poor immediately results in lower housing costs for the poor or tends to drive up the price of housing units available to the recipients of the subsidy is crucial in appraising such a program. And how such a subsidy affects prices for ineligible families who want similar housing is also of more than passing interest. Answers to these questions depend on the speed and vigor with which federal agencies implement programs and with which consumers, investors, and municipal and state officials react to new conditions.

An important adjunct of housing services not calculated in the distributional consequences of housing subsidies is the locationally fixed residential services.[12] The real benefits to families moving from unsubsidized to subsidized housing depend not only on changes in the quality of housing services, but also on the relative qualities of schools, police protection, transportation, and other urban services.

Institutional Changes

Some of the most important federal policies to improve housing conditions have altered the institutional framework within which businessmen and consumers make their decisions. These policies include the provision of mortgage insurance and loan guarantees, the creation of such financial intermediaries as the Federal National Mortgage Association (FNMA), the Government National Mortgage Association (GNMA), and the Federal Home Loan Bank Board, and the encouragement of adoption of building and housing codes by municipalities.

All of these measures except the last have widened the range of consumer choice. Mortgage insurance was not generally available before the Federal Housing Administration (FHA) provided it. The willingness of FNMA to purchase FHA mortgages under certain conditions differentiated them still further from conventional mortgages. Whatever their quantitative significance, these measures created new options for lenders to invest in mortgages and facilitated a revolution after World War II

---

11. For a discussion of filtering, see Chapter 1 above.
12. See Chapters 1 and 2.

in the mortgage terms available to borrowers. By contrast, building and housing codes prohibit the sale or rental of housing built or maintained below certain standards. Such codes are intended to reduce predatory or exploitive practices by unscrupulous builders or owners. They also deny to low income households the option of occupying housing unacceptable by middle class tastes but perhaps preferable to that the poor can afford.

Each of these public actions affects the real incomes of households by enabling them to borrow more cheaply or by compelling them to occupy better or more costly housing than they might otherwise prefer. They affect real incomes not primarily by subsidizing or taxing certain behavior, but rather by creating institutions or erecting prohibitions or requirements. Such programs may cost little or nothing, but they may provide substantial gains or inflict large losses. Though these institutional policies may entail subsidies, their consequences may bear little relation to the cost of such subsidies; their benefits are far more difficult to analyze than those of subsidies or taxes.

Estimates of Direct Benefits

Housing policies affect income distribution in a bewildering variety of ways. The process through which these effects occur is complex, even within the oversimplified model suggested in this chapter. Zoning, building and housing codes, racial discrimination, and the provision of urban services may influence who is affected by federal housing policies and how fast. In addition, institutional changes induced by federal policies produce gains and, in some cases, losses. It is not possible to measure how much these forces change real incomes of various groups. This study identifies only the direct beneficiaries of housing programs and estimates benefits to those groups. The impact of housing programs on relative payments to labor and capital receives scant attention. This course is dictated by two considerations. First, except for benefits to direct program beneficiaries, the net consequences of policies to encourage consumption of housing services are uncertain. Second, direct recipients of program benefits can be identified. Chapters 4 through 9 review six major groups of federal housing programs. Except in Chapter 6 on federal credit institutions, direct program beneficiaries are identified by income and certain other characteristics. A rough indication of the value of institutional change is presented in Chapter 5 on mortgage insurance and loan guarantees.

chapter four **Taxes**
and
Housing

The murky provisions of the Internal Revenue Code
contain the most important housing programs currently administered by
the federal government. One "program" costs the Treasury at least $7
billion per year. It subsidizes nearly every homeowner in the United States.
Others provide benefits to most renters. Despite their cost and pervasive-
ness, these programs receive negligible scrutiny within government and,
except for occasional academic analysis, almost none from outside the
government.

This chapter contains new estimates of the impact on income distribution
of personal income tax provisions relating to housing. The tax benefits to
homeowners are equivalent to a reduction in the price of housing. The
benefits rise with taxable income. Other significant tax advantages of
homeowners reinforce those provided by the personal income tax.

Favorable Treatment of Homeowners

The personal income tax encourages taxpayers to buy rather than rent
housing by making the tax bill of homeowners smaller than that of renters
who invest in other assets. Table 4-1 shows the tax liabilities of a renter and
an owner, each of whom earns $15,000 per year, occupies housing with a
market value of $3,750 per year, and has $37,500 in assets. All assets of the
renter yield taxable income. The homeowner holds $15,000 of his assets as
equity in his home. He receives no cash income from his home, but he could
have invested in other assets and earned $600, or he could have rented the
house for $3,750, netting $600 after he had paid $3,150 in housing ex-

Table 4-1. Personal Tax Liabilities of Renter and Homeowner with Equivalent Earnings, Assets, and Expenses[a]

In dollars

Item	Renter	Homeowner
Income		
Earnings	15,000	15,000
From assets of $37,500		
Interest (at 4 percent)	1,500	900
Imputed net rent on $15,000 equity in house	...	(600)
Money income	16,500	15,900
Housing cost[b]		
Money expenditure	3,750	3,150
Imputed net rent	...	(600)
Residual money income	12,750	12,750
Taxable income		
Money income	16,500	15,900
Less standard deductions and personal exemptions	5,000	5,000
Less mortgage interest and property taxes	...	2,100
Total	11,500	8,800
Tax liability	2,150	1,556

Source: Adapted from Richard Goode, "Imputed Rent of Owner Occupied Dwellings Under the Income Tax," *Journal of Finance*, Vol. 15 (December 1960), pp. 505–06.

a. Based on 1972 tax rates for a four-person household with no members age 65 or over. Renter claims standard deduction of $2,000 and personal exemptions of $3,000; homeowner itemizes and claims as deductions $2,100 in mortgage interest and property taxes, $2,000 in other deductions, and personal exemptions of $3,000.

b. Real housing costs are 25 percent of earnings for both renter and owner. Costs of homeownership include $600 net profit or net imputed rent, $1,350 in mortgage interest (6 percent on a $22,500 mortgage), $750 in property taxes, and $1,050 for maintenance and depreciation.

penses. Actually, the homeowner is playing two separable roles; he is a tenant who pays "imputed" rent to the landlord, and he is a real estate investor who receives "imputed" rental income from his "tenant." Since the same person plays both roles, no cash changes hands.

A neutral tax system would levy the same tax on the owner and renter. In fact, as Table 4-1 illustrates, the United States collects a larger personal income tax from the renter than from the homeowner. Three aspects of the Internal Revenue Code explain this differential. If the homeowner were taxed like other investors, he would have to report as gross income the rent he could have obtained on his house. He would be allowed deductions for maintenance, depreciation, mortgage interest, and property taxes as expenses incurred in earning income. The difference, or net rent, would be his taxable income. In fact, rather than paying a tax on his imputed net rent he is allowed to deduct mortgage interest and property taxes from his gross income.[1] The taxable income of a homeowner is thus below that of other investors by the sum of net rent, mortgage interest, and property taxes. This understatement—$2,700 in Table 4-1—explains the $594 difference between tax liabilities of owner and renter.

Impact on Revenues

Homeowners paid $7 billion less in taxes in 1966 than they would have if they had been governed by the rules applicable to investors in other assets. This amount is 16.7 percent of the $42 billion collected from homeowners under the personal income tax in 1966. The change in the 1966 tax liabilities of homeowners under three alternative sets of rules would be approximately as follows:[2]

Alternative rule	*Increase in revenue, in billions of dollars*
1. Disallow homeowner deductions for property tax and mortgage interest	2.9
2. Include imputed net rent in taxable income of homeowners	4.0
3. Include imputed net rent and disallow deductions for homeowners	7.0

Except for tax provisions related to accelerated depreciation, homeowners governed by rule 3 would be on a roughly equal tax footing with investors in other assets and with renters.[3]

Favorable treatment of homeowners, like many provisions of the tax code, causes tax liabilities to differ sharply within each income bracket among various socioeconomic groups.[4] In each bracket, homeowners pay

1. Symbolically, $R_N = R_G - (M + D + I + T)$, where R_N is net rent, R_G gross rent, M maintenance expense, D depreciation, I mortgage interest, and T property taxes. Homeowners may deduct $I + T$. Other investors must report R_N. The homeowners' taxable income is understated by $R_N + I + T$.

2. This and other estimates in this chapter were computed from a sample of 90,000 federal tax returns for 1966 on file at the Brookings Institution. Revenue effects are those that would occur immediately; eventually the pattern of homeownership and the size of the housing stock would change substantially, altering revenue collections.

3. The revenue effect under rule 3 is greater than the sum of the revenue effects under rules 1 and 2 because some taxpayers become subject to higher marginal tax rates when the two sets of changes are made simultaneously than they are when each is made independently.

4. See Melvin and Anne White, "Horizontal Inequality in the Federal Tax Treatment of Homeowners and Tenants," *National Tax Journal*, Vol. 18 (September 1965), pp. 225–59 (Brookings Reprint 114).

Table 4-2. Increase in 1966 Federal Individual Income Tax Collections under Alternative Rules for Reporting Homeowner Income[a]

In millions of dollars

Category	Increase under		
	Rule 1[b]	Rule 2[c]	Rule 3[d]
All homeowners	2,904	4,017	6,982
Homeowners under 65 years old	...	3,659	6,394
Itemized deductions	2,685	2,543	5,279
Standard deduction	...	1,115	1,115
Homeowners 65 and older	...	358	588
Itemized deductions	219	287	517
Standard deduction	...	71	71

Source: Estimated from a sample of 90,000 federal individual income tax returns for 1966 on file at the Brookings Institution. Figures are rounded and may not add to totals.

a. Total income equals adjusted gross income plus excluded dividends, excluded sick pay, and imputed rent. Capital gains and losses are included in income in full in the year realized, but no losses carried forward from previous years are deducted. Total income does not include unrealized capital gains, tax exempt interest, or the excess of percentage over cost depletion on income from natural resources.

b. Mortgage interest and property tax deductions not allowed.

c. Imputed net rent on owner occupied houses included in taxable income.

d. Imputed net rent included in taxable income; mortgage interest and property tax deductions not allowed.

less tax than do nonhomeowners. The aged pay less than those under 65 years old. Taxpayers with sufficient deductions to itemize pay less than those who claim the standard deduction (see Table D-1, Appendix D).

The consequences of taxing homeowners more fully are shown in Table 4-2. Adoption of any of the suggested alternatives would require other fiscal or monetary adjustments—lowered taxes, increased expenditures, or lowered interest rates—to prevent unemployment. Each compensating policy would have distributional consequences of its own. For example, if rule 3 had been adopted, an overall cut in income tax rates of about 12 percent would have left income tax collections unchanged in 1966, at $56 billion. The net loss to homeowners would be the excess of their increased homeowner taxes over their decreased general taxes. Renters would gain through the 12 percent cut in income taxes. The effects of compensatory policies are ignored in this chapter in order that the effect of current tax advantages of homeownership may stand out more clearly.

Deductibility of mortgage interest and property taxes reduced 1966 revenues by $2.9 billion.[5] Overall, 90 percent of the tax savings accrued to households with incomes above $7,000, 70 percent to families with incomes

5. Deductibility of mortgage interest alone reduced revenues by $1.6 billion, of property taxes alone by $1.5 billion. Disallowing both deductions increases revenues by only $2.9 billion because more taxpayers take standard deductions when both are disallowed than when either is disallowed separately.

over $10,000 per year (see Table D-2, Appendix D). This saving accrues entirely to homeowners who itemize deductions. As a fraction of income, tax savings rise for all homeowners with annual incomes up to $25,000. Deductibility is worth less to the aged than to those under 65 in each income bracket because they tend to have paid off more of their mortgage debt than younger taxpayers. Less than 8 percent of the revenue forgone accrues as tax savings to the aged and less than half of that to those aged with incomes under $10,000.[6]

The failure to tax imputed net rent generates tax savings worth even more—$4 billion—than the two deductibility provisions combined. Eighty percent of that savings accrues to families with incomes of more than $7,000 per year, more than 60 percent to households with incomes over $10,000 (see Table D-3, Appendix D). Less than one-tenth of the benefits accrue to the aged, only 2 percent to aged taxpayers with less than $7,000 of income. The exclusion of imputed rent helps all homeowners, for imputed rent would raise adjusted gross income and taxable income whether or not a household itemized deductions.[7] As a fraction of income, the benefits from nontaxability of imputed rent are highest for taxpayers in the lowest bracket, which includes many households with temporarily depressed incomes. The fraction rises over the income range of $5,000 to $50,000.

The full revenue loss from favorable treatment of income from homeownership is shown in Table 4-3. Most of the benefits accrue to households with incomes of more than $10,000. Less than one-tenth accrues to the aged, less than 2 percent to aged with incomes of $5,000 per year or less. In each income bracket, homeowners systematically pay lower taxes than renters. Abolition of homeowner privileges would narrow the difference in tax treatment between homeowners and other taxpayers.[8] Such narrowing occurs for virtually all taxpayers in the tax brackets between $3,000 and $25,000.[9] In the lowest and highest income brackets the pattern is more diverse, partly because households that carry forward losses and report capital gains, which crucially influence effective tax rates, are concentrated in top and bottom brackets.[10]

6. Income does *not* include social security payments.
7. Table 4-2 understates the revenue forgone by the amount that would be paid by present nonfilers whose imputed rent would force them to file returns.
8. See Melvin and Anne White, "Horizontal Inequality in the Federal Income Tax Treatment of Homeowners and Tenants."
9. The only exceptions are households headed by those 65 and older with incomes between $7,000 and $15,000 who do not itemize deductions. See Table D-4, Appendix D.
10. Homeowners would be taxed more heavily than nonhomeowners if less of their current income were realized from net long-term capital gains or their losses carried forward were smaller than those of nonhomeowners.

Table 4-3. Increase in 1966 Federal Individual Income Tax Collections If Imputed Net Rent on Owner Occupied Houses Were Taxed and Mortgage Interest and Property Tax Deductions Were Disallowed, by Income Bracket, Age, and Type of Deduction[a]

Item	Income bracket (dollars)									Total tax savings (millions of dollars)
	Under 3,000	3,000–5,000	5,000–7,000	7,000–10,000	10,000–15,000	15,000–25,000	25,000–50,000	50,000–100,000	Over 100,000	
All returns										
Increase in tax per family, in dollars	12	29	56	103	190	351	736	1,179	2,308	...
Increase in tax as percent of income	0.9	0.7	0.9	1.2	1.6	1.9	2.2	1.8	1.0	...
Tax as percent of income	4.7	7.6	9.1	10.3	12.3	15.0	19.8	26.7	30.0	...
Increase in total tax, in millions of dollars	253	328	544	1,359	1,986	1,256	770	318	169	6,982
Homeowners										
Increase in tax per family, in dollars	40	77	93	146	237	414	830	1,283	2,440	...
Increase in tax as percent of income	2.6	1.9	1.5	1.7	2.0	2.3	2.5	1.9	1.1	...
Tax as percent of income	5.5	7.4	9.0	10.2	12.3	14.9	19.9	26.8	30.1	...
Increase in total tax, in millions of dollars	253	328	544	1,359	1,986	1,256	770	318	169	6,982
Under 65 years old										
Increase in tax per family, in dollars	42	77	92	146	238	420	836	1,244	2,282	...
Increase in tax as percent of income	2.8	1.9	1.5	1.7	2.0	2.3	2.5	1.9	1.0	...
Tax as percent of income	6.1	7.9	9.1	10.2	12.3	15.0	20.0	27.0	29.8	...
Increase in total tax, in millions of dollars	226	263	486	1,291	1,913	1,190	667	247	110	6,394
Itemized deductions										
Increase in tax per family, in dollars	82	105	127	178	267	442	865	1,269	2,316	...
Increase in tax as percent of income	6.2	2.6	2.1	2.1	2.2	2.4	2.6	1.9	1.1	...
Tax as percent of income	13.0	7.5	8.1	9.7	12.0	14.9	19.9	26.9	29.8	...
Increase in total tax, in millions of dollars	38	140	302	1,023	1,668	1,117	641	242	109	5,279

Standard deduction										
Increase in tax per family in dollars	38	60	64	87	136	239	462	644	919	...
Increase in tax as percent of income	*2.5*	*1.5*	*1.1*	*1.0*	*1.1*	*1.3*	*1.3*	*1.0*	*0.5*	*...*
Tax as percent of income	*5.5*	*8.2*	*9.9*	*11.2*	*13.3*	*16.1*	*21.9*	*29.0*	*28.1*	*...*
Increase in total tax, in millions of dollars	188	123	185	268	245	73	27	5	1	1,115
65 and older										
Increase in tax per family, in dollars	31	77	105	148	210	333	790	1,441	2,804	...
Increase in tax as percent of income	*1.7*	*2.0*	*1.8*	*1.8*	*1.7*	*1.8*	*2.3*	*2.1*	*1.2*	*...*
Tax as percent of income	*2.6*	*5.0*	*7.7*	*9.6*	*11.9*	*13.9*	*19.4*	*25.7*	*30.8*	*...*
Increase in total tax, in millions of dollars	27	65	58	68	73	66	103	70	59	588
Itemized deductions										
Increase in tax per family, in dollars	55	82	117	166	231	362	804	1,465	2,832	...
Increase in tax as percent of income	*2.6*	*2.1*	*2.0*	*2.0*	*1.9*	*1.9*	*2.3*	*2.2*	*1.2*	*...*
Tax as percent of income	*3.7*	*4.9*	*7.4*	*9.0*	*11.6*	*13.8*	*19.4*	*25.9*	*30.9*	*...*
Increase in total tax, in millions of dollars	13	50	52	59	62	56	98	69	58	517
Standard deduction										
Increase in tax per family, in dollars	22	62	57	87	136	223	589	697	1,055	...
Increase in tax as percent of income	*1.3*	*1.6*	*0.9*	*1.0*	*1.1*	*1.2*	*1.8*	*1.0*	*0.6*	*...*
Tax as percent of income	*2.0*	*5.4*	*8.9*	*11.5*	*12.8*	*14.3*	*19.4*	*21.4*	*24.4*	*...*
Increase in total tax, in millions of dollars	14	15	6	9	11	9	5	1	*	71

Source: Estimated from Brookings tax file. Figures are rounded and may not add to totals.

* Less than $500,000.

a. Total income equals adjusted gross income plus excluded dividends, excluded sick pay, and imputed rent. Capital gains and losses are included in income in full in the year realized but no losses carried forward from previous years are deducted. Total income does not include unrealized capital gains, tax exempt interest, or income from natural resources in excess of cost depletion allowance.

Response to Favorable Treatment

The tax benefits to homeowners shown in Tables 4-2 and 4-3 are broken down by age and type of tax deduction of recipients. The tabulations do not relate the size of the benefits to the cost of housing. They do not indicate how many people became homeowners or increased their consumption of housing services because of tax benefits.

The Price Equivalent of Tax Benefits

Current income tax provisions understate income by the sum of imputed net rent, mortgage interest, and property taxes, and tax liability by the amount that would otherwise be collected on that income. The size of tax benefits relative to the annual cost of housing services depends on the degree to which taxable income of homeowners is understated and on the tax rate applicable to that income. The percentage reductions in homeownership costs are negligible for low bracket households who reside in houses with high maintenance and depreciation costs (see Table 4-4). The subsidy is very large for high bracket households whose maintenance and depreciation costs are low. For example, a homeowner in the 50 percent bracket whose imputed rent, mortgage interest, and property taxes equal his maintenance and depreciation costs receives a tax benefit worth one-fourth of his housing costs.

The composition of gross rents of owner occupied houses is unknown. A

Table 4-4. Reduction in Homeownership Costs as a Result of Favorable Tax Treatment, by Tax Bracket

In percent

Tax benefits as fraction of imputed gross rent[a]	Tax bracket (percent)				
	14	20	30	50	70
One-eighth	1.8	2.5	3.8	6.2	8.8
One-fourth	3.5	5.0	7.5	12.5	17.5
Three-eighths	5.2	7.5	11.2	18.8	26.2
One-half	7.0	10.0	15.0	25.0	35.0
Five-eighths	8.8	12.5	18.8	31.2	43.8
Three-fourths	10.5	15.0	22.5	37.5	52.5
Seven-eighths	12.2	17.5	26.2	43.8	61.2
One	14.0	20.0	30.0	50.0	70.0

a. Benefits are the sum of imputed net rent, mortgage interest, and property taxes.

rule of thumb of the real estate market suggests that annual rents on single-family houses run 10–12 percent of market price.[11] Maintenance plus depreciation has been estimated at 2–6.5 percent of market value.[12] The remaining, tax favored, elements (mortgage interest, property taxes, and imputed net rent) would constitute at least one-third and as much as five-sixths of gross rent; Laidler estimates tax favored elements at 68 percent of gross rent.[13] The fraction of gross rent accounted for by tax favored items probably rises with income, for as property value rises, so does the portion of that value represented by land.[14]

The plausible range of benefits runs from roughly 5 percent of gross rent in the lowest tax brackets to more than 50 percent in the highest; homeowners with no taxable income receive no benefits. The tax benefits make it increasingly likely, as taxable income moves from zero up the income scale, that ownership would be preferred to renting.

Primary Market Effects of Subsidies

The implicit subsidies to owner occupants may initially affect them in two ways. As consumers, they find that the subsidies lower the cost of homeownership relative to renting (and other consumer goods). As investors, they find that after-tax income from their housing investment is greater than that from other investments. In response to these advantages, some households that have rented will buy their own residence. Some owners will choose a more valuable residence. How many renters the tax laws have induced to become homeowners is not known.

The overall change in housing demand caused by tax benefits for homeowners can, however, be estimated. The price elasticity of demand for

11. This rule evolved when interest rates were below current levels. Whether the trend toward higher interest rates would cause that rule to be altered is not clear. To the extent that the rise in interest rates is due to anticipated inflation rather than to an increase in the real rate of time preference, anticipated depreciation would tend to fall or anticipated appreciation would tend to increase as much as interest rates change. For this reason, however, inflation raises tax benefits to homeowners.

12. See John P. Shelton, "The Cost of Renting Versus Owning a Home," *Land Economics*, Vol. 44 (February 1968), pp. 65, 67.

13. David Laidler, "Income Tax Incentives for Owner-Occupied Housing," in Arnold C. Harberger and Martin J. Bailey (eds.), *The Taxation of Income from Capital* (Brookings Institution, 1969), p. 61.

14. See Allen D. Manvel, "Trends in the Value of Real Estate and Land, 1956 to 1966," in *Three Land Research Studies*, Prepared for the Consideration of the National Commission on Urban Problems, Research Report 12 (Government Printing Office, 1968).

housing—the percentage by which the quantity of housing demanded responds to a 1 percent change in the price of housing—is in the vicinity of −1.0 to −1.5; that is, a tax benefit that reduces housing costs by 1 percent will raise the quantity of housing demanded by 1.0–1.5 percent.[15] Accordingly, tax benefits that reduce gross rent by 10–15 percent will increase demand for owner occupied housing by at least 10 percent and perhaps more than 20 percent. The benefits shown in Table 4-4 above make it virtually certain that tax subsidies substantially raise housing consumption by owner occupants, and more so for upper income than for lower income homeowners.

Other Market Effects of Subsidies

Significant tax benefits for homeowners began in the early 1940s, when personal income tax rates were raised to help pay for World War II. The proportion of the housing stock that is owner occupied has risen sharply since then for both whites and nonwhites (see Figure 4-1). The availability of mortgage credit on increasingly liberal terms after World War II helps explain the shift. The most important factor, however, is undoubtedly the personal income tax system.

If existing and new housing units were perfect substitutes for each other and if housing supply could expand promptly to satisfy demand without affecting construction costs, the consequences of tax benefits could be traced with certainty: (1) rents would tend to decline; (2) prices of housing units for sale to owner occupants would tend to rise; (3) some rental units would be sold for owner occupancy; (4) construction of rental units would fall and of homeowner units would rise. After the housing market had fully adjusted to tax benefits for homeowners, housing prices exclusive of tax benefits would be unchanged if construction costs remained constant. This situation is depicted in Figure 4-2.[16]

15. See, for example, Tong Hun Lee, "The Stock Demand Elasticities of Non-Farm Housing," *Review of Economics and Statistics*, Vol. 46 (February 1964), pp. 85–87; Margaret G. Reid, *Housing and Income* (University of Chicago Press, 1962), p. 381; Richard F. Muth, "The Demand for Non-Farm Housing," in Arnold C. Harberger (ed.), *The Demand for Durable Goods* (University of Chicago Press, 1960), pp. 72–75; H. S. Houthakker and Lester D. Taylor, *Consumer Demand in the United States, 1929–1970: Analyses and Projections* (Harvard University Press, 1966), pp. 76–77. Only Reid estimated price elasticity across a range of households in different income brackets. The reliability of all such estimates declines outside the observed price range.

16. Figures 4-2A and 4-2B measure quantity of housing services rather than number of structures. See Chapter 1 and Richard F. Muth, *Cities and Housing: The Spatial Pattern of Urban Residential Land Use* (University of Chicago Press, 1969), pp. 18–19.

Figure 4-1. Occupancy of Rental and Owner Occupied Housing, by Race, 1890–1970

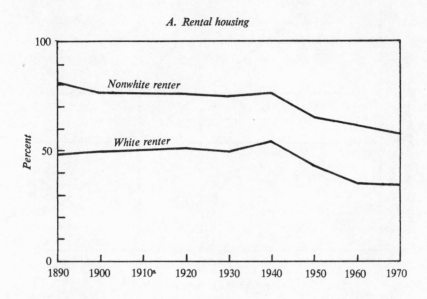

A. Rental housing

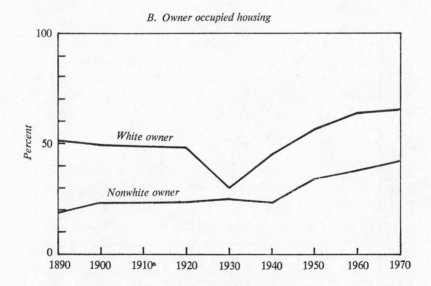

B. Owner occupied housing

Sources: U.S. Bureau of the Census, *Statistical Abstract of the United States, 1968* (1968), p. 707; *Census of Housing: 1970, General Housing Characteristics*, Final Report HC(1)-A1, *United States Summary* (1971), p. 1-16.
a. Extrapolation; data for 1910 are not available.

Figure 4-2. Impact of Favorable Tax Treatment of Homeowners on Owner Occupied and Rental Properties

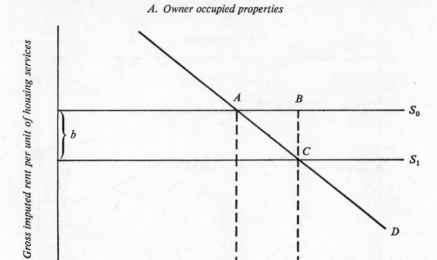

A. Owner occupied properties

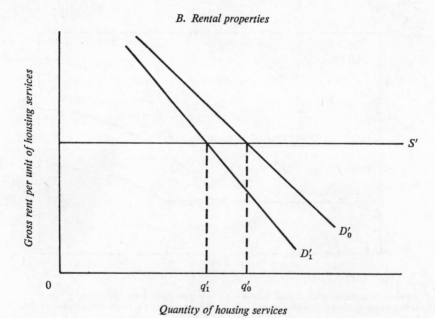

B. Rental properties

The quantity of housing owners want to own and the choice between owning and renting depend on the relative prices of the two. Accordingly, the quantity of housing is measured in units of, say, $1,000, in initial prices.

Tax benefits, like excise taxes and subsidies, may be represented either as a shift in seller perceived demand, the supply curve S fixed, or as a shift in buyer perceived supply, the demand curve D fixed. In Figure 4-2A, tax benefits b shift the supply curve for owner occupied housing from S_0 to S_1. For rental housing, Figure 4-2B, the supply curve S' is unchanged. The quantity of housing services demanded for owner occupancy rises from q_0 to q_1. The demand for rental housing declines from D_0' to D_1', reducing the demand for rental housing services from q_0' to q_1'. Until the stock falls to the equilibrium q_1' renters might derive benefits from the introduction of favorable tax treatment for homeowners.

For homeowners whose housing consumption and tenure is not affected, tax benefits are equivalent to a cash transfer of b times the quantity of housing consumed. For other homeowners the value is somewhat smaller because the tax subsidy distorts housing consumption.[17]

Neither the assumption that construction costs will not be affected by increased housing demand nor the assumption that existing units and new units are perfect substitutes is fully valid. In the short run, increased construction will tend to raise the relative cost of building materials and labor. In the longer run, an increase in the demand for a capital intensive good like housing will also raise the cost of capital relative to the cost of labor and the price of capital intensive goods relative to the price of labor intensive goods.[18] While these consequences are not analyzed in this study, they probably follow the pattern of tax savings to homeowners.

If new and used housing units prove to be imperfect substitutes, the prices of existing houses more suitable for sale than for rental will tend to rise and remain higher than they would have been in the absence of tax benefits for homeowners. Some part of the tax benefits would be capitalized into permanently higher prices, providing a lump sum gain to owners at the time the benefit became effective. If the effects of increased construction costs and of imperfect substitutability were incorporated into Figure 4-2, the supply curves would slope up and the price of housing at the unsubsidized consumption level, q_0, would be greater than shown. (The benefit

17. The difference between the value of tax benefits to the homeowner and their cost to the Treasury is deadweight loss equal to the area ABC in Figure 4-2A.
18. See Chapter 3.

estimates in Tables 4-3, and D-2 and D-3, Appendix D, would also have to be modified to account for the increased original cost of housing for current owners.) Since 1966, tax benefits to homeowners have increased by more than $2 billion. The reduction in tax due to deductibility of property taxes rose from $1.6 billion in 1966 to an estimated $2.8 billion in fiscal year 1970; the tax savings from deductibility of mortgage interest rose from $1.5 billion to $2.6 billion.[19] Large increases in the standard deduction will tend to reduce the value of those deductions to homeowners. On the other hand, increases in property taxes and in mortgage interest will increase their value. Net imputed rent has risen only slightly since 1966 according to the Department of Commerce.

Tax Benefits on Rental Property

Whether tax benefits to homeowners encourage households to buy rather than rent depends on the size and incidence of tax benefits on rental property. The major benefit available only to investors in rental property is deduction for depreciation in excess of true economic depreciation. Owners may depreciate rental property for tax purposes at a rate appreciably above the true decline in market value. Taxes on that excess are deferred until the property is sold, or they are canceled altogether at the owner's death.[20] If rental markets are competitive, property owners will over time reduce rents, thereby transferring the benefits of excess depreciation to renters (or to other owners of capital).

The analysis of the incidence of excess depreciation closely resembles that of tax benefits to homeowners. Assume that the cost of producing rental housing is constant (see Figure 4-3). Excess depreciation will increase the supply of rental housing from S_0' to S_1', causing the market price

19. *The Economics of Federal Subsidy Programs*, A Staff Study Prepared for the Use of the Joint Economic Committee, 92 Cong. 1 sess. (1972), p. 152.

20. According to the Tax Reform Act of 1969, owners of rental property may choose among an array of tax formulas that allow property to depreciate more rapidly than it does in reality. Subsequent owners are governed by more conservative formulas but may choose shorter estimated lives for their property than original owners. The Tax Reform Act provides for taxation of the excess of selling price over depreciated value as ordinary income rather than as capital gains in certain cases where capital gains treatment was formerly allowed. The earlier advantage of claiming capital gains has been further reduced by the increase in tax rates on capital gains and the imposition of a minimum tax on tax favored income. The act also allows five-year depreciation of the cost of major improvements to housing for families with low and moderate incomes.

Figure 4-3. Impact of Excess Depreciation on Rental and Owner Occupied Housing

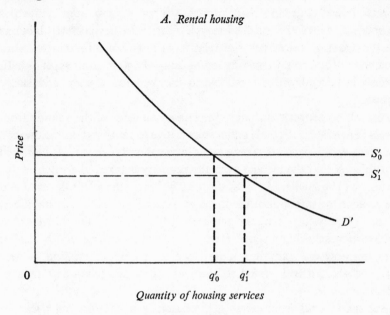

A. Rental housing

Quantity of housing services

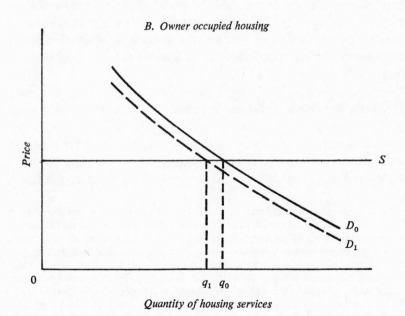

B. Owner occupied housing

Quantity of housing services

of rental housing services to decline, the amount of rental housing demanded to rise, and the amount of other housing to fall from D_0 to D_1. If total housing demand rises, capital will move from other industries to housing, where the yield of capital relative to payments to labor is greater. Housing prices will rise relative to prices of other commodities because of the capital intensity of housing. Factor earnings of wealth holders in general will rise relative to the incomes of wage and salary earners.

As with homeowner subsidies, the impact on rents of the subsidy from excess depreciation depends on its size relative to rents and on the owner's tax bracket. The percentage reductions in rental costs can vary as indicated in Table 4-5.[21] If the income from the property is taxed, the value of the subsidy will be smaller than that shown. The longer the sale is deferred and the smaller the importance the taxpayer attaches to future tax liabilities, the more nearly correct are the figures in Table 4-5. The value of the excess depreciation subsidy on rental property is almost certainly much smaller than homeowners' subsidies, unless true economic depreciation is near zero and there is little or no recovery of excess depreciation at time of subsequent sale.

The tax benefits from excess depreciation to a high bracket owner of rental property, however, may easily be greater than the benefits to a low bracket homeowner for similar property (but not to a high bracket homeowner). Tax factors help explain why the fraction of households renting apartments or houses declines sharply as incomes rise.

Property and Corporate Income Taxation

A fair comparison of taxes levied on housing and on other industries must include the property tax and the corporation income tax. The property tax is levied principally on real property, although some jurisdictions

21. The table assumes that taxpayers can deduct the full value of excess depreciation. Complete avoidance would occur only if the owner died before selling the property or donated it to charity; if the owner traded the property for another, the depreciated value of the original property would be carried over to the new one. This process could go on indefinitely. See Martin David, *Alternative Approaches to Capital Gains Taxation* (Brookings Institution, 1968), p. 18; Richard E. Slitor, *The Federal Income Tax in Relation to Housing*, Prepared for the Consideration of the National Commission on Urban Problems, Research Report 5 (Government Printing Office, 1968), pp. 16–17; and Commerce Clearing House, *Explanation of Tax Reform Act of 1969* (CCH, 1969), pp. 158–68.

Table 4-5. Reduction in Rental Housing Costs as a Result of Favorable
Tax Treatment, by Tax Bracket

In percent

True depreciation (percent)ᵃ	Tax bracket (percent)			
	14	25	50	70
4.5	0.0	0.0	0.0	0.0
4.0	0.4	0.8	1.6	2.2
3.0	1.3	2.3	4.7	6.6
2.0	2.2	3.9	7.8	10.9
1.0	3.1	5.5	10.9	15.3
0.0	3.9	7.0	14.1	19.7

a. Benefits are the difference between true depreciation and depreciation that rental property owners may deduct from taxable income. Property is assumed to have a useful life of forty years. Gross rents are assumed to equal 16 percent of market price. Depreciation at double declining-balance (twice the annual value of equal reductions over the life of the property) is taken to be the unweighted, undiscounted average of the first five years, 4.5 percent.

try feebly to tax tangible personal property of individuals and more ener-getically and successfully to tax business inventories and equipment.[22] Because housing services are attributable almost entirely to real property, the property tax falls more heavily on them than on any other major category of consumer goods, much of whose value comes from labor. On the other hand, housing largely escapes the corporation income tax because individuals or unincorporated businesses own all owner occupied housing and many rental dwellings.

These two taxes fall less heavily on housing than on most other indus-tries.[23] The combined rate, averaged for 1953–59, on nonfarm residential dwellings was 28 percent, on all nonfinancial industries except housing 40 percent, and on manufacturing 47 percent. Of the forty-six major industry groups, only five were taxed more lightly than housing.[24] The favorable treatment of housing in business income taxation only increases advantages of homeownership under the personal income tax.

22. See Dick Netzer, *Economics of the Property Tax* (Brookings Institution, 1966), pp. 138–63.
23. See Leonard G. Rosenberg, "Taxation of Income from Capital, by Industry Group," in Harberger and Bailey (eds.), *The Taxation of Income from Capital*, pp. 174–77.
24. The five were farms (17 percent), crude petroleum and natural gas (20 percent), petroleum and coal products (25 percent), personal services (slightly under 28 percent), and business services not elsewhere classified (25 percent).

Alternative Policies

The Internal Revenue Code contains massive tax subsidies for housing. The largest accrue to homeowners through exemption from taxation of net imputed rent and deductibility of mortgage interest and property taxes. Smaller benefits accrue to owners of rental housing to the extent that accelerated depreciation exceeds true depreciation by a greater margin on real estate than on other properties.

These tax subsidies affect allocation of resources, distribution of income, and the form of legal tenure of housing. Consumption of housing services is greater than it would be in the absence of tax benefits. The increase cannot be gauged precisely, but is about 20 percent in the aggregate.[25] Homeowners in particular reap large benefits—especially those subject to high tax rates, for whom implicit subsidies equal 30 percent or more of the cost of housing services.

The impact on income distribution is large. The direct benefits accrue primarily to upper income homeowners. By increasing demand for housing services, a highly capital intensive commodity, they raise yields on capital in general. Furthermore, the price of capital intensive commodities, such as housing, rises relative to the price of other commodities. Thus those with high income from capital—primarily upper income homeowners— benefit most. Since tax benefits on rental property are much smaller than those available to homeowners, they may do little more than offset the price increasing effects, through capital costs, of the homeowner subsidies.

With respect to any conceivable policy objective, the pattern of tax benefits seems to be capricious and without rationale. Apart from the alleged, but unsubstantiated, benefits accruing to the community when households come to own their own homes, there appears to be no reason for subsidizing homeownership rather than other investments or sub- sidizing homeownership rather than renting or the consumption of other commodities.[26]

25. This estimate presumes that the mean marginal tax rate among homeowners is 22 percent (in 1966 the rate among all taxpayers was 19 percent), that imputed rent plus deductible expenses averages five-eighths of gross rent, and that the price elasticity of demand for housing is -1.5.

26. A vast literature exists that purports to show the beneficent effects of good housing or of homeownership or the harmful effects of slums on households or on society. For bibliographies, see Daniel M. Wilner and others, *The Housing Environment and Family Life* (Johns Hopkins Press, 1962); Jerome Rothenberg, *Economic Evaluation of Urban*

Even if property ownership reduced family instability and antisocial behavior, the tax benefits are ill designed to extend property ownership. The largest benefits go to recipients of the largest incomes whose experience with wealth typically is not limited to their own houses. A negligible amount of aid goes to low income households, most of whom have not been vouchsafed the salutary discipline of property management.

The obvious remedy for the problems raised in this chapter is to require homeowners to report gross imputed rent and expenses on their residences in the same way that businesses report income and expenses and to award housing subsidies on more plausible grounds. Though such a remedy may be politically unthinkable, it is workable despite significant administrative problems. The estimation of net imputed rent could be approached in at least two ways. Appraisers could make direct appraisals of gross imputed rent, much as they now estimate fair market values for property tax offices and banks, insurance companies, savings and loan associations, and other financial intermediaries. Deductions from these estimates for maintenance expense, depreciation, and interest would determine net rent. Alternatively, the appraised fair market value of the house minus the balance of any outstanding debts secured by the house could be used to determine the owner's equity interest. Net imputed income could be estimated by multiplying owner's equity by a rate of return equal to that on such investments as long term government bonds, high grade corporate bonds, passbook savings account rates, or other forms of security.

On balance, the latter method seems preferable, since under the first procedure the homeowner, by discretionary behavior, could keep net rent artificially low. Because each dollar he spent for maintenance or noncapital improvements would reduce his tax liability, he might be encouraged to make more improvements than he would choose to make if tax considerations were absent. Even partial recovery through capital gains taxation at time of sale would be far from certain since effective tax rates on gains from sale of owner occupied homes are even lower than those on other assets.

Renewal (Brookings Institution, 1967), pp. 58–60; and Alvin L. Schorr, *Slums and Social Insecurity*, U.S. Department of Health, Education, and Welfare, Research Report 1 (1963). No study has shown both that the beneficial effects of housing are due to housing itself rather than adequate income—that is, that the composition, rather than the level, of consumption matters—and that correlations between homeownership and socially or personally desirable characteristics (or the absence of antisocial characteristics) are not the joint results of other psychological, sociological, or economic characteristics. The issue of which way causation runs is frequently troublesome.

This avenue of tax avoidance would be narrowed under the latter procedure.

Success in the equitable taxation of net imputed rent would rest on reasonably accurate property valuation. The administrative problems are real but manageable. Financial intermediaries now make appraisals before approving loans, but considerable inaccuracy is tolerable because conventional loans usually are much below property value. Property tax valuations are likewise inaccurate, for rather different reasons. While the cost of making property tax appraisals sufficiently exact to support taxation of net imputed rent would probably be significant, such a course would generate major collateral benefits through improvement in the administration of the property tax.

If full taxation of income from housing were politically unacceptable, deductions could be disallowed for mortgage interest, property taxes, or both.[27] If deductions for mortgage interest were disallowed, homeowners would be encouraged to borrow on assets other than their homes. To the extent that they could substitute other credit instruments, disallowance of deductions for mortgage interest would have no tax consequences. The impact would be massive on markets for financial assets, however. For financial intermediaries, such as savings and loan associations, which are restricted by law to investing in home mortgages, the result would be catastrophic.[28] Clearly, mortgage interest deductions could not be disallowed unless major changes were made in laws regulating savings and loan associations.

If deductions for property taxes paid were disallowed, no valuation problems would arise, nor would credit markets be disturbed. Fiscal distortions would occur, however, since increases in property taxes would raise costs to taxpayers more than would increases in other taxes. Disallowance of all state and local tax deductions would not appear to be politically acceptable unless massive financial aid, through revenue sharing or other fiscal devices, were offered state and local governments. As a means of removing the inequities between homeowners and renters, it would be possible to introduce benefits for renters, perhaps by allowing tax deductions for some

27. Secretary of Housing and Urban Development George Romney suggested that deductibility of mortgage interest be disallowed (*New York Times*, Oct. 24, 1969, p. 18); the suggestion did not become official administration policy.

28. If net imputed rent were taxable, this problem would not arise. As mortgage debt was reduced, equity interest would rise. The homeowner–investor would face the conventional choice of portfolio balance.

part of rental payments. But that remedy would introduce new inequities. Households whose tastes ran to housing would gain relative to those that preferred other goods. Even if greater housing outlays by renters were considered in the national interest, deduction of part of rental payments, like all other deductions, would help most those households in the highest tax brackets. The social utility of such an approach is obscure.

Complete reform in tax treatment of homeowners seems the most attractive course, particularly if it were combined with overall tax reductions to offset the increases homeowners would experience. The reform would develop a common interest among the federal government, municipal governments, and school districts in accurate property appraisal. It would reduce the substantial horizontal inequality resulting from the anomalous treatment of homeowners. And it would cause the personal income tax to generate substantially larger revenues, which could support direct expenditures for housing or other purposes, reductions in tax rates, or lowering of interest rates.

chapter five **Mortgage**
Insurance
and
Guarantees

Most people borrow money when they buy a house.
Some homebuyers borrow against assets other than the newly purchased
house. Others sell their assets or run down cash balances in order to purchase a house outright. Most homebuyers, however, can buy a house only
if they can float a loan secured by the newly purchased house.[1] For them
one of the costs of homeownership is the series of periodic payments necessary to pay off the loan. The more stringent the terms on such loans, the
higher the cost of housing.

The federal government undertakes a number of programs designed to
help homebuyers borrow on less stringent terms. The largest and most
important are the programs of mortgage insurance administered by the
Federal Housing Administration (FHA) and the system of loan guarantees
administered by the Veterans Administration (VA). Both protect lenders
against loss from default by borrowers. Since their introduction, the terms
of most home financing have been radically relaxed.

The Market for Home Loans

Homebuyers borrow from many kinds of lenders under a wide variety
of conditions. In all home loans, however, the borrower sells, and the
lender buys, a set of future payments. The price is the amount of cash the

1. More than five out of six houses sold in 1959 carried mortgages in 1960 (U.S.
Bureau of the Census, *U.S. Census of Housing, 1960*, Vol. 5, *Residential Finance*, Pt. 1,
Table 1).

borrower receives. The certainty with which the lender expects the borrower to repay the loan depends on many circumstances that also affect the terms of the loan. If the borrower falls behind in his payments, the lender may foreclose and sell his collateral, the house. The collateral may sell for less than the outstanding balance on the loan. In any case, the lender will incur certain foreclosure and selling costs. He will require, therefore, that the loan payments yield him a return at least as great as the safe yield he could obtain on other assets plus a premium to compensate him for the risk of loss from delinquency or foreclosure that he foresees. If the market for home loans is competitive, competition will prevent the yield on risky loans from exceeding this minimum. The crucial factor in the lender's calculations is his estimate of loss risk.

Among the most important influences on loss risk is the fraction of the value of the collateral that the lender is willing to lend—the loan-to-value ratio. The higher that ratio, the less likely is the selling price to cover the outstanding debt in the event of foreclosure. The repayment period, the size of the payments in relation to borrower's income, the interest rate, the term of the loan, and the occupation, health, wealth, age, and family size of the borrower also affect the probability that he will be unable to meet his payments or that the property will be worth less than the unpaid balance of the loan. The procedures by which lenders may obtain possession in the event of default, any penalties to be charged if the loan is paid ahead of schedule, and the steps subsequent buyers must take to assume the loan also affect the risk of loss and the attractiveness of the mortgage to the borrower.

A homebuyer usually has some choice about loan terms. He may normally trade off more stringent terms of one kind for more liberal terms of another. For example, lenders frequently charge higher interest rates for loans with high loan-to-value ratios and long repayment periods than for those with low ratios and short repayment periods. Borrowers with low or uncertain incomes have to pay higher interest rates or agree to easier foreclosure procedures than do borrowers with high or steady incomes.[2]

The loan terms available to homebuyers influence their ability to purchase a house and bear the financial burdens of ownership. For example, a

2. Certain "high risk" customers seeking to buy housing in "high risk" areas may be able to borrow only under a "land purchase contract" under which foreclosure is easier than under a mortgage (or trust deed). These contracts are not eligible for FHA or VA protection. They are used chiefly by individuals rather than by financial intermediaries. Some state courts have extended to borrowers under land purchase contracts the same protection mortgagors enjoy.

would-be purchaser who cannot make a downpayment greater than 10 percent, but can borrow only 80 percent, must wait until he has doubled his cash or must secure a second loan (frequently at a high interest rate). The growth of VA and FHA loan protection accompanied a substantial increase in loan-to-value ratios and extension of repayment periods so that homebuyers need less cash today than they did in the 1930s and earlier.

Most home mortgages are provided by institutional lenders—savings and loan associations, mutual savings banks, commercial banks, and life insurance companies. During the 1920s, savings and loan associations (S&Ls) held one-half of outstanding home mortgage debt. Their mortgages averaged 58 percent of estimated property value and ran for eleven years; 95 percent were fully amortized.[3] Roughly three-fifths of other home mortgages were held by life insurance companies and commercial banks. Repayment periods were six years and two to four years, respectively, and loans ranged from 46 to 52 percent and 48 to 54 percent of property value, respectively; less than one-fifth of these mortgages were fully amortized.[4] Throughout the 1920s banks and insurance companies charged about 1 percent less than did savings and loan associations.[5] Partially amortized or nonamortized loans were typically renegotiated at their expiration. Those mortgages more closely resemble contemporary intermediate term commercial loans than present day mortgages.

Today all FHA and VA and most conventional mortgages are fully amortized and run for twenty years or more. Loan-to-value ratios on VA and FHA mortgages exceed those on conventional mortgages (98 and 93 percent, respectively, versus 72–73 percent) largely because VA and FHA protect lenders against loss from default by the borrower.

Houses can be acquired for smaller downpayments relative to income than was formerly possible; carrying costs relative to income have changed little (see Table 5-1). FHA (and VA) default protection clearly has enabled would-be homebuyers with adequate income but few savings to enter the housing market. Relatively young households are most likely to be in such a position; in fact, in 1960 the average age of homeowners with FHA mort-

3. Many mortgages in the 1920s were not self-amortizing. J. E. Morton, *Urban Mortgage Lending: Comparative Markets and Experience* (Princeton University Press for the National Bureau of Economic Research, 1956), App. C, Tables C-2, C-6, and C-7, pp. 170, 174–75; Leo Grebler, David M. Blank, and Louis Winnick, *Capital Formation in Residential Real Estate* (Princeton University Press for the National Bureau of Economic Research, 1956), Table 66, p. 231.

4. Grebler, Blank, and Winnick, *Capital Formation*, p. 231.

5. Morton, *Urban Mortgage Lending*, Table C-5, p. 173.

Table 5-1. Relative Burden of Loan Terms, 1920s and 1960s[a]

Decade and lender	Terms	Percent of annual income	
		Down-payment	Annual payment
1920s			
Savings and loan association	60 percent of house value loaned for 11 years at 7 percent; fully amortized	100	20
Bank or insurance company	50 percent of house value loaned for 5 years at 6 percent; unamortized	125	7.5 plus 125 in fifth year
1960s			
Conventional lender	75 percent of house value loaned for 20 years at 7 percent; fully amortized	62.5	17.7
FHA	95 percent of house value loaned for 30 years at 7.5 percent; fully amortized	12.5	20.1

a. For a house equal to approximately two-and-a-half times the purchaser's annual salary.

gages and VA loan guarantees was four and six years lower than the age of those with conventional mortgages.[6]

FHA Programs

The Federal Housing Administration was established by the National Housing Act in 1934[7] primarily to help restore prosperity to the construction industry and the general economy and only secondarily to promote other changes in housing markets.[8] Over time, such goals as improvement in the quality of the housing stock have become prominent.

Under a variety of programs FHA has insured loans issued by private lenders to private (or semiprivate) borrowers for the purchase of new or existing single-family houses or multifamily dwellings. Between 1935 and 1969, 19 percent and since 1965, 15 percent of all privately financed nonfarm dwelling units were started under FHA programs (see Table 5-2).[9]

6. Bureau of the Census, *U.S. Census of Housing, 1960*, Vol. 5, Pt. 1, pp. 21, 25, 29.
7. 48 Stat. 1246, 12 U.S.C. 1701 and following.
8. Sherman J. Maisel, *Financing Real Estate: Principles and Practices* (McGraw-Hill, 1965), p. 100.
9. Department of Housing and Urban Development, *1969 HUD Statistical Yearbook* (1970), p. 26.

**Table 5-2. Use of FHA, VA, and Conventional Mortgages,
Selected Years, 1950–70**

| | Nonfarm housing starts | | | | Mortgage credit outstanding[a] | | | |
| | Thousands of mortgages | Percent of total mortgages | | | Billions of dollars | Percent of total credit | | |
Year		FHA	VA	Conventional		FHA	VA	Conventional
1950	1,908	26	10	64	45.2	19.0	22.8	58.2
1955	1,627	17	24	59	88.2	16.2	27.9	55.9
1960	1,230	21	6	73	141.3	19.0	21.0	60.0
1965	1,451	14	3	83	212.9	19.7	14.6	65.7
1970	1,434[b]	29	4	67	279.7	21.3	13.3	65.4

Sources: U.S. Department of Housing and Urban Development, *1969 HUD Statistical Yearbook* (1970), pp. 28, 367, and *1970 HUD Statistical Yearbook* (1971), pp. 307, 323, except for VA guaranteed units for 1950 and 1960 which are from *Housing and Home Finance Agency, Fourteenth Annual Report, 1960*, p. 368, and VA guaranteed units, other years, which are from a tabulation supplied by the Veterans Administration. Percentages are rounded and may not add to 100.

a. Mortgage debt outstanding on nonfarm properties for one to four families.

b. Includes farm housing.

Under FHA insurance contracts the agency promises to pay most of the losses the lender may incur if he forecloses. Payment is limited to the amount of insurance plus some additional allowances for administrative costs and is made initially in debentures rather than cash.[10]

Most FHA mortgage insurance has been written on one- to four-family houses under the basic mortgage insurance program, section 203 of the National Housing Act of 1934, as amended. Mortgages may cover as much as 97 percent (100 percent for veterans) of the appraised value of both new and existing houses; value includes closing costs (other than brokers' commissions) which average about 3 percent of purchase price. The maximum allowable ratio of loan to appraised value is higher the lower the price of the housing. The bulk of FHA insurance is written on moderately priced housing, for purchasers in the middle income ranges (see Appendix B, Tables B-4 and B-5).

Section 221 of the National Housing Act is intended to help low and moderate income families, particularly those displaced by such federal action as urban renewal. On one- to four-family houses and multifamily projects owned for profit, FHA mortage insurance provides no subsidy to owners. But on multifamily projects owned by public agencies, coopera-

10. See Appendix B for a description of loss reimbursement by FHA, VA, and the Farmers Home Administration.

tives, and limited dividend or nonprofit corporations, some mortgages have been made at interest rates as low as 3 percent. To induce commercial lenders to lend at less than market rates, the Government National Mortgage Association (GNMA) purchases such mortages at par from private lenders and FHA waives its usual 0.5 percent mortgage insurance premium.[11]

Many lenders sell FHA insured mortgages to the Federal National Mortgage Association (FNMA) or to other purchasers. FHA has aided the development of the secondary financial market for home mortgages by establishing standards regarding the quality and condition of the structure, the relation between mortgage payments and borrower income, and reputability of the lender. Investors who have never seen the property securing a mortgage and know little of it or of the borrower may nevertheless be willing to purchase FHA mortgages. Thus they may buy mortgages in distant states or regions where the demand for mortgage funds exceeds the amount supplied at prevailing interest rates. Only those mortgages issued under the basic FHA program have been widely accepted by private investors. GNMA purchases many other kinds of FHA mortgages, including those carrying below-market-interest rates.

Basic FHA mortgage insurance, handled under the mutual mortgage insurance fund, is designed to be financially self-supporting. Income from premiums, from prepayment and other fees, and from rent or sale of acquired properties is intended to cover all operating costs. In recent years, income has substantially exceeded outlays; in fiscal year 1970, receipts were $317 million and expenses $70 million. On other 1970 operations FHA ran a $56 million surplus.[12] FHA's solvency depends principally on trends in property values and general economic conditions that influence the job and earning prospects of homeowners. In determining financial soundness, it is possible only to determine whether or not the home mortgage insurance fund will provide adequate default protection under certain assumed economic and real estate market conditions. Since these conditions cannot be forecast accurately, neither can the financial self-sufficiency of mortgage insurance be forecast.[13]

11. See Appendix B for a description of basic FHA credit terms and characteristics of FHA transactions.

12. Table B-7, Appendix B.

13. See Ernest M. Fisher and Chester Rapkin, *The Mutual Mortgage Insurance Fund: A Study of the Adequacy of Its Reserves and Resources* (Columbia University Press, 1956).

The VA Program

The Servicemen's Readjustment Act of 1944 established guaranteed home loans for veterans—the GI loan program. The Veterans Administration guarantees approved lending institutions against losses suffered on approved loans made to veterans.[14] The guarantee is limited to $12,500 or 60 percent of the mortgage, whichever is less.[15] Since the guarantee exceeds typical foreclosure losses (even if the borrower has made no down-payment) for all but relatively high priced houses, most VA guaranteed loans cover 100 percent of the selling price, exclusive of closing costs.

Although the VA program is limited to veterans and servicemen, its guarantee persists if a nonveteran buyer assumes the loan. The number of nonveterans holding VA guaranteed loans is unknown.

Despite technical differences between VA and FHA procedures and clientele, the general function of both is to transfer loss risk from the lender to the government. No fee was levied for VA's loan guarantees until 1966, when the "cold war GI bill" required veterans whose service began after 1955 to pay a one-time fee of 0.5 percent of the loan. In other words, the program is federally subsidized. Direct appropriations were used through fiscal year 1961 to cover losses under the program. On July 1, 1961, a loan guarantee revolving fund was established. Through sale of loans, participation certificates, transfers of income and excess capital from the direct loan revolving fund, and other receipts, VA avoided any need for further appropriations until fiscal year 1969.

Effect on Mortgage Markets

Typical home mortgage terms have changed radically since loss protection offered by FHA and VA was introduced. VA and FHA loans carry higher loan-to-value ratios and lengthier repayment periods than does conventional credit. In addition, terms on conventional mortgages have become more liberal. Terms on conventional mortgages may have changed because the government's ability and willingness to prevent severe economic slowdown have made home mortgages safer. On the other hand, conventional terms may have been liberalized because the FHA and VA

14. The VA makes a limited number of direct loans (8,500 in fiscal year 1970).
15. Before 1968 the maximum guarantee was $7,500.

programs revealed that more liberal mortgage terms increased risk only slightly, or because borrowers have come to prefer FHA or VA options. Most homeowners do not use FHA insurance (see Table 5-2 above), presumably because the improvement over conventional terms that FHA insurance makes possible is worth less than the 0.5 percent insurance premium charged by FHA.[16] Moreover, federal ceilings on interest rates have made FHA mortgages unattractive to lenders when conventional rates have risen above those limits. The drop in VA guarantees from the late 1940s to 1966 is due to the decline in the number of veterans eligible for benefits; veterans have every incentive to use the guarantee, since they receive it at little or no cost.

Benefits from Loss Protection

Mortgage insurance and loan guarantees affect income distribution in two ways. The first is widely diffused, impossible to measure accurately, and probably very important; the other is concentrated on identifiable beneficiaries, measurable, and not very important.

Loss risk depends on many factors in complex ways. As a result, all lenders use rules of thumb for choosing among loan applicants: borrowers must have steady employment; monthly payments may not exceed a stipulated fraction of family income; blacks, Spanish-Americans, and Indians need not apply; loans in certain neighborhoods will not be approved; loans may not exceed a certain percentage of appraised value; repayment periods may not exceed a certain number of years. These and other rules reflect the judgments (and sometimes the prejudices) of bank officers, based on limited information, about how best to distribute loanable funds. For many years, banks had no information about the difference between loss risk on 50 percent ten-year mortgages and the untested 90 percent thirty-year mortgage, and the belief that long-term, high loan-to-value mortgages were unsound persisted.

Mortgage insurance and loan guarantees transformed this situation. The

---

16. The cost of the increase in loan size or repayment period may be quite steep. A homebuyer who can obtain a 75 percent thirty-year loan conventionally at 7 percent or a 90 percent thirty-year loan through FHA at 7.5 percent (7 percent interest plus 0.5 percent insurance on the entire loan) is paying 9.9 percent interest for the extra 15 percent of purchase price he can borrow because of FHA insurance. He would be better off with the conventional loan if he could obtain a second mortgage at less than 9.9 percent interest.

lender's risk, it appeared, might be smaller on lenient insured or guaranteed loans than on stricter loans without loss protection, since the government assumed much of the loss risk. As banks acquired delinquency and foreclosure information on such loans, financial intermediaries liberalized terms on conventional mortgages.

By enabling lenders to adopt new practices and to broaden their knowledge, loss protection may have perfected the market for home mortgages. Borrowers could now obtain loans they regarded as preferable; and lenders, to their surprise, could offer them at little added risk. The benefits of the liberalized mortgage market accrued to all homebuyers and lenders, not just those who used mortgage insurance or loan guarantees. Just as any technological change or modification in institutions that improves economic efficiency affects the distribution of income, so also this improvement raised real incomes and altered the distribution of income.

The second effect on income distribution from FHA or VA loss protection arises because some borrowers may be charged a price for such protection different from the expected loss transferred from the lender to the government. Lenders or borrowers (and possibly others) enjoy a subsidy if FHA or VA premiums are less than the actuarial value of the risk the government assumes.

Both of these benefits are portrayed in Figure 5-1. Each equity-value ratio E/V represents the mortgage terms that affect the loss risk lenders are willing to undertake. The curves L indicate combinations of equity-value ratios and interest rates i among which lenders are indifferent. The curve L_1 indicates the most liberal combinations of mortgage terms and interest rates at which lenders will make loans if no loss protection is available and they are uncertain about loss risk on loans to various classes of borrowers. L_2 shows the most liberal combinations of terms that lenders would accept if they knew the loss risk precisely. L_3 shows the most liberal combination that lenders will accept if loss protection is available.

Lenders are willing to accept more liberal terms when loss protection is available than when it is not because it enables them to avoid the risk of large loss from unusually frequent or costly foreclosures. Furthermore, loss protection insulates lenders from losses due to such unpredictable events as increased unemployment, declines in property values, or slowdowns in economic growth. FHA's actuarial calculations are probably more optimistic than those that even well-informed lenders could prudently adopt if they operated without any protection against economic adversity. Loss protection enables lenders to exchange a definite cost, the premium

Figure 5-1. Lender and Borrower Tradeoffs between Interest Rates
and Downpayments[a]

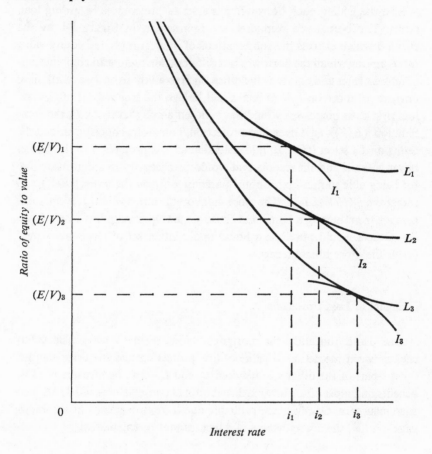

a. L curves express lenders' preferences, I curves borrowers' preferences.

for loss protection, for the risk of greater loss which has equal expected
value.[17] If lenders are averse to risk, this exchange will be beneficial and
lenders will be willing to accept lower E/Vs at each i. Accordingly, curve
L_3 is drawn as if the provision of loss protection at actuarial cost increases

17. If continuous supply and demand curves exist for mortgage funds, the fact that
FHA charges the borrower, not the lender, for loss protection is irrelevant because of
the well-established principle that in such a case it does not matter whether a tax (or
subsidy) is imposed on buyer or seller.

the willingness of lending institutions to make low E/V risky loans. In fact, however, FHA's premiums do not always equal the risk it assumes.

Like the lender, each borrower has a set of preferences regarding loan terms. The borrower's responses are represented in Figure 5-1 by the curves I which express the combinations of interest rates and equity-value ratios among which the borrower is indifferent. He prefers all combinations of interest rates and equity-value ratios on I_3 to all those on I_2, and all those on I_2 to all those on I_1.[18] If banks had known the true impact of E/V on loss risk, then borrowers would have chosen among terms on L_2 the combination $[(E/V)_2, i_2]$. Given loss protection, borrowers choosing among the terms on L_3 select $[(E/V)_3, i_3]$. The value of loss protection to the home-buyer is the change in income that would be necessary to compensate him for being able to finance his home purchase only on the terms $[(E/V)_1, i_1]$ rather than $[(E/V)_3, i_3]$.[19] The more unfavorable terms would prevent some persons from buying a home and cause some to purchase less costly housing. Others would purchase a house under either set of terms but would prefer the more liberal terms.

Impact of Loss Protection

Loss protection alters the mortgage market in many ways. The difference between the actuarial value of loss protection and the price charged for it—part of the difference between L_2 and L_3—can be measured. Most benefits and most of the income distributional consequences of FHA mortgage insurance, however, are probably due to improvements in the mortgage market, the consequences of which cannot be calculated.

Improvement in Mortgage Market

The increase in loan-to-value ratios and repayment periods has lowered the downpayment required on homes and left the monthly amortization costs roughly unchanged. As a result families with much smaller savings can become homeowners at an earlier age than in the 1920s. They gather

18. The curve is also drawn to indicate that the higher the equity-value ratio, the larger the decline in interest rates necessary to compensate for any further increase in the ratio—that is, a diminishing marginal rate of substitution.

19. See Appendix C for an application of the concept of the income equivalent of commodity subsidies.

substantial tax benefits and such other benefits as the reduced borrowing costs that improvements in the mortgage market bring.

Unfortunately there is no practicable way of measuring these benefits. If as few as 10 percent of the 32 million nonfarm owner occupied housing units change hands annually and reduced downpayments are worth only $300, benefits are $960 million per year. The tax benefits and other advantages of homeownership may be worth far more than $300 for young families (for estimates of tax benefits see Chapter 4).[20] To some extent the increased tax advantages are offset by higher tax rates, lower government expenditures, tighter monetary conditions, or some combination of all three. How much of the liberalization in mortgage terms was triggered by VA and FHA is not clear. It is possible, however, that substantial benefits, approaching $1 billion per year, flow from liberalized mortgage terms.

Pricing of Loss Protection

Loss risk differs from one borrower to another. On the basis of recent estimates of loss risk it is possible to estimate the income redistribution that occurs through FHA mortgage insurance and VA loan guarantees.

FHA MORTGAGE INSURANCE. Home mortgages insured under FHA's basic program carry widely divergent terms. Loan-to-value ratios range from less than 70 percent to 100 percent. Most prices of homes, like the incomes of most insured buyers, fall in the lower and middle brackets; more than two-thirds of FHA insured sales covered houses valued at $12,000 to $25,000 in 1970. The overwhelming majority of repayments were scheduled for thirty years. More than three-fourths of all newly insured mortgagors were under age forty, and slightly less than half under thirty; the average age was thirty-three.[21]

The most striking difference between FHA and conventional loans is in loan-to-value ratios. In a study of nearly 13,000 conventional, FHA, and VA mortgages, the probability of default and foreclosure was found to be greater the higher the loan-to-value ratio.[22] Such variables as secondary

---

20. If a family of four with annual income of $12,500 is enabled to buy a house five years before it otherwise could have, tax benefits might exceed $1,000. Assuming a 10 percent subsidy through reduced taxes and one-fifth of family income devoted to housing, the tax benefits equal $250 per year. The present value of $250 for five years discounted at 6 percent is $1,053.

21. *1970 HUD Statistical Yearbook*, pp. 198–200.

22. John P. Herzog and James S. Earley, *Home Mortgage Delinquency and Foreclosure* (Columbia University Press for National Bureau of Economic Research, 1970).

financing, occupation and family size of the mortgagor, and the region in which he lived were of considerable importance in predicting delinquency or foreclosure. Other studies based on FHA data alone found that foreclosure rates depend on the loan-to-value ratio, the income of the borrower, the repayment period, and the age of the mortgage.[23] Variations in the loan-to-value ratio and in household income explained roughly half the variation in mean default rates among the mortgages examined.[24]

The differences between premium payments and anticipated default losses for various income classes within the FHA program are shown in Table 5-3.[25] Default losses are equivalent to the discounted value of insurance premiums on all mortgage insurance written in 1966 (assuming that mortgages were repaid on the average at the end of ten years and that the system is actuarially sound).

If FHA's basic mortgage insurance program is actuarially sound, only a moderate amount of progressive intraprogram redistribution occurs. This redistribution arises because FHA charges identical premiums to insure mortgages with widely different default probabilities. But if the insurance is not financially self-supporting, varying, say, 20 percent in either direction, the redistribution pattern is radically different.[26] The 20 percent deviations from actuarial soundness in Table 5-3 indicate the distributional consequences of a financial deficit or surplus.

23. See George M. von Furstenberg, "Default Risk on FHA-Insured Home Mortgages as a Function of the Terms of Financing: A Quantitative Analysis," *Journal of Finance*, Vol. 24 (June 1969), pp. 459–77, and "Risk Structures and the Distribution of Benefits within the FHA Home Mortgage Insurance Program," *Journal of Money, Credit and Banking*, Vol. 2 (August 1970), pp. 303–22 (reprinted in George M. von Furstenberg, *Technical Studies of Mortgage Default Risk* [Cornell University, Center for Urban Development Research, 1971], Chaps. 3, 4).

24. The impact of repayment periods and age of the mortgage on default rates is not examined here because data are not sufficient to evaluate the four factors simultaneously. Loans with long repayment periods have higher default rates than do short-term loans. Furthermore, default rates on home loans decline precipitously about the sixth year and become negligible after eight to ten years (George M. von Furstenberg, "The Investment Quality of Home Mortgages," *Journal of Risk and Insurance*, Vol. 37 [September 1970], pp. 437–45). If interest rates remained roughly constant, borrower and lender could profitably dispense with default protection on seasoned loans, settling on an interest rate rise of up to 0.5 percent, to their mutual benefit.

25. It is assumed that the mortgage insurance is actuarially balanced and thus that no income redistribution occurs between FHA insured homeowners and all other households. The equations that explain the impact of loan-to-value ratios and household income on default rates appear in Appendix C.

26. Fisher and Rapkin considered that the mutual mortgage insurance fund was adequate in 1956 to cover anticipated losses on the portfolio then insured by FHA if a depression occurred as severe and lengthy as the Great Depression of the 1930s (*The Mutual Mortgage Insurance Fund*, pp. 146–56). Since then, the loan-to-value ratio

Table 5-3. Income Redistribution among Single-Family Homeowners Benefiting from FHA Mortgage Insurance Program, 1966[a]

In dollars

	Present value of FHA benefits, assuming					
	Actuarial soundness		20 percent actuarial deficit		20 percent actuarial surplus	
Income bracket	Total (thousands)	Per house-hold	Total (thousands)	Per house-hold	Total (thousands)	Per house-hold
Under 4,000	625	162	1,029	267	220	57
4,000–4,999	2,194	137	3,802	237	587	37
5,000–5,999	4,310	110	8,278	211	341	9
6,000–6,999	5,528	82	12,680	187	−1,623	−24
7,000–7,999	2,760	46	9,179	152	−3,658	−61
8,000–8,999	416	9	5,361	114	−4,529	−97
9,000–9,999	−1,669	−36	3,101	66	−6,438	−138
10,000–11,999	−4,556	−86	677	13	−9,788	−185
12,000–14,999	−6,033	−172	−2,670	−76	−9,396	−268
15,000 and over	−3,574	−263	−2,376	−175	−4,773	−352
All classes	0	0	39,059	+102	−39,059	−102

Sources: Derived from indexes in Table C-2, Appendix C. Figures are rounded and may not add to totals.
a. Loans insured under section 203 of the National Housing Act.

VA LOAN GUARANTEES. VA guaranteed loans resemble FHA insured mortgages; both require property appraisals and are larger fractions of final selling prices than are conventional loans. Which program provides the lender superior protection is unclear.[27] One obvious difference is that

distribution has risen so significantly that FHA default protection might be unable now to weather the economic circumstances it could weather in the 1950s. In fact, crude default rates (defaults as a percent of mortgages outstanding) rose spectacularly in the early 1960s (the upward trend was arrested in 1967, perhaps because of the accelerated increase in housing prices accompanying the Vietnam inflation and economic boom). These rising loan-to-value ratios suggest a weakening in the financial strength of default protection. On the other hand, the capacity of governmental officials to regulate economic activity makes severe recession appear less probable than it appeared during the 1950s and the hurdles that the insurance fund may be called upon to clear thus less formidable.

27. Maisel (*Financing Real Estate*, pp. 114–15) asserts: "The VA guarantee has been thought to be worth slightly more than the FHA insurance. The claim procedure is simpler. No debentures are involved. The VA guarantee covers all costs and expenses incurred up to the time of claim, in contrast to the FHA settlement of only part of those included in the certificate of claim." Charles M. Haar (*Federal Credit and Private Housing: The Mass Financing Dilemma* [McGraw-Hill, 1960], p. 334) states, "A survey of builders indicated that by and large they considered VA the less efficient and more costly to deal with."

Table 5-4. Income Redistribution among Homeowners Benefiting from VA Loan Guarantee Program, 1966[a]

In dollars

| | Present value of VA benefits, by loan program[b] | | | | | |
| | Total | | Without fee | | With fee | |
Income bracket	Total (thou-sands)	Per house-hold	Total (thou-sands)	Per house-hold	Total (thou-sands)	Per house-hold
Under 4,000	4,562	619	3,131	638	1,431	583
4,000–4,999	19,636	724	13,466	744	6,170	682
5,000–5,999	31,872	832	21,861	856	10,011	784
6,000–6,999	28,818	945	19,791	973	9,027	888
7,000–7,999	21,064	1,008	14,479	1,039	6,585	945
8,000–8,999	14,080	1,055	9,687	1,089	4,393	988
9,000 and over	21,300	1,102	14,691	1,140	6,609	1,026
Total	141,332	901	97,106	928	44,226	846

Source: See Appendix C.
a. Loans guaranteed under Servicemen's Readjustment Act of 1944, as amended.
b. Effective in 1966, some veterans were required to pay a one-time loan guarantee of 0.5 percent of the face amount of the loan.

all VA borrowers are veterans or members of the armed forces, while many FHA borrowers are not. Default probabilities on VA loans are approximately the same as those on FHA mortgages and appear to be related to loan-to-value ratio and income in approximately the same way. The principal difference between the estimates of the value of VA loan guarantees by income class, shown in Table 5-4, and those of FHA mortgage insurance is that some VA borrowers pay little or nothing for default protection and, as a group, receive substantial benefits while FHA borrowers must pay a sizable premium approximately equal in cost to the default risk the government assumes.

CONTRAST IN VA AND FHA BENEFITS. If FHA mortgage insurance is financially balanced, it redistributes income from program users with incomes of $9,000 or more per year to program users with incomes below $9,000. The transfers equal the difference between the present discounted value of premium payments and the anticipated cost of mortgage defaults. Because default rates are highly sensitive to loan-to-value ratios and to income, they are low among high income groups, whose downpayments are high. A total of approximately $16 million was redistributed in this manner among FHA homebuyers insured in 1966.

Because VA charges little for its loan guarantees, the transfers to households are far larger than under FHA. The VA transfers increase as income rises because house values rise with income and loan-to-value ratios decline at a slower rate. The total present discounted value of the default protection provided to households newly covered by VA in 1966 was approximately $141 million. Redistribution of income within the program is negligible.

The pattern of FHA benefits contrasts sharply with those provided by VA. The largest VA benefits accrue to the middle income brackets ($7,000 to $9,000 and over) for whom FHA provides default protection approximately at cost. The contrast arises because VA charges little or nothing for its loan guarantee and because high loan-to-value ratios are more common in VA at all income brackets.

The reason why veterans and home purchasers with little cash participate in these programs is clear. They receive positive transfers, as measured by default risk assumed by a government agency. Higher income households or those with low loans in relation to value receive default protection worth less than the premium charged for it. It would appear that lending institutions could profitably offer such borrowers conventional loans with an interest charge greater than the current conventional rate but less than the FHA premium. Their failure to do so may reflect a judgment that in the absence of price inflation and attendant rises in property values, FHA home mortgage insurance would be severely underfinanced, perhaps by considerably more than 20 percent, so that virtually everyone would realize a net benefit under FHA mortgage insurance.

Summary

Following the introduction of FHA mortgage insurance and VA loan guarantees, a revolution in home mortgage practices occurred. Loan-to-value ratios rose and repayment periods lengthened. Liberalization in mortgage practices quite probably enabled lenders to learn about the real relationship between loss risk and mortgage terms. Families were enabled to buy homes sooner than they otherwise could have and to pay more than they otherwise could have afforded. These families secured access to tax benefits and other advantages homeownership provides. While these benefits may well be large, it is impossible to measure them precisely, and their distribution is unclear. The less significant benefits that accrue because the price of loss protection differs from actuarial cost probably did not exceed $180 million in 1966, most of which accrued to VA borrowers.

The rationale for public provision of loss protection hinges on the degree to which FHA and VA enabled lenders to make loans previously regarded as "unsound." Whatever improvement in mortgage markets FHA and VA could bring to general borrowers has already occurred. The useful role of those institutions now is to underwrite other forms of loans traditionally regarded as unsound—for example, to homebuyers who live in run-down areas, rural areas, or minority enclaves. Today's judgments of the riskiness of such loans may be no more reliable than were the judgments about 95 percent thirty-year loans in the 1920s. FHA has undertaken to insure some mortgages by high risk borrowers in high risk areas. In order to protect the basic mortgage program from heavy losses, it has not used that program to insure such loans. FHA has encountered rather substantial default rates in certain cities. Whether these foreclosures are the inevitable consequences of insuring properties in decaying neighborhoods or are due to remediable faults in insurance methods is still unclear.[28]

The value to the public from provision of loss protection at a price other than actuarial cost is obscure. The implicit subsidy through VA loan guarantees, like other veterans' benefits, presumably rests on a desire to make partial financial amends to men who served in a socially useful, but underpaid, occupation. Why veterans who own their residences deserve such a subsidy, while those who rent do not, is far from clear. Why the subsidy should be tied to housing or, even more restrictively, to loans secured by houses veterans occupy, and why the guarantee should be transferable even if the veteran sells his home to a nonveteran are equally obscure. The small FHA subsidy to low income mortgagors may be justified if homeownership is regarded as desirable. The general public rather than higher income mortgagors should bear the cost, however. In addition, when interest rates stop rising, the FHA may well be compelled to reduce premiums on mortgages older than, say, ten years, or to increase prepayment penalties. Otherwise, many borrowers will refinance with conventional loans to avoid the FHA insurance premium. To maintain actuarial balance, FHA would have to raise premiums during the first and riskiest years of a mortgage's life or secure an explicit public subsidy. In any case, a lengthy period of stable or declining interest rates could raise difficult problems for FHA.

28. William Lilley III and Timothy B. Clark, "Urban Report/Federal Programs Spur Abandonment of Housing in Major Cities," *National Journal*, Vol. 4 (Jan. 1, 1972), pp. 26–33.

chapter six **Federal**
Credit
Institutions

The federal government has established four major institutions designed to increase the flow of credit to housing. The Federal National Mortgage Association (FNMA or Fannie Mae) and the Government National Mortgage Association (GNMA or Ginnie Mae) buy mortgages from, and on occasion sell them to, a variety of private financial organizations. The Federal Home Loan Mortgage Corporation, created in 1970, principally buys mortgages from and sells them to savings and loan associations (S&Ls). The Federal Home Loan Bank (FHLB) system provides various kinds of support to S&Ls and a few savings banks, which in turn invest predominantly in home mortgages. Only GNMA gives explicit subsidies. The other organizations, created to improve the operation of the home mortgage market, have since 1966 sought to insulate housing from the full effects of monetary policy and thus to alter income distribution as well as resource allocation.

Federal National Mortgage Association

With the public sale of its stock in 1968 the Federal National Mortgage Association emerged from thirty years as an active but obscure agent in the market for home mortgage credit.[1] Beginning in 1934 Congress had sought to encourage private establishment of national mortgage associations that would buy and sell the new and unfamiliar insured mortgages of the Federal Housing Administration (FHA). By creating a secondary market for

1. See Jack M. Guttentag, "The Federal National Mortgage Association," in George F. Break and others, *Federal Credit Agencies*, Prepared for the Commission on Money and Credit (Prentice-Hall, 1963), pp. 67–158; and Charles M. Haar, *Federal Credit and Private Housing: The Mass Financing Dilemma* (McGraw-Hill, 1960), pp. 74–125.

these assets, they would increase the willingness of primary lenders to make such mortgages. No private associations were formed, however. After liberalizing terms under which associations could be organized, but still with no success, Congress established the Federal National Mortgage Association in 1938. Federal action was precipitated by concern over the acceptability of new FHA 90 percent twenty-five-year loans authorized that year.

At first the association operated on a small scale, but its willingness to buy FHA mortgages encouraged lenders to make them.[2] A 1948 authorization to purchase mortgages guaranteed by the Veterans Administration led the association to make purchases, commitments, loans, and investments that soon approached the congressionally authorized limit of $2.5 billion. Since the maximum interest rate on VA mortgages was below the market rate, FNMA's advance commitments to buy VA-guaranteed mortgages at par assured windfall gains to private borrowers or lenders.

Congress in 1950 removed the right to issue advance commitments, restricting FNMA to over-the-counter purchases of existing mortgages. Congress soon authorized advance commitments, however, for mortgages on cooperative housing and housing in critical defense areas and for members of the armed forces. In 1953 these programs dominated all others; FNMA suspended over-the-counter purchases but began to exchange seasoned mortgages from its portfolio for unseasoned mortgages under the "one-for-one" program. Lenders benefited from the exchange since risk of loss on seasoned mortgages is negligible.

The Housing Act of 1954 modified FNMA's charter and specified three financially discrete functions. First, the agency was to manage its existing portfolio with the objective of liquidating loans acquired before 1954. Second, while it was to continue to maintain a secondary market for FHA and VA loans, these operations were to be purged of all subsidies.[3] The association began to pay market prices for mortgages rather than par value or more. FNMA refused to sell mortgages below par, assuring growth of its portfolio since FHA and VA loans persistently sold below par. To limit growth, FNMA established numerous eligibility requirements. Third, FNMA was to provide special assistance for certain types of mortgages specified in legislation or by the President by paying more than market value for mortgages. The growth of its portfolio is shown in Figure 6-1.

2. Haar, *Federal Credit and Private Housing*, p. 86.
3. Certain exceptions were introduced in 1969, under which FNMA and GNMA provide joint assistance for special FHA programs.

Figure 6-1. Portfolio of Federal National Mortgage Association, Selected Years, 1956–70[a]

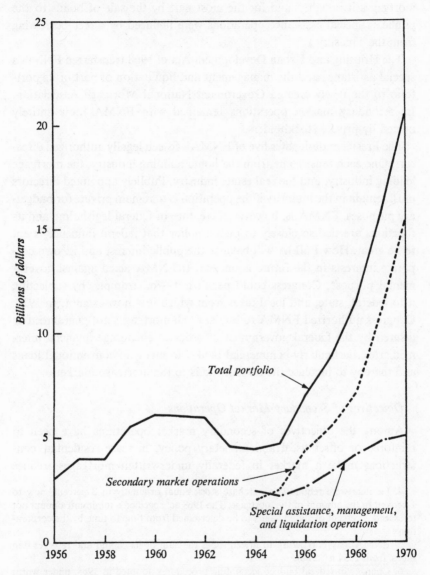

Source: *Federal Reserve Bulletin*, Vol. 50 (March 1964), p. 375; Vol. 55 (January 1969), p. A51; Vol. 57 (May 1971), p. A53.

a. Since 1968 FNMA has performed only secondary market operations; special assistance, management, and liquidation operations are now performed by the Government National Mortgage Association.

FNMA financed these operations through sale of its preferred stock to the U.S. Treasury; through sale of its common stock to lenders whose mortgages it bought;[4] and for the most part by the sale of bonds to the public.[5] (Special assistance operations were financed by direct borrowing from the Treasury.)

The Housing and Urban Development Act of 1968 transferred FNMA's special assistance and the management and liquidation of part of its portfolio to the newly created Government National Mortgage Association. Its secondary market operations remained with FNMA, now entirely owned by private stockholders.[6]

The President designates five of FNMA's fifteen legally authorized directors. One each must come from the home building industry, the mortgage lending industry, and the real estate industry. Publicly appointed directors must remain in the minority if the operation is to remain private for budgetary purposes. FNMA is, however, a creature of federal legislation, and its functions are tied so closely to public policy that federal influence is apt to be great. How FNMA will balance the public interest and its own corporate interests in the future is unclear. If FNMA acted against governmental purpose, Congress could penalize it—for example, by subjecting it to federal, state, and local taxes from which it is now exempt. In 1970, Congress authorized FNMA to buy and sell mortgages not guaranteed or insured by the federal government in order to encourage financial intermediaries, particularly commercial banks, to invest in conventional loans and thereby to increase the flow of funds to the mortgage market.

Objectives of Secondary Market Operations

Among the objectives of secondary market operations have been to reinforce or offset fiscal and monetary policy, increase residential construction, make a market in federally underwritten mortgages, reduce

4. Lenders were required to purchase stock equal originally to 3 percent, now to 1 percent of the amount of the mortgage. The 1968 act specified a minimum amount not to exceed 2 percent of stated value, to be determined from time to time by the corporation.

5. FNMA may borrow up to fifteen times the sum of its capital and reserves (ten times, from 1954 to 1966).

6. Changes in federal budget accounting procedures adopted in 1968, under which all net additions to the FNMA portfolio would have been recorded as federal expenditures, led to this reorganization. Since expenditures of privately owned corporations were to be excluded from the budget, the secondary market operations were transferred to private ownership. Special assistance was kept within the budget, since private investors would have found most of this portfolio unattractive at the prices paid by FNMA.

regional yield differentials, and act as a mortgage lender of last resort.[7] Their relative importance has never been clear, and on occasion they have conflicted with one another. Since the mid-1960s, for example, FNMA has sought to insulate the housing market at least partially from the effects of stringent monetary policy. Since tight monetary policy is undertaken to reduce excess demand in the economy at large, other industries or the economy as a whole must experience greater instability as a price of FNMA's success.

In 1966, for example, when the Federal Reserve curtailed growth in the money supply, FNMA responded with modest increases in secondary market purchases (see Figure 6-1) and the Federal Home Loan Banks with reduced advances to their members (see Figure 6-2, p. 102). Investment in nonfarm residential structures plummeted from $26.5 billion in the first quarter of 1966 to $21.1 billion in the fourth. By early 1967, economic prospects had become so bearish that steps were taken to spur investment and general economic activity.

When the Federal Reserve once again curtailed growth in the money supply in 1969, FNMA and the Home Loan Banks sharply expanded net secondary market purchases and advances to members. This time, investment in nonfarm residential structures fell much less sharply, from $32.4 billion in the first quarter to $29.8 billion in the fourth. An economic slowdown followed in 1970, but only after greater delay than in 1966–67, and after a more stringent application of tight money for a more extended period; the change in FNMA and FHLB behavior may have accounted for part of the difference in economic events.

Consequences of Secondary Market Operations

Any important consequences of FNMA flow from its very existence and from the fact that on balance it adds to its portfolio. The existence of FNMA increases the marketability of mortgages and may cause lenders to accept lower interest rates than if mortgages were less salable. The net increase in the flow of funds to mortgage markets due to FNMA's operations is probably smaller than FNMA purchases. Purchasers of FNMA common stocks and bonds may pay for these securities with previously idle cash or with proceeds from the sale of other assets, including mortgages. The net direct increase in mortgage demand equals FNMA mortgage purchases less sale of mortgages by purchasers of FNMA bonds. If FNMA

7. Guttentag, "The Federal National Mortgage Association," p. 67.

bonds were perfect substitutes for mortgages and paid for by the proceeds from sale of mortgages, the volume of mortgage credit would be unchanged. But in private financial markets, FNMA bonds closely resemble bonds of the federal government and blue chip corporations, and it is likely that a substantial number of them are paid for by the sale of assets other than mortgages or from previously idle cash.

The demand for mortgages thus goes up, and for other assets (including FNMA bonds) goes down. As yields on mortgages subsequently drop relative to yields on other assets, investment in mortgages except by FNMA will fall. The size of this decline and the speed with which it occurs depend on the sensitivity of asset holders to changes in the relative yields of different assets, and on the frequency with which financial intermediaries adjust their investment plans, the size of free bank reserves, and other institutional factors.

One investigator has suggested that half of each dollar diverted from other assets to FNMA assets results in increased mortgage demand;[8] another that the fraction may have been as high as 77 percent in 1969.[9] Yet another believes that the demand increases only temporarily and that within two years private financial intermediaries cut back mortgage holdings by the full amount of FNMA's purchases.[10]

The need to estimate accurately the impact of FNMA operations on residential construction or, one step removed, on the price of housing services has grown sharply in recent years, for FNMA acquired 17 percent of all mortgages in 1966, 24 percent in 1969, and 44 percent in the fourth quarter of 1969 alone.[11] Unfortunately, existing data can only support the conclusion that FNMA probably generates some benefits for homebuyers and homeowners and may also help stockholders of financial intermediaries.

Government National Mortgage Association

Congress transferred the special assistance program and management and liquidation of the existing portfolio from FNMA to the newly created

8. Ibid., p. 102.

9. Craig Swan, "Homebuilding: A Review of Experience," *Brookings Papers on Economic Activity* (1:1970), p. 64.

10. Dwight M. Jaffee, "An Econometric Model of the Mortgage Market: Estimation and Simulation" (Princeton University, April 1, 1970; processed), pp. 54–58, 81.

11. Swan, "Homebuilding: A Review of Experience," p. 63.

Government National Mortgage Association in 1968.[12] To be eligible for special assistance, mortgages were to "be of such quality as to meet, substantially and generally, the purchase standards imposed by private institutional mortgage investors but which, at the time of submission of the mortgages to the Association for purchase, are not necessarily readily acceptable to such investors."[13] This language is essentially meaningless as virtually any financial instrument can be sold at some price. In practice, GNMA pays more than market prices, thereby according concealed subsidies to borrowers or lenders. With minor exceptions, the price GNMA pays is 99.5–100 percent of par regardless of market value of the mortgage.

Most special assistance is provided for mortgages on low and moderate income housing (see Table 6-1); almost 80 percent of the portfolio fell into that category at the end of 1970 and the fraction was rising sharply. Other purchases include seasoned mortgages eligible because of such extraordinary events as natural disasters and the FHA-insured 3 percent mortgages that GNMA is obligated to buy at par.

The subsidy that accrues to the lender on GNMA mortgages is estimated in Table 6-1 for 1966–70. GNMA paid over $300 million per year more than market value for the mortgages it purchased under special assistance in 1969 and 1970. Most of this went to the below-market-interest-rate mortgages insured by FHA, a program for low income families, three-fourths of whom have incomes of $4,000 to $9,000. The subsidies on all other FHA or VA mortgages, which typically bear interest at rates near current market rates and are frequently paid in full before maturity, are smaller than those on 3 percent loans.

Federal Home Loan Banks

The Federal Home Loan Banks deal only with savings and loan associations and a few mutual savings banks. The Federal Home Loan Bank Board (FHLBB) governs the twelve regional banks[14] and regulates the

12. For simplicity, in this section GNMA is credited with services FNMA performed until late 1968.

13. 68 Stat. 617. GNMA's function is the same, under the Housing and Urban Development Act of 1968 (82 Stat. 538).

14. The FHLBB presided over the Home Owners' Loan Corporation from 1933 to 1951 and has governed the Federal Savings and Loan Insurance Corporation since 1934.

Table 6-1. Purchases, Portfolio, and Estimated Subsidy in GNMA Special Assistance Program, 1966–70[a]

In millions of dollars

| Item and year | Single-family homes | | Multifamily homes | | Total mortgages |
	FHA[b]	VA	FHA, subsidized[c]	FHA, other	
Purchases					
1966	15.7	0.2	180.7	4.7	201.3
1967	108.8	50.2	159.7	21.2	339.9
1968	236.2	121.0	234.5	45.8	637.4
1969	35.8	4.9	604.8	71.9	717.4
1970	32.8	0.4	538.3	17.0	588.6
Portfolio[d]					
1966	522.7	290.4	379.1	277.2	1,469.5
1967	601.3	320.3	533.9	286.5	1,742.0
1968	804.0	419.8	756.2	322.8	2,302.8
1969	806.0	403.8	1,342.5	384.8	2,937.0
1970	804.8	385.3	1,823.1	388.3	3,401.5
Subsidy[e]					
1966	2.1	*	71.6	0.7	74.3
1967	10.8	4.8	66.6	3.5	85.6
1968	34.1	18.0	105.2	9.4	166.7
1969	10.7	0.5	305.4	19.4	335.9
1970	12.2	*	291.2	5.2	308.6

Source: Federal National Mortgage Association and Government National Mortgage Association, unpublished tabulations. Figures are rounded and may not add to totals.

* Less than $50,000.

a. Portfolio belonged to FNMA before GNMA was created in 1968.

b. Principally under the basic home mortgage program (sec. 203, National Housing Act) and low to moderate income program (sec. 221).

c. Under the below-market-interest-rate program (sec. 221 [d] [3]).

d. End of year.

e. Estimates computed assuming mortgages would sell at par; below-market-interest-rate mortgages would mature in 40 years; all other mortgages would mature in 30 years.

4,600 member organizations (with estimated combined assets of $190.5 billion in mid-1971).[15]

From a system established by the federal government in 1932 to sustain the viability of savings and loan associations, the banks have passed into a member-owned instrument for regulating and aiding its membership.[16]

15. *The Budget of the United States Government—Appendix, Fiscal Year 1972*, p. 194.

16. On the history of FHLBs, see Thomas B. Marvell, *The Federal Home Loan Bank Board* (Praeger, 1969); and Ernest Bloch, "The Federal Home Loan Bank System," in Break and others, *Federal Credit Agencies*, pp. 159–257. Members have acquired $1.6 billion in FHLB stock through adherence to the requirement that their stock holdings

The FHLBs also carry out many of the supervisory activities that the Federal Reserve Banks and the Comptroller of the Currency perform for commercial banks; they charter new federal savings and loan associations, approve or disapprove mergers, and establish accounting regulations. They most affect the flow of mortgage credit through their authority to establish reserve ratios, to set maximum interest rates payable on deposits, and to provide advances to members.

Liquidity Requirements and Deposit Interest Rates

Members of the FHLB system must maintain reserves adequate to assure "meaningful and flexible liquidity . . . which can be increased when mortgage money is plentiful . . . and reduced to add to the flow of funds to the mortgage market in periods of credit stringency."[17] The FHLBs can set the requirement at 4 to 10 percent and vary the rate by class of institution. In 1968 the FHLBB had the upper limit raised to enable it to compel member associations to build up reserves in years when deposits were plentiful as a cushion for years when they were scarce.[18] The board has not used this authority because concern about a housing shortage has led it to encourage investment in mortgages rather than reserves. It has customarily set one rate for all S&Ls and, until recently, adjusted it infrequently, as the following percentages of savings accounts required held in liquid assets show:[19]

Date	Percent of savings	Date	Percent of savings
Before Dec. 27, 1950	None	Dec. 1, 1969–Mar. 31, 1971	5.5
Dec. 27, 1950–Feb. 28, 1961	6.0	Apr. 1, 1971–Apr. 30, 1971	6.5
Mar. 1, 1961–July 31, 1968	7.0	May 1, 1971–Aug. 26, 1971	7.5
Aug. 1, 1968–June 11, 1969	6.5	Aug. 27, 1971–	7.0
June 12, 1969–Nov. 30, 1969	6.0		

Between July 1 and October 31, 1966 the FHLBB allowed members flexibility in meeting the percentage requirement; individual associations could deviate from 7 percent by the percentage of actual withdrawals to total

---

equal at least 1 percent of their mortgage portfolio (until 1962, 2 percent). Since no member can obtain advances equal to more than twelve times his FHLB stock holdings, some members have purchased extra stock.

17. Federal Home Loan Bank Board, *Annotated Manual of Statutes and Regulations* (March 1970), p. 2.

18. See Marvell, *The Federal Home Loan Bank Board*, pp. 233–34.

19. Office of the General Counsel, Federal Home Loan Bank Board.

savings or by 1 percent, whichever was smaller. In recent years the FHLBB has greatly broadened the definition of assets acceptable as part of the liquidity reserve.

The liquidity ratio discourages S&Ls from operating with dangerously small liquidity, a practice that would increase risk of failures by S&Ls. Among other things, such defaults would raise costs of the Federal Savings and Loan Insurance Corporation (FSLIC), the insuring agency that FHLBB also administers. The reserve requirement has the additional function of determining the loan volume that can be built on any given deposit base.

Deposit Rate Ceilings

Since 1966 the FHLBB has set maximum rates that S&Ls may pay depositors to prevent competitive rate increases that might be individually attractive but collectively destructive. Rising interest rates push up costs on all deposits but increase income only on a small proportion of assets. Long-term mortgages cannot be converted to higher yielding assets but depositors can withdraw funds at will. Each association might attempt to woo deposits from competitors in order to increase investments in mortgages at high prevailing interest rates. If each made this attempt, all (or nearly all) would fail. Fear that S&Ls might be faced with ruinously higher costs and little added scope for higher income caused the FHLBB to establish interest ceilings. By 1970 the board had begun to set different rates for different kinds of depositors. The FHLBB recognized that large depositors are more sensitive to interest rate differentials than are small depositors by establishing seven classes of deposits, with maximum rates graduated according to the size of the deposit and the period the depositor agreed in advance to leave his funds with the S&L.[20] These ceilings were still in effect in early 1972, after other interest rates and many actual passbook rates had declined from the highs of 1970.

One indisputable consequence of these regulations and a host of complementary actions has been to hold down the interest income of small investors. In March 1970 when the interest rate on Treasury bills far exceeded passbook savings rates, the minimum denomination on Treasury bills was increased from $1,000 to $10,000. The interest rate payable on

20. Rates ranged from 5 percent to 6 percent for deposits of under $100,000 and from 6.5 percent to 7.5 percent for certificates of deposit of $100,000 or more. *Journal of the Federal Home Loan Bank Board*, Vol. 3 (January/February 1970), p. 2.

United States savings bonds has remained below most commercially determined rates; by December 1969 the rate (4.25 percent) was more than 1 percent below the rise in consumer prices in 1968. The yields on FNMA debentures also rose far above 5 percent, but the minimum denomination of these securities is $10,000.[21] This artificial stratification of capital markets imposes the burdens of tight money policies on depositors with few assets and typically with modest income.

Advances to Members

The FHLBs, with board approval of each action, lend money to member organizations whose reserves threaten to become inadequate. Advances may not exceed twelve times the member's holdings of FHLB stock or 50 percent of its savings accounts. Those issued to assist in expansion are limited to 12.5 percent of the member's savings accounts, or less if excessive proportions of the member's assets are badly delinquent or foreclosed. The FHLBs also make advances to help members weather heavy withdrawals. Most advances have been for expansion. Total FHLB advances have risen sharply since 1960, as the FHLBs have helped channel funds to S&Ls (see Figure 6-2).

Advances help S&Ls deal with the seasonal, regional, and cyclical discrepancies between growth in mortgage demand and that of deposits. Seasonal problems are met in the following fashion:

In late summer and fall, the bulge in takedowns of prior commitments [by lenders] is financed in part by a rise in FHLB advances. Toward the end of the calendar year, the growing surplus on current account is sufficient to pay down the small volume of takedowns then coming due, and the continuation of the surplus into the new year permits the repayment of the previous year's seasonal jump in advances. Meanwhile, as spring approaches, new commitments are being let once more, and toward midyear, new commitments and housing starts accelerate and build toward a peak. As completions bunch up in summer and fall, so do takedowns, mortgage loans, and advances from the Home Loan Banks.[22]

Regional problems arise because housing demand responds to changes of population and income while savings flows depend on the level of population and income. The difference between demand for mortgage credit

21. For a sharp attack on this range of policies, see Edward J. Kane, "Short-Changing the Small Saver: Federal Government Discrimination against Small Savers During the Vietnam War," *Journal of Money, Credit and Banking*, Vol. 2 (November 1970), pp. 513–22.

22. Bloch, "The Federal Home Loan Bank System," p. 187.

Figure 6-2. Federal Home Loan Bank Lending Operations, 1932–70

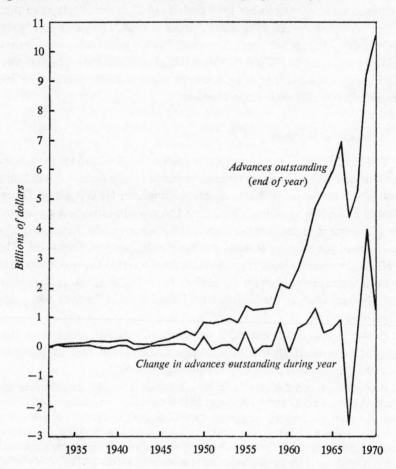

Sources: *Report of the Federal Home Loan Bank Board for the Year Ending December 31, 1966,* pp. 114–15; Board of Governors of the Federal Reserve System, *Federal Reserve Bulletin,* Vol. 57 (May 1971), p. A51.

in rapidly and slowly growing areas typically is far greater than the difference in their supply of savings. The advances made to keep pace with demand in rapidly growing regions—San Francisco in the 1950s, for example, received about one-third of total FHLB advances[23]—frequently represent almost permanent additions to the capital of recipient members.

Cyclical problems have caused most advances made since 1965. Only once before then—in 1959 when mortgage commitments were undertaken

23. Marvell, *The Federal Home Loan Bank Board,* pp. 73–74.

in anticipation of very large increases in deposits that turned out to be only modest—had they required FHLB action.

The growth in deposits was so robust that FHLB advances were made primarily to meet seasonal imbalances or special problems and to channel funds to the most rapidly growing regions.[24] Between 1945 and 1965 the growth in net deposits of savings and loan associations averaged 14.5 percent per year and fell below 11 percent only in 1965, when the increase was 8.4 percent.

As the situation began to change in the early 1960s, the flow of FHLB advances rose markedly. The credit "crunches" of 1966 and 1969 and the 1968 housing goal signaling heightened national concern with housing encouraged a more active FHLB role. During 1966, despite a sharp decline in the growth of assets of savings and loan associations, including an absolute drop during the third quarter, FHLB advances fell from the previous years. FHLBs had exhausted their liquid reserves and could raise funds for advances only by selling their own obligations, thereby adding to already severe money market pressures. Mortgage lending by savings and loan associations slackened abruptly. Once again in 1969 and early 1970, tight monetary conditions placed S&Ls at a disadvantage; interest rates on alternative assets rose, and the net growth in S&L deposits fell. This time the FHLBs aggressively encouraged S&Ls to accept advances, more than three times as large a volume as in any previous year and more than four times as much as in 1966. One expert has estimated that the $4 billion in net advances by FHLBs that year added 140,000 to 160,000 housing starts, well over 10 percent of the U.S. total.[25] Then, in 1970, as the prospect of relaxed monetary conditions appeared, the FHLBB took steps to discourage S&Ls from using increased deposits to repay advances. To keep these funds invested in mortgages, they offered S&Ls the option of converting all advances at 8.5 percent interest into special advances at 7.25 percent interest but with a penalty for prepayment.[26]

24. Most savings and loan associations are members of the FHLB system. Since 1955, savings and loan associations in the system have held more than 95 percent of total assets of all savings and loan associations.

25. Swan, "Homebuilding: A Review of Experience," p. 62. Jaffee estimates that FHLBB advances result almost dollar-for-dollar in increased mortgage holdings by private financial intermediaries, principally S&Ls; after very long periods (over eight years) this effect tends to waste away ("An Econometric Model of the Mortgage Market," pp. 58–59, 81).

26. *Journal of the Federal Home Loan Bank Board*, Vol. 3 (June 1970), p. 1. Authorization for federal expenditures to accomplish this purpose was contained in the Emergency Home Finance Act of 1970.

The Housing Opportunity Allowance Program

Congress in 1970 also empowered the Federal Home Loan Bank Board to administer a program of subsidies to middle income homebuyers. A subsidy of $20 per month for five years against mortgage payments is allowed on home mortgages of $25,000 or less to homebuyers whose incomes are less than 150 percent of the limits set under FHA's homeownership assistance program.[27] In some areas, families with incomes of up to $16,335 per year are eligible.

The declared purpose of the program is "to assist the 'Forgotten American,' the prospective home buyer whose present annual income is either (1) too high to allow him to obtain home purchase assistance under various subsidy programs of [HUD] and other agencies, or (2) insufficient to permit him to obtain a mortgage loan [on an] . . . unsubsidized basis." How assistance for the forgotten middle income American can be justified at the same time that HUD's homeownership program for low and lower middle income families is being criticized for helping some who could have obtained unsubsidized housing is puzzling. Since the middle income subsidy applies to 100 percent mortgages, which S&Ls do not otherwise accept, the real beneficiaries will probably be households in the $7,000–$12,000 income range who lack sufficient cash to make a downpayment.

Federal Home Loan Mortgage Corporation

Only since 1970 has the Federal National Mortgage Association been authorized to deal in conventional mortgages. Congress simultaneously created the Federal Home Loan Mortgage Corporation (FHLMC), under the control of the Federal Home Loan Bank Board,[28] to deal in reasonably secure conventional mortgages as well as those insured or guaranteed by the government. The new institution puts the secondary market facility for S&Ls under the same board that regulates them. By so doing Congress intended to avoid the conflict that might arise between regulatory organizations and to enable the board to choose between secondary market purchases and direct loans to members, a potentially significant distinction if

27. See Chapter 8 for a description of the homeownership program (sec. 235 of the National Housing Act).
28. Emergency Home Financing Act of 1970, Public Law 91-351, 91 Cong., July 24, 1970.

S&Ls ever receive authority to invest a substantial part of their resources in assets other than mortgages.

The Future Role of FNMA, GNMA, and FHLBs

The events of 1966 and 1969 reconfirmed that tight monetary policy chokes off the flow of mortgage credit. Because of restrictions on their activities, thrift institutions cannot compete effectively with commercial banks or other financial intermediaries or with securities directly offered in financial markets. FNMA secondary market operations and FHLB advances reduce this handicap. Should still other measures be taken to insulate the flow of mortgage credit from the effects of tight money? Should FNMA, GNMA, and the FHLBs attempt to increase the average flow of mortgage credit; and if so, how?

The most basic recommendations call for new types of home mortgages. Under one proposal, interest rates on mortgages would vary with current interest rates. If interest rates rose, monthly payments would increase or the term of the loan would lengthen. Alternatively, home mortgage terms might be renegotiated periodically. Or the federal government might pay interest subsidies to S&Ls for the difference between the average yield of their portfolio and the marginal yield on home mortgages. Such a procedure would shift the risk of loss due to higher interest rates to the government from the lender (as at present) or the borrower (as under the variable interest rate arrangement).[29]

Other recommendations deal with the structure of savings and loan associations. During neither 1966 nor 1969 did commercial bank deposits drop as much as those of S&Ls, nor were commercial banks driven to limit seriously their investments in mortgages. Part of their strength was due to FNMA purchases. Commercial banks, however, could compete effectively for funds by raising interest rates payable on some deposits and by borrowing abroad for short periods, often at very high interest rates. Their portfolio was liquid or short term, and as it matured or was sold, proceeds could be reinvested at high rates. One method of reducing the sensitivity

29. For a review of alternative mortgage arrangements, see Roger G. Noll, "Current Mortgage Finance Problems," in President's Task Force on Suburban Problems, "Final Report, Policy Papers" (1968; processed). Noll also describes how mortgages might be designed so that mortgagors would not be deterred from moving by the prospect of losing a favorable mortgage.

of S&Ls to tight money would be to allow them to invest in assets other than mortgages and to accept demand deposits.[30] A gradual relaxation of present restrictions would protect S&Ls against extreme vulnerability to monetary restraint. On the other hand, mortgage credit would lose the undivided attention of its most ardent supporter.

Within the present system S&Ls could be given greater flexibility in meeting unexpected withdrawals of funds. The President's Commission on Mortgage Interest Rates proposed that the liquidity requirement set by the FHLBB for S&Ls be made flexible when S&Ls experience net withdrawals of deposits.[31] For example, the required liquidity reserve might be allowed to drop one dollar for each dollar of net withdrawals until it reached some minimum level. This recommendation closely resembles FHLBB practice in late 1966. There are a number of ways by which the FHLBB could liberalize its policies in making advances. It could make long-term advances to S&Ls, particularly in rapidly growing areas where mortgage demand is strong.[32] S&Ls have indicated strong interest in such credit.[33] The FHLBB would have to increase sale of its bonds and pay higher interest rates than formerly, or design new financial instruments to appeal to investors not presently interested in FHLB bonds. By driving up general interest rates, such a course would make it somewhat more difficult for S&Ls to compete for funds.

The Federal National Mortgage Association has also been concerned with how to raise sale of its own bonds to support enlarged operations without driving up interest rates. The Housing and Urban Development Act of 1968 authorized GNMA to guarantee FNMA bonds. Although FNMA bonds have been backed by federally insured mortgages, lenders have not been spared all loss risk. Holders of FHA insured and VA guaranteed mortgages also bear some liquidity risk, since payment in case of default is usually made in debentures, not cash. The GNMA guarantee relieves investors of even these remote risks. This added security was designed to attract funds from sources such as pension funds or trusts that do not normally invest in mortgages or in FNMA or FHLB bonds. It

30. See "Savings and Loan Study Recommendations," *Journal of the Federal Home Loan Bank Board*, Vol. 2 (September 1969), pp. 5, 24, 25.
31. *Report of the Commission on Mortgage Interest Rates to the President of the United States and to the Congress* (Government Printing Office, 1969), pp. 78–80.
32. Ibid., pp. 82–83.
33. See "Returns from Bank Survey Show Big Demand for Long-Term Credit," *Journal of the Federal Home Loan Bank Board*, Vol. 2 (July 1969), pp. 6–7.

grows in importance as FNMA begins secondary market operations in conventional mortgages.[34]

Summary

The three established financial institutions discussed in this chapter crucially influence the level and flow of mortgage credit. Secondary market purchases of FNMA and net advances of FHLBs probably have added to mortgage credit, although less than dollar for dollar. But for them, monetary restraint in 1969 almost certainly would have compelled even greater cutbacks than occurred in mortgage lending.[35]

The only one of these institutions that provides direct subsidies supported by the federal budget is GNMA. Both FNMA and the Federal Home Loan Bank have customarily made profits, but have not used the profits to subsidize unprofitable operations. They have probably lowered interest rates on mortgages and increased them on other assets by diverting funds to mortgages. Whether lower mortgage rates help homebuyers, sellers, or lenders depends on how they influence homebuyers' offers and final sales prices. Homeowners as a class probably have benefited relative to nonhomeowners, though the benefits may be quite unevenly distributed. These institutions are part of a system that suppressed increases in interest rates on small investors' holdings during periods of tight money or anticipated inflation. They have thus encouraged the tendency to distribute the consequences of inflation regressively. The most important consequences of these institutions, however, have been to alter the allocation of resources and to promote stability in the residential construction industry.

34. In addition, GNMA is authorized to guarantee mortgage-backed securities issued by the Federal Home Loan Mortgage Corporation (Emergency Home Financing Act of 1970, section 306[a]).

35. The Federal Home Loan Mortgage Corporation will perform a similar function for S&Ls.

chapter seven **Low Rent**
Public
Housing

The major federally supported program intended solely for low income Americans is low rent public housing. State and local governments have been cooperating in this federal program for more than three decades, and a few have built additional public housing without federal aid. In June 1970, 2.5 million people lived in 800,000 federally supported units. The number of public housing residents is about one-tenth of the poor, but not all public housing residents are poor.

Over the years public housing has acquired a vile image—highrise concrete monoliths in great impersonal cities, cut off from surrounding neighborhoods by grass or cement deserts best avoided after dark, inhabited by large, mostly black, families, exhibiting the full range of social and economic difficulties. This image suggests that any benefits inhabitants derive from physical housing amenities are offset by the squalid surroundings.

In contrast, actual and prospective tenants seem to regard public housing as a better buy than any housing available to them on the free market. Most projects have extremely low vacancy rates and long waiting lists for admission.[1] The public image ignores the extremely heterogeneous architecture, tenant population, management efficiency, social service provisions, and other amenities of public housing.[2] Despite its unfavorable

1. Waiting lists exceeded vacancies in public housing in 47 of the 49 largest cities with programs in November 1967. They were more than ten times the number of vacancies in 32 of those cities. *Building the American City*, Report of the National Commission on Urban Problems, H. Doc. 91-34, 91 Cong. 1 sess. (1969), p. 131. The vacancy rate for all public housing units on June 30, 1970, was 2.5 percent; it was 1.5 percent or less in 23 states including New York and California. U.S. Department of Housing and Urban Development, *1970 HUD Statistical Yearbook* (1971), p. 103.

2. See George Schermer Associates, *More than Shelter: Social Needs in Low- and Moderate-Income Housing*, Prepared for the National Commission on Urban Problems, Research Report 8 (Government Printing Office, 1968).

image, public housing has weathered political opposition, and in recent years, construction of public housing has been accelerated.

Development of Low Rent Public Housing

The motives for public housing, as for much social legislation, have been mixed. The housing program established in 1937 expressed a desire to improve deplorable housing conditions and a concern over the depressed state of the economy and the construction industry.[3] When World War II superseded depression as the nation's foremost problem, public housing emerged as a legislative device to build housing for defense workers.

The political fortunes of public housing in the two decades following World War II were decidedly mixed.[4] The program narrowly escaped extinction during consideration of the Housing Act of 1949, but then Congress accorded it a major role in meeting the anticipated postwar housing shortage; 810,000 units were to be built in six years. The Korean war forced postponement of that goal, and an unfriendly administration in 1953 deferred it indefinitely. Not until the late 1960s, as concern about poverty and an imminent housing shortage grew, did public housing again obtain substantial political support. These political fortunes are reflected in the fluctuating number of public housing units started or leased and the annual change in the number of units under management, particularly since 1948 (see Figure 7-1).

The uneven political fortune of public housing expresses a continuing lack of consensus about its objectives. Which poor people should get housing assistance when there isn't enough to go around? The poorest, who can pay little for their own housing, or the not-quite-so-poor, who can pay more rent and get along with smaller subsidies? The mostly white aged who might otherwise be a burden on their probably middle class children? Fatherless, frequently black, families with many dependent children? Intact families with heads unable to earn an adequate income? The one

3. The United States Housing Act of 1937—the Wagner-Steagall act—sought to "alleviate present and recurring unemployment and to remedy the unsafe and insanitary housing conditions and the acute shortage of decent, safe, and sanitary dwellings for families of low income . . . that are injurious to the health, safety, and morals of the citizens of the Nation" (50 Stat. 888).

4. For a history, see Robert Fisher, *Twenty Years of Public Housing* (Harper, 1959); and Gilbert Y. Steiner, *The State of Welfare* (Brookings Institution, 1971), Chap. 4.

Figure 7-1. Low Rent Public Housing Units under Management and in Process, 1946–70[a]

A. Units under management

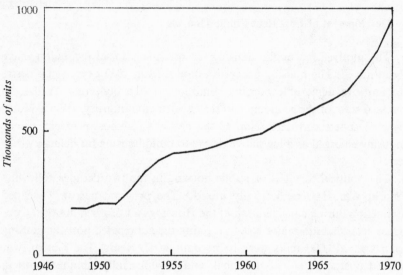

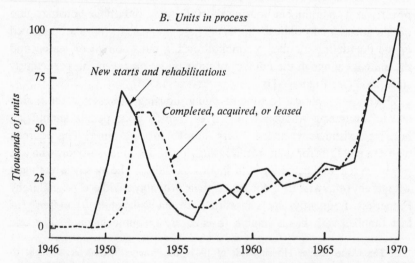

B. Units in process

Sources: Units under management: 1950, 1955, 1960, 1965–70, U.S. Department of Housing and Urban Development, *1970 HUD Statistical Yearbook* (1971), p. 135; other years, *Second Annual Report, Housing and Home Finance Agency, Calendar Year 1948*, and subsequent reports. Units completed, acquired, or leased: 1946–66, *A Decent Home*, Report of the President's Committee on Urban Housing (1969), p. 61; 1967–70, *1970 HUD Statistical Yearbook*, p. 135. New starts and rehabilitations: 1949–67, HUD, *Housing and Urban Development Trends, Annual Summary*, Vol. 22 (May 1969), p. 66; 1968–70, *1970 HUD Statistical Yearbook*, p. 135.

a. Excludes farm labor camps.

alternative clearly eliminated by the modest size of the program is that all poor people should be eligible.

Should public housing be used to clear "slums" or to augment the supply of "low cost" housing? Should tenants be provided housing alone or housing plus social services? Should racial segregation be eliminated, accepted, or reinforced by public housing? Less basic questions, such as how large public housing projects should be, where they should be located, and why they take so long to get built, have sometimes masked the more essential concerns.

Procedures for Establishing Public Housing

The United States Housing Act of 1937 established the principle, still honored, that each community should decide whether or not public housing will be built in it. Local authorities may enter public housing contracts with the federal government only in states where enabling legislation has been enacted. (By 1971 all states except Wyoming had enacted such legislation, and Congress had acted on behalf of the District of Columbia, Puerto Rico, and the Virgin Islands.) Municipal governments then create local housing authorities to construct public housing and to obtain federal subsidies. However, Congress bars such subsidies unless the municipal governments approve the authorities' preliminary applications and agree to exempt public housing projects from property taxes. The authorities in turn agree to pay a stipulated fraction of gross rents in lieu of taxes. In addition, under the Housing Act of 1949 any community in which public housing was to be built had to have "a workable program for community improvement";[5] that requirement was removed by the Housing and Urban Development Act of 1969.

Public housing is developed, owned, and operated by local housing authorities that operate within a municipality, county, several counties, or a

---

5. The workable program is an outline of the community's building, plumbing, electrical, housing, and fire prevention codes and enforcement procedures; its arrangements for evaluating and planning physical, social, and economic development; its plan for meeting housing needs, especially of low and moderate income families, including a schedule of assistance programs to be used, sponsors of projects, and starting and completion dates for construction; and its means of involving citizen groups, especially the poor, in development and execution of the program. See U.S. Department of Housing and Urban Development, *Workable Program for Community Improvement*, A HUD Handbook, RHA 7100.1 (HUD, October 1968). As of September 1969 about half of the U.S. population lived in communities with workable programs.

group of cities. They are legally distinct from local governments to avoid
limitations on bonded indebtedness. Their day-to-day operations are
usually administered by a permanent staff. A board of commissioners determines the need for public housing, selects sites, carries through the planning, development, and management of projects, and sets rents, income
limits (for entrance and continued occupancy), and other eligibility requirements.

Federal Assistance

The federal government offers four kinds of assistance to local authorities. The Department of Housing and Urban Development (HUD) can
make direct loans "to assist the development, acquisition, or administration of low-rent-housing or slum-clearance projects."[6] This power is often
used to assist local authorities in planning projects and in financing other
work before construction loans can be obtained commercially. Before construction begins, HUD enters into an annual contributions contract (not
to exceed forty years) covering interest and amortization on long-term
bonds issued by the authority after construction is completed; the bonds
are almost as secure as obligations of the federal government. The annual
contributions contract is the government's largest form of assistance. Yet
another is the exemption from federal income taxes, which makes interest
rates lower on these bonds than on taxable federal securities. Finally, HUD
makes certain additional payments to local housing authorities on behalf
of elderly, disabled, and handicapped tenants, families displaced by such
federal actions as urban renewal, and unusually large and especially poor
families.

Before 1969, local housing authorities were required to meet current
operating expenses out of rents and utility charges collected from tenants
and to remit any excess over current operating expenses to the federal
government. More than 84 percent of annual contributions were offset by
such remissions in 1948 and 1949,[7] but only about 2 percent in the aggregate in fiscal year 1971.[8] Many housing authorities, particularly in large
cities, could not cover operating expenses out of rents.[9] As a result, Con-

6. Housing Act of 1937, sec. 9 (50 Stat. 891).
7. Fisher, *Twenty Years of Public Housing*, p. 159.
8. *The Budget of the United States Government, 1971—Appendix*, p. 482.
9. On the reasons for this cost squeeze, see Frank de Leeuw, assisted by Eleanor L.
Jarutis, *Operating Costs in Public Housing: A Financial Crisis* (Urban Institute, 1970).

gress in 1969 and 1970 specifically authorized payments to defray them.[10] In addition, Congress stipulated that public housing rents should not exceed 25 percent of tenant income and agreed to appropriate additional funds to reimburse housing authorities for the resulting loss of revenues. Such supplementary payments are anticipated to add $170 million during fiscal year 1973 to the approximately $950 million in fixed annual contributions. Due to various offsetting amounts, total annual contributions are estimated at 1.1 billion.

The form of the federal subsidy offers local housing authorities little incentive for efficient planning and operation. Before 1969 the federal willingness to bear all capital costs but no operating costs encouraged local authorities to minimize maintenance through construction design, even if additional capital costs outweighed future savings in maintenance. Construction guidelines issued by HUD probably narrowed opportunities for abuse. The 1969 and 1970 provisions reduced this problem but created a new one. They commit the federal government to pay the excess (up to a certain maximum) of operating expenses over rents, offering little incentive to efficient management. A subsidy equal to some proportion of total (capital plus operating) expenses or a subsidy directed to tenants in housing projects would correct this deficiency; in either case, the requirement that all residual receipts be returned to HUD would have to be relaxed if profit incentives were to have any effect.

Public Housing Population

The number of families eligible for public housing on the basis of income so vastly exceeds the number of units available for occupancy that local housing authorities have broad discretion in screening applicants. How these powers are exercised determines the characteristics of public housing tenants, the size of federal subsidy required, and the distribution of benefits.

Incomes and Rents of Public Housing Tenants

Both the maximum income of public housing tenants and the rents they are charged depend on local rent levels. At time of his admission the ten-

10. The previous federal practice of limiting its contributions to capital costs was not legally required, but the strength of custom deterred HUD officials from subsidizing operating costs without specific congressional authorization.

ant's income may not exceed five times the rental charged for standard housing.[11] In practice, standard housing refers to the lowest cost private housing available in substantial supply and inhabited by blue collar workers. Most newly admitted tenants have incomes below the maximum. Although practice varies, most housing authorities require tenants to move out if their incomes rise above the maximum allowed for admission by about 25 percent.[12]

Public housing rents must be one-fifth lower than rents charged privately for standard housing, but the authorities themselves determine what the minimum rents on standard housing are. Some authorities set rents at a flat percentage of income; some allow rents as a fraction of income to decline as incomes decline. Many authorities establish minimum rents to protect their solvency. Others set maximum rents for admission below rents acceptable for continued occupancy. The New York City authority has based rents for units that have become available for occupancy since 1961 on the size and amenities of the unit, not the income of the tenant. Most housing authorities make special arrangements with welfare agencies for tenants receiving welfare; many agencies, however, pay recipients less than the minimum needs standards. If local housing authorities attempt to set rents at the needs standards to assist solvency, some welfare agencies reduce clients' payments for items other than rent.

Local housing authorities have had to decide whether to stay financially solvent or to help only the neediest families. They have aimed for solvency. Accordingly, they balance the very poor families who cannot afford rents sufficient to cover even maintenance costs with those who can pay rents that more than cover maintenance costs. Many authorities stipulate the fraction of tenants that can be admitted from each income bracket. Most refuse admission to or evict families with undesirable characteristics. As a result, public housing tenants constitute a very small fraction of each low income bracket (see Table 7-1).[13] Indeed the admissions policy largely determines the character of tenants in a project and the project's solvency.

The diversity of rent formulas and allowable deductions causes a wide

11. Nearly all authorities exempt certain income—for example, Veterans Administration benefits, antipoverty payments, certain special costs, deductions for children—in deciding whether families are eligible to enter or to remain in public housing. Rules for continued occupancy may differ from those for initial eligibility.

12. See Appendix B for a review of income and other limitations for admission to low rent public housing and for receipt of other housing subsidies.

13. On the subject of tenant characteristics, admission procedures, tenant rights or lack thereof, and other policies that affect who gets to live in public housing, see Steiner, *The State of Welfare*, Chap. 5.

Table 7-1. Percentage of Households in Low Rent Public Housing, by
Income Bracket, 1970

| Income bracket (dollars) | Thousands of households in U.S. | Public housing households | |
		Thousands	As percent of households in U.S.
Under 1,000	2,058	43	2.1
1,000–1,999	4,437	306	6.9
2,000–2,999	4,051	201	5.0
3,000–3,999	3,859	135	3.5
4,000–4,999	3,666	86	2.3
5,000–5,999	3,794	51	1.3
6,000 and over	42,508	75	0.2
Total	64,373	897	1.4

Sources: Public housing numbers derived from U.S. Department of Housing and Urban Development, *1970 HUD Statistical Yearbook* (1971), Tables 107, 112, 147; others from U.S. Bureau of the Census, *Current Population Reports*, Series P-60, No. 80, "Income in 1970 of Families and Persons in the United States" (1971), p. 27. Figures are rounded and may not add to totals.

variation in rent-to-income ratios among public housing tenants. Similarly, the gap between public housing rents and minimum rents of private standard housing differs widely. The only consistent objective of pricing policy is to assure local officials considerable autonomy over a politically touchy issue.

The decision by Congress in 1969 and 1970 to limit rents to 25 percent of tenant income and to make extra payments on behalf of low income tenants reflected a realization that available public housing could be more than filled with families too poor to sustain current operating expenses. It also reflected an awareness that some present residents pay more of their incomes in rent than is conventionally acceptable. By setting a ceiling over rent-to-income ratios but not a floor under rents and by agreeing to cover operating losses, Congress has left local authorities free to accept households even poorer than in the past.

The Public Housing Tenant

The typical public housing tenant is desperately poor and, relatively, he is getting poorer. Median income of tenants under 65 years old reexamined for continued occupancy in the year preceding September 1970 was $3,636. Adjusted for price changes, incomes of public housing tenants rose slowly during the 1960s (see Table 7-2). They rose more slowly than the median incomes of all families partly because tenants who "make it" move out

Table 7-2. Median Income of Public Housing Tenants under 65 Years
Old, Selected Years, 1961–70

		Public housing tenants		
Year	All families (current dollars)	Current dollars	Constant 1957–59 dollars	As percent of median family income
1961	5,737	2,704	2,595	47.1
1963	6,249	2,919	2,736	46.7
1965	6,957	3,132	2,850	45.0
1967	7,974	3,462	2,977	43.4
1968	8,632	3,537	2,938	41.0
1969	9,433	3,712	2,984	39.4
1970	9,867	3,636	2,726	36.9

Sources: HUD, Office of Program Development, "Families in Low-Rent Projects: Families Reexamined for Continued Occupancy, Twelve Months Ending September 30, 1970," HMS-225.1 (September 1971; processed), and issues of April 1968, February 1970, January 1971; Bureau of the Census, *Current Population Reports*, Series P-60, No. 80, "Income in 1970 of Families and Persons in the United States" (1971), p. 18, and preceding relevant issues.

voluntarily or are evicted when their income exceeds limits for continued occupancy.

Seventy percent of the tenants were nonwhite in 1970 although just under half of *new* tenants are white. This paradox arises because whites move out of public housing faster on the average than do nonwhites (see Table 7-3). Nonwhite families contain more children than do white families, but each has about the same number of adults on the average. This pattern holds for households headed by persons over 65 years old as well.

The elderly form a growing proportion of the public housing population and this trend will continue. The proportion of new public housing units designed exclusively for them far exceeds the average among existing units. Among new entrants to public housing during the six months preceding March 1970, 52 percent of white households and 19 percent of nonwhite were headed by persons 65 or older.[14] It may be that elderly white poor are more readily accepted in neighborhoods than the younger black poor. Also, legislation makes it easier for housing authorities to build and maintain public housing for the elderly: the maximum cost per room on units designed for them is $4,000, compared with $2,800 for other units,[15] and HUD pays up to $120 a year per family extra for elderly tenants.

Contrary to popular belief, nearly half of all nonelderly public housing residents—48 percent—are not on relief or receiving any other public trans-

14. *1970 HUD Statistical Yearbook*, p. 107.
15. Housing and Urban Development Act of 1969, section 215 (83 Stat. 389).

Table 7-3. Race and Other Characteristics of Public Housing Families, by Age of Head of Family, 1970[a]

Characteristic	Family head under 65 White	Family head under 65 Nonwhite	Family head 65 or older White	Family head 65 or older Nonwhite
Median income (dollars)				
All	3,479	3,425	1,767	1,792
No earners	2,457	2,466	1,693	1,609
One earner	4,540	4,437	3,406	3,361
Two or more earners	7,788	7,703	7,673	6,956
Racial composition within age group (percent)				
Reexamined for continued occupancy	25.7	74.3	62.2	37.8
Newly admitted	37.1	62.9	72.5	27.5
Labor force status (percent)				
No earners	39.5	39.0	89.8	77.4
One earner	54.4	54.6	9.6	20.4
Two or more earners	6.1	6.4	0.6	2.2
Income from public sources (percent)				
None	51.9	47.1	3.4	7.5
Public assistance	35.9	46.1	30.9	51.6
Social security or other transfers but no public assistance	12.2	6.8	65.7	40.9
Family size (percent)				
One person	8	4	68	53
Two persons	18	14	25	26
Three or four persons	39	36	5	13
Five or more persons	36	46	2	8
Average number of persons				
All	3.97	4.58	1.46	2.01
Adults	1.50	1.43	1.32	1.42
Minors	2.47	3.15	0.14	0.59
Admitted to public housing (percent)				
1970	2	2	2	1
1969	21	15	15	10
1968	18	16	18	14
1967–65	28	29	31	29
1964–62	12	14	15	15
1961–58	9	11	9	11
1957 or before	10	13	9	18

Sources: HUD, Office of Housing Management, "Families in Low-Rent Projects: Families Reexamined for Continued Occupancy, Twelve Months Ending September 30, 1970," HMS-225.1 (September 1971; processed); and *1970 HUD Statistical Yearbook*, p. 106 (for families newly admitted during six months ended March 31, 1970).

a. Characteristics differ from true characteristics of all public housing tenants to the extent that households reexamined during 1970 are unrepresentative of the whole public housing population. Data on year of admission are most seriously affected since few households admitted in 1970 would be reexamined in that year.

fer payments. Nineteen elderly household heads in twenty, however, are receiving public assistance, social security, or some other public benefit. Most elderly tenants are not employed, although one-fourth of the non-white and one-tenth of the white households in this group have at least one earner. The majority of younger households have at least one earner (about 60 percent for both nonwhite and white families). However, the median earning capacity of public housing tenants is depressingly low. The median family with head under age 65 and with one earner has income about $2,000 more than that of a family with no earners, elderly whites $1,700 more, and elderly nonwhites $1,750 more.

These statistics tell nothing of the social problems or poor health or lack of education that explain the abnormally high rates of dependency or the meager earnings prospects. The failure of the median income of public housing tenants to rise as fast as the per capita income of the general population suggests that public housing families are even more likely than in the past to suffer from one or more of the handicaps that cause dependency or poor earnings prospects.

Public Housing Construction

Until recent years, local housing authorities purchased sites and directly supervised planning, construction, and management of nearly all public housing. This procedure involved the authority intimately in all phases of the project and exposed each step to intensive political scrutiny and considerable delay. One of HUD's recent alternatives to such involvement is the turnkey project, introduced in late 1965. Private realtors, builders, or contractors propose their designs for suitable structures on sites they specify. The housing authority selects the most appropriate and awards a contract for a completed project. Not only are the problems of site acquisition and preparation avoided, but groups within the real estate and construction industries traditionally opposed to public housing are brought into the process.

In a move designed to cut down management headaches and costs, HUD introduced a Turnkey II program to employ private management. This experiment with private managers who receive their expenses plus a fixed fee appears to have been unsuccessful in cutting costs.[16]

16. For possible reasons, see de Leeuw, "The Financial Crisis of Public Housing Operation." Also see C. Peter Rydell, *Factors Affecting Maintenance and Operating Costs in Federal Public Housing Projects*, New York City Rand Institute (Rand Corp., 1970).

Local housing authorities have also begun to purchase and lease existing housing. Units that must be rehabilitated may be purchased and repaired by the authority or they may be rehabilitated before sale under a turnkey plan. Such units in fiscal year 1971 cost on the average $1,242 in annual contributions as contrasted to conventionally supplied new units at $1,424 and new turnkey units at $1,478. A shorter life or higher maintenance expense may eventually offset this reduced initial cost. One advantage of these units is their rapid availability for occupancy. Relatively small, scattered buildings can be bought, thereby preventing public housing from creating neighborhoods of the poor. Some of these buildings are purchased from private owners, many from the stock of foreclosed properties held by the Federal Housing Administration or the Veterans Administration.

Leases on existing units or new turnkey structures also permit relatively rapid additions to the public housing stock and enable dispersion rather than concentration of the poor. Leasing appears to be more expensive than other methods, in part perhaps because leased units are larger than conventional or turnkey units. Also, owners of leased units do not enjoy tax exemption of their interest payments. They do, however, enjoy such other tax benefits as accelerated depreciation.

Since 1965, public housing tenants have been able to purchase units that can be separated from the rest of the project.[17] The price is the unamortized debt or the appraised value of the unit, with repayment in up to forty years at the average interest rate of outstanding loans on the project. The purchaser must pay local taxes and for services performed by the housing authority. Though these terms are superior to any the borrower could obtain commercially, this program and a 1968 version[18] have been slow in getting started because housing costs are higher than many tenants can afford.

Slum Clearance

Congress has taken all positions, including indifference, on the question of whether public housing should be used to increase the supply of low cost housing or as an offset to "slum clearance."

The Housing Act of 1937 required that for each unit of public housing constructed, an existing unit of slum housing had to be destroyed. In 1949

17. United States Housing Act of 1937, sec. 15(9), added by the Housing and Urban Development Act of 1965 (79 Stat. 488).

18. Housing Act of 1937, sec. 23(g), added by Housing and Urban Development Act of 1968 (82 Stat. 504).

Table 7-4. Distribution of Housing Programs and Units, by Size of City, 1970

In percent

Population of city	Distribution of programs[a]	Distribution of units[b]	Distribution of population inside SMSAs[c]
Under 2,500	49	7	7.8
2,500–9,999	26	11	14.5
10,000–49,999	18	19	27.1
50,000–99,999	4	10	11.6
100,000–249,999	2	11	9.9
250,000–499,999	1	14	7.2
500,000–999,999	*	13	9.0
1,000,000 and over	*	15	13.0

Source: HUD, Division of Research and Statistics, Statistics Branch, "Publicly Financed Low-Rent Housing: Population Size Comparison of Localities with Local Housing Authority Programs, as of December 31, 1970," tabulation; Bureau of the Census, *U.S. Census of Population: 1970, Number of Inhabitants*, Final Report PC(1)-A1, *United States Summary* (1971), p. 1-44.
* Less than 0.5 percent.
a. Based on 4,399 programs.
b. Based on 1,270,007 units.
c. Standard metropolitan statistical areas.

the requirement was modified to apply only to new urban public housing units. In 1969 the terms were reversed: for every low income unit eliminated by an urban renewal project, a new low cost unit must be constructed to take its place.

Location and Size of Project

Contrary to popular conceptions, most public housing is in small and medium sized cities; just over one-fourth of all units are in cities of 500,000 or more (see Table 7-4). More housing units are located in southern states than in any other region, as the following percentage distribution in 1970 shows:[19]

Region	Distribution of units
West	11
South	36
Central, except Chicago	18
North, except New York City	24
New York City and Chicago	12

19. Calculated from *1970 HUD Statistical Yearbook*, p. 136, and unpublished data from the Department of Housing and Urban Development.

Nearly half of all public housing is in large projects in Chicago or New York or small projects in small or medium sized southern cities and towns. Among the most important factors causing this distribution of public housing has been the political economy of racial segregation. Housing authorities in large cities have concentrated housing in densely populated projects because land is costly and large parcels are difficult to amass. Reasonably priced land is available in the suburbs, but suburbanites have successfully resisted the influx of large clusters of the poor who are often black. In small communities land is reasonably priced and the public housing population is drawn locally.[20]

Measuring the Subsidy in Public Housing[21]

Public housing redistributes real incomes in two different ways. Tenants buy housing services at a "bargain" and their real incomes thus increase. The real incomes of owners and tenants of other housing also change. If the availability of public housing reduces demand for unsubsidized housing more than it reduces supply, rents paid for low cost, unsubsidized housing will tend to decline. Thus the real incomes of tenants in unsubsidized housing will tend to be higher and the incomes of owners lower. If public housing construction raises construction costs, the price of unsubsidized housing services may rise. Moreover, the amount people are willing to pay for unsubsidized housing may be altered by the introduction of public housing. Untangling these rather complex interrelationships would be hard enough even if such obstacles to the smooth operation of the housing market as racial discrimination and zoning restrictions did not exist. Because they do, only benefits to public housing tenants are measured.

20. See Steiner, *The State of Welfare*, Chap. 6.
21. See Robert L. Bish, "Public Housing: The Magnitude and Distribution of Direct Benefits and Effects on Housing Consumption," *Journal of Regional Science*, Vol. 9 (December 1969), pp. 425–38; James R. Prescott, "Rental Formation in Federally Supported Public Housing," *Land Economics*, Vol. 43 (August 1967), pp. 341–45, and "The Economics of Public Housing: A Normative Analysis" (Ph.D. thesis, Harvard University, 1964); Eugene Smolensky, "Public Housing or Income Supplements—The Economics of Housing for the Poor," *Journal of the American Institute of Planners*, Vol. 34 (March 1968), pp. 94–101; Edgar O. Olsen, "A Welfare Economic Evaluation of Public Housing" (Ph.D. thesis, Rice University, 1968); Eugene Smolensky and J. Douglas Gomery, "Efficiency and Equity Effects in the Benefits from Federal Public Housing Program in 1965," paper prepared for the Joint Economic Committee (University of Wisconsin, n.d.; processed).

Table 7-5. Distribution of Benefits from Public Housing, by Income Bracket, Race, and Public Assistance Status, 1966

Income bracket (dollars)	Total benefits (millions of dollars)		Percent of total benefits		Benefits per family, by race (dollars)		Benefits per family, by public assistance status (dollars)	
	White	Nonwhite	White	Nonwhite	White	Nonwhite[a]	Receiving public assistance	Not receiving public assistance
0–1,000	15.1	12.2	3.0	2.4	784	753	767	818
1,001–1,500	36.3	32.9	7.1	6.5	778	775	764	848
1,501–2,000	32.6	35.7	6.4	7.0	804	824	805	846
2,001–2,500	29.1	36.3	5.7	7.1	821	827	826	827
2,501–3,000	26.7	35.9	5.2	7.1	845	821	869	800
3,001–4,000	35.8	55.3	7.0	10.9	801	826	890	771
4,001–5,000	20.6	36.0	4.0	7.1	776	818	884	773
5,001–6,000	12.9	24.6	2.5	4.9	752	805	808	779
6,001–7,500	6.9	15.8	1.4	3.0	677	808	768	750
7,501–10,000	2.1	5.2	0.4	1.0	564	745	694	665
Over 10,000	0.7	0.9	0.1	0.2	653	495	357	614
Total or average	219.0	290.6	43.0	57.0	790	809	817	784

Source: Derived from data supplied by HUD (see Appendix C). Figures are rounded and may not add to totals.
a. Nonwhite omits Indians and Spanish Americans, includes only blacks.

The Level and Distribution of Public Housing Subsidies

Public housing obviously raises the living standard of its tenants. If it did not, they would not have chosen it, or if they had blundered in, would have moved out. Most tenants probably occupy better housing than they would occupy if they paid commercial rents.[22] The costs the federal government incurs and the property taxes municipal governments forgo do not equal the unrestricted cash transfer that would bring the same improvement in living standards as public housing.

The benefits from public housing are estimated here to equal the difference between public housing rents and rents on equivalent unsubsidized units; they are presumed to accrue to public housing tenants only. The possible social benefits, discussed in Chapter 1, are ignored.

The Distribution of Public Housing Benefits

The difference between rents charged public housing tenants and rents charged privately for equivalent housing totaled $510 million in 1966 (see Table 7-5). More than half of the benefits accrued to households with incomes of $3,000 per year or less, 86 percent to households with incomes of $5,000 per year or less.[23] Public housing is clearly aimed at low income households. The large proportion of benefits going to low income families arises from admissions policies alone, for benefits per family vary little among income brackets except for the thinly populated "high" income brackets over $7,500 per year. Of total benefits, 45 percent accrue to households receiving no public assistance, social security, or other federal, state, or local assistance.

For several reasons the size of the estimated benefits is open to some question. The benefits shown in Table 7-5 are equal to the difference between rents tenants actually pay and the rents local housing authorities estimate would be charged for the lowest cost standard housing in substantial supply.[24] These "gap rents" are reduced by 20 percent in calcu-

22. It is conceivable that some tenants may occupy public housing, inferior to commercial units they would otherwise have chosen, in order to obtain the subsidy.

23. If society at large gains from improved housing for some of the poor, benefits to low income groups would be decreased slightly, while those to upper income groups would be increased considerably. See Henry Aaron and Martin McGuire,"Public Goods and Income Distribution," *Econometrica*, Vol. 38 (November 1970), pp. 907–20 (Brookings Reprint 202).

24. For a description of sampling methods, see Appendix C.

lating maximum public housing rents. Local housing authorities are allowed considerable latitude in determining them, and thus in setting maximum public housing rents and the size and income of eligible households. Even if local housing authorities lacked all discretion in setting gap rents, public housing is unlike any unsubsidized housing available to the poor. Physically similar private housing would cost more and be inhabited by higher income households. Because the tenants would be richer, the environment would differ. Or put another way, the private market provides no unsubsidized housing comparable in quality to public housing inhabited entirely by people like public housing tenants.

The rents charged by local housing authorities are negotiated with welfare agencies for many tenants who receive welfare. Some agencies that must meet public housing rents greater than their normal allocations reduce payments for food, clothing, and other goods accordingly. In these cases, public housing "subsidies" are an arbitrary part of a larger transfer payment.

The Table 7-5 total of $510 million in benefits received by tenants compares with annual contributions against housing loans by the federal government of $232 million in fiscal year 1966 and of $261 million in fiscal year 1967. These contributions are of course determined by historical costs and interest rates, often much below current rates. Moreover, they are only one part of the package of federal aids that housing authorities receive. The figures in Table 7-5 may be much higher than annual contributions because of unrealistically high gap-rent estimates. Or the inefficiency of housing authorities relative to private landlords may generate costs without corresponding benefits. The National Commission on Urban Problems found delays in public housing were at times "disgraceful," that cost reducing techniques were not used, and that administrators failed to train personnel adequately.[25] No direct evidence on the efficiency of public housing management is available, but indirect evidence is disquieting.

The annual capital subsidy necessary to amortize low rent public housing placed under construction in 1966 was about $790 per unit.[26] The numerous other federal subsidies to low rent public housing and the property taxes forgone by municipal governments are worth several hundred dollars additionally. These figures indicate that the average benefit to

25. *Building the American City*, p. 119.
26. Average total development cost was $16,037 in 1966. The interest rate on high grade municipals was 3.82 percent. Amortization over forty years requires annual outlays of $788.69.

tenants through rent reduction is smaller than the incremental social cost of public housing. They do not prove the program inefficient, since the true subsidy on older units may be smaller than on new units, and since these estimates ignore benefits that may accrue to families outside public housing. They also ignore the consequences of other housing and related programs, particularly urban renewal.

Summary

After three decades of a now-she-loves-me-now-she-hates-me relationship with Congress and the President, public housing seems to have secured the grudging acceptance of lawmakers. The President's *Second Annual Report on National Housing Goals* projects increases in public housing starts and rehabilitations from 100,000 in 1970 to 145,000 in 1975. Even a program of 100,000 units per year is high by historical standards.

Since the requirement that local housing authorities cover operating costs out of rents was removed in 1969, the relative incomes of tenants are likely to continue to decline. The character of the public housing tenant population is likely also to change, in predictable ways. Since blacks are poorer than whites, the fraction of residents who are black is likely to continue rising. Race has been and will remain a touchy issue in public housing, as elsewhere. Of probably greater significance, however, is the fact that the poverty population increasingly consists of female-headed families and households with persistent problems. They will constitute an ever increasing proportion of public housing tenants. Unless housing authorities successfully diffuse units in small decentralized projects, problems caused by clusters of problem families will grow.

The willingness of the federal government to pay part of operating costs and the limitation of rents to 25 percent of income change the relationship between low rent public housing and other federal housing programs. These changes reduce substantially the difference between public housing, on the one hand, and rent supplements and rental assistance for low income families on the other.[27] The latter programs require tenants to pay one-fourth of income in rent, while public housing permits them to pay less. Only public housing requires tenants to vacate units if their incomes rise above a certain limit.

27. See Chapter 8.

The low rent public housing program provided low income Americans with $510 million in reduced rental costs in 1966. This benefit level has risen further and will continue to rise as new units are added. If the relationship between benefits as estimated in this chapter and federal annual contributions has remained roughly constant, benefits will approach $2 billion in fiscal year 1972.

A number of issues concerning public housing remain unsettled. The most important is the fairness of giving a sizable subsidy—$800 per year on the average—to a small fraction of low income households and nothing to most of the rest. Another is whether the large variation in rent-to-income ratios should be permitted to continue. Answers to both questions depend on other housing subsidy programs described in Chapter 8 as well as public housing. The reason for different rules under programs with similar purposes is unclear. The administration recognized this issue in its proposed Housing Act of 1970 by calling for a single rent formula under all rental assistance programs. Congress took no action in 1970. A similar bill was introduced in 1971.

Should social services be provided along with public housing? Should the trend toward greater use of existing housing, through lease or acquisition, be continued? Should public housing be used as an instrument to combat racial segregation or should it accommodate to existing residential patterns? Answers to these and other policy questions will determine the character of the growing low rent public housing program.

chapter eight **Housing
Assistance
Programs**

Over the years the federal government has experimented with a variety of programs intended to help low or middle income households buy or rent adequate housing. This effort, shaped by conflicting objectives of various influential groups in and out of government, has zigzagged toward a form of housing assistance that incorporates features the Congress and the President appear to have thought desirable, not necessarily the characteristics that other standards would have dictated.

The program has relied heavily on private builders and developers since their opposition could have retarded the program politically, as it did with publicly owned housing. More positively, the active cooperation and support of the construction industry could greatly aid the growth of any program of housing assistance tied to new construction. Another aim in the design of programs has been to defer the impact of assistance on the federal budget as long as possible. If its costs were not concentrated in the year the assistance was first undertaken, the program would be politically more attractive to both the executive and legislative branches, whose concern over next year's budget outlays seems more passionate than their worries about commitments two or three decades hence. Yet another important goal has been to relate the amount of assistance to the economic circumstances of the aided households.

At the federal level, and particularly within the Department of Housing and Urban Development (HUD), a consensus has developed that housing assistance should not reinforce economic and racial segregation, but rather contribute to the development of economically and racially heterogeneous neighborhoods. Dispersion of assisted households throughout the community would provide them with a salutary environment and might be

127

acceptable to the more privileged. Suburban communities, angry at being chosen for reformist moves, have repeatedly frustrated these hopes. Most housing programs have sought to increase housing supply as well as demand in order directly to upgrade the housing stock and to offset demolition under such programs as urban renewal and highway construction. The degree to which housing assistance should be tied directly to additional housing construction remains unresolved.

Low rent public housing has quite successfully removed program costs from the federal budget or spread them over a long period. The program has also increased both the supply of and the demand for housing. On the other hand, it has until recently given developers a subsidiary role; it has not consistently matched rents to tenant incomes; and its projects have contributed more often to economic or racial segregation than to integration.

Four programs offering purchase and rental aid have attempted to embody wider objectives. Programs of below-market-interest-rate loans on housing designated for lower middle income families and rent supplements have been in operation for several years. Two newer programs promote homeownership and rental and cooperative housing for lower income families.

Below-Market-Interest-Rate Loans

In 1961, Congress authorized loans at low interest rates to nonprofit or limited dividend corporations or cooperatives for the construction of modest housing for lower middle income households. By the end of fiscal year 1970, 135,000 units had been completed under this program. The program never worked quite as intended. It was plagued by administrative delays, and the myth grew up that it assisted households with higher incomes than Congress or the administration originally intended; the coup de grace came from accounting reforms that increased the current budget cost of the program.

Under the program, qualified builders could obtain loans at 3 percent interest from banks and other lenders. Lenders made such loans only because the Government National Mortgage Association[1] immediately purchased the mortgage at par. Under this arrangement, GNMA was the real lender, the bank merely a middleman or broker. Limited dividend

1. The Federal National Mortgage Association before 1968. See Chapter 6.

corporations, nonprofit corporations, and cooperatives have built 98 percent of all units under this program.

The program's benefits are the reduced rents for tenants made possible by below-market-interest rates. The reduction in cost from such loans clearly depends on the rate at which the developer otherwise would have to borrow. With market interest rates at 6.5 percent, a 3 percent loan makes possible an estimated 27 percent reduction in rents.[2] With market interest rates at 9 percent, a rate prevailing during the later years of the program, a rent reduction of 37 percent is possible. Estimates of the amount of government subsidy provided by interest rate support for low income housing in the years 1966–70 are shown in Table 6-1 (p. 98); they represent the present discounted value of the benefits generated over forty years by projects started in a particular year. The annual flow of benefits from all units was roughly $11.8 million in fiscal year 1968 and $27.9 million in 1970 and will be $50.1 million at the end of fiscal 1972.[3]

The below-market-interest-rate program was aimed at households with incomes of $4,000 to $6,000 for a family of four. Most households with lower incomes would find the housing too expensive, and those with higher incomes would be excluded by income limits (which vary geographically). Although the limits for admission range from about one-third to nearly two times more than those for low rent public housing, prospective tenants must include all family income in determining eligibility.

The typical family seeking such housing in 1968 had an income of $5,678, had three members including one child, and paid between $110 and $120 per month for a walk-up apartment in a small or medium sized metropolitan area; most were white. As Table 8-1 suggests, the program served precisely the group for which it was designed, contrary to a fairly widespread belief that it primarily served higher income brackets.[4]

2. George von Furstenberg and Howard R. Moskof, "Federally Assisted Rental Housing Programs: Which Income Groups Have They Served or Whom Can They Be Expected to Serve?" in *The Report of the President's Committee on Urban Housing: Technical Studies* (Government Printing Office, 1967), Vol. 1, p. 153.

3. Based on an average annual subsidy of $207 on units built before 1971 and $376 on units built in 1971 and 1972 (*Independent Offices and Department of Housing and Urban Development Appropriations for 1971*, Hearings before a Subcommittee of the House Committee on Appropriations, 91 Cong. 2 sess. [1970], Pt. 3, pp. 654–65); the numbers of units completed are taken from Table D-8, Appendix D.

4. In 1965 Robert C. Weaver, then director of the Housing and Home Finance Agency, later secretary of housing and urban development, testified that "from the very start this program only took the top of the moderate-income market, it did not take it

Table 8-1. Distribution of Tenants in Homeowner and Rental Assistance Programs, by Income and Other Characteristics, Various Dates, 1968–71

	Percentage of all tenants in program			
Characteristic	Below-market-interest-rate loans (1968)	Rent supplements (1969)	Home-ownership assistance (1971)	Rental assistance (1970)
Income bracket (dollars)				
Under 1,000	0.3	7.7	...	...
1,000–1,999	2.5	41.1	...	...
2,000–2,999	4.7	27.3	1.1ᵃ	10.7ᵃ
3,000–3,999	10.1	17.0	4.2	13.5
4,000–4,999	17.0	5.7	15.2	23.5
5,000–5,999	22.6	1.2	25.7	25.6
6,000–6,999	21.6	0.1ᵇ	25.0	17.6
7,000–7,999	12.5	...	16.8	6.6
8,000–8,999	5.3	...	7.7	1.9
9,000–9,999	1.9	...	2.8	0.4
10,000 and over	1.5	...	1.5	0.2
Age of head				
Under 20	n.a.	3.0	2.7	7.5
20–29	n.a.	26.0	50.1	61.7
30–39	n.a.	14.5	29.2	14.1
40–49	n.a.	7.4	11.8	6.3
50 and over	n.a.	49.1ᶜ	6.2	10.4
Family size				
1 person	9.5	32.8	0.2	13.6
2 persons	30.3	13.4	10.7	24.9
3 persons	29.4	15.4	24.9	31.6
4 persons	17.3	13.3	21.2	17.2
5 persons	8.2	12.5	17.2	7.9
6 or more persons	5.1	12.5	25.8	4.9
Monthly mortgage payment or rent (dollars)				
Under 40	...	32.9	0.2	n.a.
40–49	...	25.8	0.2	n.a.
50–59	...	14.2	1.9	n.a.
60–69	...	10.3	6.9	n.a.
70–79	3.8ᵈ	10.6	16.1	n.a.
80–89	10.2	3.4	22.7	n.a.
90–99	12.8	1.9	20.0	n.a.
100–109	14.6	0.9ᵉ	13.9	n.a.
110–119	18.9	...	9.2	n.a.
120–129	17.2	...	5.1	n.a.
130–139	11.1	...	2.0	n.a.
140–159	9.0	...	1.2ᶠ	n.a.
160 and over	2.4	...	...	n.a.

Table 8-1. (*continued*)

	Percentage of all tenants in program			
Characteristic	Below-market-interest-rate loans (1968)	Rent supplements (1969)	Home-ownership assistance (1971)	Rental assistance (1970)
Subsidy per month (dollars)				
Under 20	n.a.	...	0.4	n.a.
20–29	n.a.	...	0.5	n.a.
30–39	n.a.	...	1.3	n.a.
40–49	n.a.	10.5ᵍ	3.0	n.a.
50–59	n.a.	6.3	6.5	n.a.
60–69	n.a.	13.8	13.5	n.a.
70–79	n.a.	16.2	23.8	n.a.
80–89	n.a.	17.2	29.3	n.a.
90 and over	n.a.	36.1	21.7	n.a.

Sources: For below-market-interest-rate loan program, U.S. Department of Housing and Urban Development (HUD), Federal Housing Administration (FHA), Division of Research and Statistics, machine tabulations, May 25, 1970. For rent supplement program, derived from HUD, "Report of Rent Supplement Tenant Characteristics," with data for June to December 1969 (processed), and "Rent Supplement Tenant Characteristics," with data for May 31, 1969 (processed). For homeownership program, *1971 Housing and Urban Development Legislation*, Hearings before the Subcommittee on Housing and Urban Affairs of the Senate Committee on Banking, Housing and Urban Affairs, 92 Cong. 1 sess. (1971), Pt. 1, pp. 13–16, 27. For rental assistance program, HUD, Housing Management, Statistics Branch, unpublished tabulations, Feb. 8, 1971, and April 2, 1971. Percentages are rounded and may not add to 100.

n.a. Not available.
a. Less than $3,000.
b. $6,000 and over.
c. Those 60 and over accounted for 43.2 percent.
d. Less than $80.
e. $100 and over.
f. $140 and over.
g. Less than $50.

The distribution of benefits in 1970 by income class and color is shown in Table 8-2.[5] Nearly three-quarters of benefits accrue to households with incomes between $4,000 and $8,000 a year.[6] Despite the program's success in reaching its intended beneficiaries, no new projects were to be started after fiscal year 1971.

---

all of the way down" (*Housing Legislation of 1965*, Hearings before a Subcommittee of the Senate Committee on Banking and Currency, 89 Cong. 1 sess. [1965], p. 16); and, again, that the program "has served only the top of the moderate-income families and it has not gotten down to the people who are still between it and public housing. It serves a little bit of the layer between public housing and private but you have a whole lot left in there and this whole lot is getting larger as the interest rate goes up" (*Housing and Urban Development Act of 1965*, Hearings before the Subcommittee on Housing of the House Committee on Banking and Currency, 89 Cong. 1 sess. [1965], Pt. 1, p. 229).

5. The distribution of benefits by income bracket differs slightly from the distribution of tenants by income bracket because the distribution of benefits is assumed to be proportional to the distribution of rent paid by income bracket.

6. The term "benefits" refers to the federal subsidy.

Table 8-2. Distribution of Benefits from Below-Market-Interest-Rate Program, by Income Bracket and Race, 1970

Income bracket (dollars)	Total benefits (millions of dollars)		Percent of total benefits	
	White	Non-white	White	Non-white
Under 1,000	0.1	*	0.2	0.1
1,000–1,999	0.4	0.2	1.6	0.9
2,000–2,999	0.7	0.6	2.6	2.1
3,000–3,999	1.5	1.3	5.3	5.8
4,000–4,999	2.6	2.2	9.1	7.9
5,000–5,999	3.5	2.8	12.7	10.0
6,000–6,999	3.5	2.5	12.7	8.9
7,000–7,999	2.0	1.5	7.1	5.3
8,000–8,999	0.7	0.8	2.6	2.7
9,000–9,999	0.3	0.3	1.0	0.9
10,000 and over	0.2	0.2	0.8	0.7
Total	15.5	12.4	55.7	44.3

Sources: Data provided by FHA, Division of Research and Statistics, and *Independent Offices and Department of Housing and Urban Development Appropriations for 1971*, Hearings before a Subcommittee of the House Committee on Appropriations, 91 Cong. 2 sess. (1970), Pt. 3, pp. 654–65.
* Less than $50,000.

One important reason for the program's demise was its limited appeal to profit-oriented developers or investors. Nonprofit and cooperative developments were sponsored by various civic, religious, charitable, or public service organizations, whose motives for building housing were varied but not confined to thirst for profit. Limited dividend corporations, restricted to a 6 percent annual yield on equity investment before taxes, must reduce rents if their profits go higher. Why would profit-oriented builders, developers, or investors be willing to participate in a program with such stringent limitations?

One of the program's major attractions was the fact that the 10 percent equity investment it required could represent forgone development fees or other services in kind. Builder-developers could "mortgage out"—that is, borrow enough to cover all out-of-pocket costs—and sell to final owners having made little or no investment in cash. In addition, there was no profit limitation on companies that sold such services as architectural design or general contracting to the limited dividend corporation or on the capital gain that previous owners of project sites could earn. The limited dividend incorporator could also own these companies and have been the previous landowner.[7] A number of important tax advantages that raised the after tax return much above 6 percent on below-market-interest-rate projects also made the program appealing.

The advantages were offset by long delays by federal and local government agencies in processing applications. Although the program was enacted in 1961, not until 1969 were as many as 15,000 units completed in any single year. Moreover, the cumulative backlog in units on which reservations had been made, but which were not completed, reached 120,000 in 1968 (see Table D-8, Appendix D). Many builders and developers felt the program was a morass best avoided unless firm commitments were available.

Another major fault of the program was the inflexibility of the subsidy. Subsidies available on behalf of families with incomes of $10,000 and $2,000 were the same. The amount is unrelated to need as measured either by income of tenants or by management costs.

For decision makers anxious to defer budgetary impacts, the budgetary accounting procedures for the program were a severe drawback. The face value and initial budget cost of the below-market-interest-rate loan exceed the subsidy value, since the lender must make some repayments to the government. The subsidy accrues to tenants over the life of the project, but the budget costs are incurred as soon as GNMA buys the mortgage. The search for a way of putting off until tomorrow the budgetary consequences of housing assistance undertaken today led to a new program in 1965.

Rent Supplements

The rent supplement program requested by President Lyndon Johnson in 1965 was designed to correct the shortcomings of the subsidized loan program. The initial proposal called for subsidies to eligible families with low incomes above public housing limits provided that they paid 20 percent of income in rent. The federal government would pay property owners the difference between the tenant's share and fair market rents; under no cir-

7. Periodically, newspaper stories expose how these techniques were used to make "fabulous" or "exorbitant" profits despite the limited dividend framework. Leonard Downie, Jr., in "FHA Helps Developers Strike it Rich," *Washington Post*, July 21, 1970, reports that one developer bought land for $8,000 an acre which FHA appraised at $26,000 per acre for purposes of calculating the mortgage it would insure. This developer "not only invested no cash but got back $206,000, which FHA records say was for land."

cumstance was the rent to be above market rates, nor was the government to pay more than the subsidy incurred for public housing. Robert Weaver, then administrator of the Housing and Home Finance Agency, testified that the administration hoped to support construction of 500,000 housing units in four years if this program were adopted.[8]

In fact, the program barely passed; Congress restricted eligibility for rent supplements to families with incomes below, rather than above, public housing limits; tenants were to pay one-fourth, rather than one-fifth, of their income in rent and at least 30 percent of fair market rents.[9] Nearly five years after enactment of the program, fewer than 46,000 units had been started, less than one-tenth the number envisaged in the original program (see Table D-9, Appendix D). The program has not been a congressional pet.

The chief innovation of the rent supplement program was to vary assistance systematically with tenant income in order to focus federal outlays on the neediest. As the tenant's income rose, his rent would increase until it reached market level, but he would not be compelled to move. Rent supplement projects were to develop into nests of economic diversity, populated by newly admitted families with low incomes and older families whose incomes had grown. The salutary example of successful neighbors would replace the supposedly baneful atmosphere of public housing where low income tenants were exposed to others like themselves.

The designers of rent supplements hoped to enhance its political appeal by spreading its costs over the life of the project, so that payments would appear in the federal budget only as made. Representative Leonor Sullivan exposed that intention during congressional hearings:

MRS. SULLIVAN: In other words, I have a suspicion that one of the reasons you were able to "sell" your program to the Budget Bureau was because of the fact that this program would have a minimum initial impact on the Federal annual budget in contrast to section 221(d)(3) below-market interest rate mortgages, for example, where the whole cost of the mortgage is an immediate charge to the budget the minute FNMA buys it. I would like your comments on that.

MR. WEAVER: Two things. Obviously, it did not hurt the program with the Bureau of the Budget, and I think certainly the President has a concern for this and I think the Congress has, too. It has merit.[10]

The designers also hoped to prevent cities and towns from vetoing projects designed for low income tenants. They explicitly excluded the work-

8. *Housing Legislation of 1965*, Hearings, p. 6.
9. This provision appears in regulations, not in the law.
10. *Housing and Urban Development Act of 1965*, Hearings, pp. 233–34.

able program for community improvement as a requirement, thus removing a favorite local device for excluding low income families.[11] By locating some projects in middle and upper class areas, providing flexible assistance, and authorizing overincome tenants to remain in projects, HUD hoped to disperse low income households. Since a disproportionate number of low income households are black, Mexican-American, and Puerto Rican, this provision would have promoted racial and ethnic, as well as economic, integration.

Even the promotion of residential integration through assistance to middle income families would have aroused considerable opposition. Combined with aid to the very poor, it was political poison. While the whole rent supplement program eventually gained narrow acceptance, relaxation of the workable program requirement never did. Until 1969, appropriation acts consistently stipulated that "no part of the rent supplement contract authority . . . may be used for incurring any obligation in connection with any dwelling unit or project which is not either part of a workable program for community improvement, or which is without local official approval for participation in the rent supplement program."[12]

The program works as follows: HUD agrees with a contractor to make rent supplement payments at a stipulated maximum per year for forty years. Having secured this commitment, the housing developer then begins construction. Rent supplement payments start only after units are completed and occupied. Since some tenants pay more than the basic 30 percent of market rents, actual payments do not reach the contracted maximum; HUD estimates that over the life of projects authorized from 1967 through 1971, payments were about 83 percent of the maximum obligation.[13] Rent supplements may be provided for those in housing programs for the elderly and handicapped and for lower income families, in below-market-interest-rate projects, or in state-aided projects.

Families benefiting from rent supplements have lower incomes but are smaller than those living in low rent public housing (see Table 8-1). The median income of families in the program is $2,089; their median rent is $127 a month, with the tenant paying $46 and receiving a subsidy of $81.

11. Section 101(f) of the Housing and Urban Development Act of 1965.

12. *Basic Laws and Authorities on Housing and Urban Development, Revised Through January 31, 1970*, House Committee on Banking and Currency, 91 Cong. 2 sess. (1970), pp. 268–69.

13. *Independent Offices and Department of Housing and Urban Development Appropriations for 1971*, Hearings before a Subcommittee of the House Committee on Appropriations, 91 Cong. 2 sess. (1970), Pt. 3, pp. 654–55.

The annual benefits, amounting to nearly two-thirds of market rents on assisted units, are approximately equal to government expenditures on the program—$44.4 million in fiscal year 1971. The present value of benefits over a forty-year project life to tenants in 21,000 rent supplement units estimated to be completed during fiscal year 1972 will be approximately $300 million, or about $14,381 per unit.[14]

Homeownership and Rental Assistance

Three years after Congress rewrote the rent supplement program as a price for approval, it enthusiastically enacted two new programs for homeownership and rental assistance structurally similar to the original rent supplement proposal and aimed squarely at lower middle income homeowners and renters (sections 235 and 236 of the National Housing Act, respectively). Congress authorized construction of units under these programs in communities with or without a workable program, and it did not nullify this authorization in its appropriation bills.

The striking change in congressional mood between 1965 and 1968 was due in part to a developing sense that housing demands in the 1970s would be strong and that, without federal assistance, many families not otherwise considered in need of aid would find themselves unable to secure adequate housing. It may also have been due to a developing interest in middle America. In any case, Congress has made generous appropriations for both programs, and they are off to a much faster start than any other federal housing program.

The homeownership assistance program requires participants to pay at least one-fifth of their adjusted income toward mortgage amortization; they may deduct 5 percent of gross income in lieu of social security and $300 for each minor child from income. If the homeowner's payment is less than amortization, the Department of Housing and Urban Development pays the lender the difference (not to exceed the difference between amortization over thirty years at market rates and amortization at 1 percent interest). In 1968 when the program was enacted and mortgage interest rates were about 6.5 percent, plus 0.5 percent insurance premium, the maximum subsidy was about 50 percent of mortgage payments. By 1970 with FHA rates at 8.5 percent, the maximum subsidy was about 60

14. This estimate presumes that undiscounted payments are spread equally over the life of the project and that the appropriate discount rate is 7 percent.

percent. For a family of five or more persons in a high cost area with a $24,000 mortgage, the subsidy would be more than $117 a month.

The rental assistance program requires renters to pay one-fourth of adjusted income as rent. HUD pays the difference between this sum and fair market rents or the difference between amortization over forty years at market interest rates and amortization at 1 percent, whichever is less. Since market rents include maintenance costs, taxes, vacancy allowances, and depreciation, the maximum subsidy at time of enactment was an estimated 35 percent.[15] By 1970, when interest rates on FHA mortgages including insurance premiums had risen to 9 percent, the maximum subsidy had risen to 44 percent of market rents. HUD has induced developers of many projects begun under the below-market-interest-rate program to convert to this program. It provides a larger subsidy for projects not designed to serve households with relatively high incomes, and because of its flexibility provides potentially greater protection for all projects against possible future drops in the incomes of tenants.

Most families in the homeownership program have annual incomes in the $4,000–$8,000 range (see Table 8-1), the same group served by the below-market-interest-rate program. The median family entering the homeownership program in early 1971 was composed of four persons headed by a twenty-nine-year-old with a $6,150 income; their mortgage subsidy was $80 and their own payment $91 per month. Most of those in the rental assistance projects have slightly lower incomes; the median family is composed of only three persons, with an annual income of $5,089. However, the larger family size in homeowner units more than offsets the small amount of extra income.

Housing under both programs is too costly for very low income households. However, up to 20 percent of the rental assistance units in a project may be occupied by tenants who also receive rent supplements. Annual federal payments under the two programs are projected to reach $299 million and $151 million respectively by fiscal year 1972 and to rise rapidly thereafter.

During early 1971 a congressional report exposed corruption and inefficiency in the administration of the homeownership program.[16] The most

15. von Furstenberg and Moskof, "Federally Assisted Rental Housing Programs," p. 153.

16. *Investigation and Hearing of Abuses in Federal Low- and Moderate-Income Housing Programs*, Staff Report and Recommendations, House Committee on Banking and Currency, 91 Cong. 2 sess. (1970).

serious abuses occurred in the part of the program based on existing housing. Some speculators had made extraordinary profits.[17] A few appraisers had been involved with incriminating frequency in such cases. Some construction was shoddy. The reported abuses raised other questions concerning the basic structure of the program, the desirability of promoting homeownership for very low income households, and the role FHA should play in such transactions.[18] Some buyers did not know that in addition to making mortgage payments they had to pay maintenance and utility expenses. Others were innocent of the simplest methods of maintenance and repair. Clearly, many low income purchasers require counseling and assistance.

But even if administrators acted with scrupulous honesty, even if they were charged with responsibility for guarding ignorant or gullible buyers against all consequences of their own folly, and even if all FHA financing and construction regulations were perfectly drawn,[19] the basic structure of

17. Perhaps the most malodorous case, among a bumper crop of fetid abuses, deserves to be reported in detail. "One house visited by the staff . . . had previously been a tavern. City records show that an order was issued by the city on October 6, 1969, to remove the refuse and board up the house. On November 18, 1969, the house was sold to a speculator for $1,800. A permit was obtained for electrical repairs at an estimated cost of $450. On March 24, 1970, the house was sold [under the homeownership program] for $20,000—an increase of over 1,100 percent. The tavern bar covering one side of what is now the living room still remains. In order to enter the remainder of the house, one has to go up two steps to the area where tables had been in the tavern. The walls are rough and uneven where fresh paint was placed over old paint without adequate preparation. The bedroom floors are warped and buckling. The front door has been moved from the center to the side of the home and a small bathroom-type window placed where the front door used to be." Ibid., pp. 11–12. FHA foreclosed a $20,595 mortgage on another house, paid $4,784 for repairs, and sold the house for $16,000. Three days after the sale, the city housing inspector found 122 building code violations; the city housing authorities declared the house not suitable for occupancy. The purchaser of this FHA approved house is still forced to make monthly payments. Ibid., p. 12.

18. Reports of corruption and inefficiency have appeared concerning FHA's role in other programs of mortgage insurance designed to promote homeownership in neighborhoods where private lenders were loath to provide credit (William Lilley III and Timothy B. Clark, "Urban Report/Federal Programs Spur Abandonment of Housing in Major Cities," *National Journal*, Vol. 4 [Jan. 1, 1972], pp. 26–33). See Appendix A for a description of these relatively modest programs under secs. 221(d)(2) and 223(e) of the National Housing Act.

19. The difficulty with construction regulations is illustrated by the case of Frontier Homes in Everett, Washington. "Without exception, every townhouse visited had floors that could best be described as trampolines. It was possible in the townhouses to stand in the kitchen and move your weight from foot to foot and rattle objects in closets in the other side of the house.

"An inspection of the crawl space underneath the townhouses quickly indicated the reason for the sagging floors. . . . There are no cross beams or any support pillars on any of the beams. . . . The townhouses also had another common condition. The second

the homeownership assistance program would encourage abuses. The buyer who qualifies for assistance has little incentive to bargain for a good selling price. He must pay 20 percent of adjusted income toward his mortgage; the government pays the rest. Unless he expects his income to fall so low that the maximum federal payment is reached or to rise so high that no federal subsidy would be required, he pays the same amount regardless of the selling price. An eligible family is unlikely to delay its move from squalid housing by haggling over price. This problem is inherent in a formula that leaves discretion in the hands of recipients but offers them no incentive for frugality. The problem would vanish if the recipient were denied discretion—for example, were not allowed to select his house—or were given some reason to be frugal—for example, if he received supplements to his income rather than to his capacity to demand housing alone. A compromise solution might involve extensive counseling of eligible households by FHA together with active interest in real estate transactions by community action agencies, neighborhood legal services, or other organizations that try to protect the interests of the poor. Such care and attention might render harmless the structural flaw in the design of homeownership assistance.

The program has been criticized also for aiding some households while denying aid to other, no less needy, households. As one man wrote to his senator:

One other thing struck my eye today. An ad for new houses in the $17,000 class being offered to low-income families for $200 down and $100 a month. This made possible by Government subsidy. In the meantime my wife and I both work to make the payments on our 30-year-home of $136 a month and support our family without the aid of the government. Can you explain to me why I should be taxed to help someone else buy a home that I myself could not afford to live in?[20]

---

floor is supported by a series of beams roughly equivalent to those that support the first floor. The majority of the houses have pitched flooring from cracks in the beams and all of the townhouses had large cracks in the ceiling beams. In many cases, these cracks were as deep as 2 inches into a 4-inch piece of wood and extended in length from 6 inches to 6 feet. Some of the beams were badly bowed. *FHA officials did not seem alarmed by any of these conditions, and once again explained that all of the wood used met minimum specifications.*" Ibid., pp. 32, 33. Emphasis supplied.

20. Statement of Senator Carl T. Curtis, in *Housing and Urban Development Legislation of 1970*, Hearings before the Subcommittee on Housing and Urban Affairs of the Senate Committee on Banking and Currency, 91 Cong. 2 sess. (1970), Pt. 1, p. 706. See also the questions posed by Senator John G. Tower in *1971 Housing and Urban Development Legislation*, Hearings before the Subcommittee on Housing and Urban Affairs of the Senate Committee on Banking, Housing and Urban Affairs, 92 Cong. 1 sess. (1971), p. 4.

This criticism arises in part because some of the families who received homeownership assistance could have afforded acceptable housing without federal subsidy and would have qualified for mortgage insurance under the Federal Housing Administration's basic program for middle income families. But the criticism reflects the serious dilemma of whether to use limited funds to aid a few very needy households or many somewhat less poor households. The homeownership program expresses the latter choice. The constituent's letter to his senator is the inevitable result. The secretary of housing and urban development in March 1971 confirmed charges of abuse in the part of the program dealing in existing housing, called it "too complicated . . . to administer," and asked Congress to examine "alternative methods of helping low-income families to better housing."[21]

Tax Provisions and Housing Assistance

Most profit-oriented investors would be driven away from the major housing assistance programs by the 6 percent ceiling on before-tax profits if other generous tax provisions were not available. Accelerated depreciation generates deductions much in excess of true depreciation on most structures. This excess depreciation offsets ordinary income and reduces tax liabilities. The reduction is largest for taxpayers with large incomes: "In this upside-down tax expenditure world for rental housing, the investor in the seventy percent tax bracket has a better *after-tax* rate of return than an investor in the fifty percent bracket—the complete negation of a progressive tax system."[22]

The Tax Reform Act of 1969 increased the relative attractiveness of investment in rental housing in general and federally assisted or low income housing in particular. It tightened depreciation formulas for most assets other than housing; for most assets other than federally assisted housing it lengthened the period that assets must be held before excess depreciation is treated as a capital gain rather than as ordinary income; it allows taxes on gains from sale of lower income rental housing to be deferred if the house is sold to the occupants and the proceeds are reinvested in similar housing; and it allows fast amortization of rehabilitation expenditures on

21. George Romney, *National Journal*, Vol. 3 (April 10, 1971), p. 811.
22. Stanley S. Surrey, "Federal Income Tax Reform: The Varied Approaches Necessary to Replace Tax Expenditures with Direct Governmental Assistance," *Harvard Law Review*, Vol. 84 (December 1970), p. 403.

housing occupied by low or moderate income families.[23] According to the assistant secretary of the treasury, Murray L. Weidenbaum, the excess depreciation on rental housing alone reduced federal revenues by $255 million in 1971.[24]

Summary

Gradually, as the variety of federal housing assistance programs has grown, the relation between assistance and household income has become closer, the budget impact of assistance has been reduced and deferred, and builders, developers, and investors have become eager participants, partly because of tax avoidance provisions of the income tax code. The absence of the workable program requirement for the latest programs may represent a new congressional willingness to let housing assistance programs be vehicles for economic and perhaps racial integration. The courts have held that public housing cannot be used to reinforce patterns of segregation. Whether federally assisted housing will be dispersed is problematic, however, since numerous legal and quasi-legal devices exist to hinder projects to which local authorities strongly object.[25]

To an increasing extent, new housing programs permit the government to "buy-now-pay-later," as shown in Table 8-3. Under each of the programs depicted, $100 million of contract authority will generate about $100 million in expenditures during the first full year after all housing units built with that contract authority are completed and occupied. Under rent supplements and rental and homeownership assistance, additional payments will be made for many years. As a result, these programs induce construction of many more housing units than does the below-market-interest-rate program. The number of units built depends on the size of the subsidy per unit. The relevant number here is not the simple total of federal expenditures over many years, but the discounted present value of such outlays. Because tenants in rent supplement projects are far poorer

23. Ibid., pp. 402–3.

24. *The Economics of Federal Subsidy Programs*, A Staff Study Prepared for the Use of the Joint Economic Committee, 92 Cong. 1 sess. (1972), p. 206.

25. Cities can prohibit multifamily dwellings or require such low densities that construction costs exceed federal limits, and then grant variances, if at all, only to approved projects. Building inspectors may be slow and extraordinarily meticulous in checking for compliance with building codes. Municipal water, sewage, gas, and electric companies can impose high fees for, or delay, installation of utilities. The scope for imaginative "sand-bagging" is limitless.

Table 8-3. Estimated Budget Outlays per $100 Million of Contract Authority under Housing Programs for Lower Middle Income Families

| Program | Number of units built | Budget outlays first full year of operation (millions of dollars) | Budget outlays over life of program | | | | Number of units built per million dollars of discounted present value spent |
| | | | Total (millions of dollars) | | Per unit (dollars) | | |
			Undis- counted	Dis- counted	Undis- counted	Dis- counted	
Below-market-interest-rate loans	6,250	100	32	18	5,168	2,894	346
Rent supplements	90,800	100	3,907	1,302	43,020	14,338	70
Homeownership assistance	106,071	99	1,439	688	13,558	6,483	154
Rental assistance	97,724	100	1,707	776	17,467	7,945	126

Sources: Based on data in *Independent Offices and Department of Housing and Urban Development Appropriations for 1971*, Hearings before a Subcommittee of the House Committee on Appropriations, 91 Cong. 2 sess. (1970), Pt. 3, p. 655, except for below-market-interest-rate loans, for which total budget outlays were independently estimated.

and are expected to remain poorer than those in units built under other programs, but despite the lower average cost of rent supplement units, the subsidy per unit under that program is more than twice as large as that under the two assistance programs.

For the same reason the rent supplement program has a direct impact on fewer families per $1 million of federal expenditures than do homeownership and rental assistance. The latter two programs, according to a study of Columbus, Ohio, reach more households indirectly through filtering than either rent supplements or low rent public housing.[26] As recipients vacate units, other households replace them and vacate still other units, and so on. Homeownership assistance affected more than three times as many households and more than one and a half times as many poor households as did the rent supplement program per dollar spent.

To the extent that the Columbus case is representative, it illustrates the brutal choice of housing assistance—whether to concentrate assistance on the poorest households whose need is presumably greatest or to spread assistance among more households whose deprivation is less severe. The first course assures that given outlays will provide significant benefits to a few households and that the chain of filtering will be short; the second course provides small amounts of assistance to more families but courts the inequity of aiding some who are less needy than others who are ineligible. The homeownership program, in some areas at least, seems to have managed the worst aspects of both choices.

Does it make sense to award housing subsidies to families whose incomes are so high that they are nowhere eligible for cash assistance before giving housing subsidies or cash assistance to all families with lower incomes? America has a long tradition of awarding financial aid on criteria other than, or in addition to, income. Under the rent supplement program, for example, those families eligible for aid must not only have incomes below public housing limits, but must also fall into the category of those who are elderly, handicapped, or victims of disasters, or who were displaced by public actions or resided in substandard housing, or whose head is a member of the armed services. The homeownership and rental assistance programs, however, are so structured that the majority of those with very low incomes cannot afford housing built under these programs.

26. William B. Brueggeman, "The Impact of Federally Subsidized Housing Programs: The Columbus, Ohio Case," in Stephen D. Messner and Maury Selden (eds.), *Proceedings, American Real Estate and Urban Economics Association, 1970*, Vol. 5 (1971), pp. 51–65.

Among issues that are bound to arise under these programs is the cost ceiling on units eligible for subsidy, which may preclude construction in cities except in urban renewal areas. Pressure may arise for increasing the income limits for recipients of assistance. If the limits rise faster than personal income, both programs might be converted from devices to aid households who cannot afford adequate housing into a broad system of middle class housing subsidies. Such a development would dilute the effectiveness of the program in achieving its original objectives.

chapter nine Rural Home Loans

        The Farmers Home Administration (FmHA) runs one of the federal government's largest, but least noticed, housing programs. Between 1967 and 1972, FmHA will have provided more than $5 billion in loans and grants for the purchase, rehabilitation, or construction of new or existing housing. The largest of the agency's programs is a system of loans to low and moderate income households in rural areas. Despite the magnitude of FmHA's housing activities, they are seldom accorded attention in discussions of federal housing policy.

        Perhaps the character of rural housing problems and programs explains their neglect. Rural areas have a large legacy of housing built when income and housing standards were lower than they are today (see Chapter 2). The gradual decline in rural population reduces the need for new construction. These factors and the low population density in rural areas make their housing problems difficult to grasp and undramatic.

        The impact of FmHA activities on the federal budget is concealed by devices not employed by other federal agencies. Persistently tight staff budgets have prevented the agency from issuing the deluge of statistics provided by various agencies of the Department of Housing and Urban Development (HUD), particularly the Federal Housing Administration (FHA). In addition, rural problems appear to have been intellectually unfashionable; no books[1] and few journal articles have been published in recent years on FmHA's activities.

        The breadth of FmHA's jurisdiction is not commonly recognized. Its

---

1. A possible exception is Sidney Baldwin's *Poverty and Politics* (University of North Carolina Press, 1968), a study of the Farm Security Administration, FmHA's administrative forebear.

borrowers are concentrated on farms and in small towns, but the Farmer's Home Administration may make loans against housing located in open country or any place with 10,000 or fewer inhabitants. Such areas encompass many small suburbs and unincorporated areas near large cities or within standard metropolitan statistical areas.[2] Inhabitants of certain nonrural areas who are planning to move into rural areas are also eligible for loans.[3]

The importance of nonfarm activities has increased sharply since 1961, when they were introduced into FmHA's coverage; in 1969, farmers received fewer than 7 percent of FmHA insured homeownership loans. The agency's jurisdiction expanded to include nonfarm areas as farming population dwindled. It also grew in response to the dearth of credit agencies in rural areas. Agrarian interests have traditionally resented their dependence for credit on urban-based financial intermediaries. The difficulty of obtaining credit in sparsely settled areas where financial intermediaries find it unprofitable to operate affects most open areas and small towns. As FmHA's farm constituency shrank, its programs were extended principally in housing since the Small Business Administration was responsible for lending to small nonfarm businesses in rural as well as urban areas.[4]

The jurisdictional question of whether HUD or the Department of Agriculture should administer federal housing policies in sparsely settled areas raises the very practical problem of the Federal Housing Administration's ability to provide services. Most FHA loans are made through private lenders who, if they do operate in sparsely settled areas, make loans on very stiff terms.[5] FmHA is accustomed to operating in such areas. Most housing programs, other than the guaranteed loan program of the Veterans Administration and tax benefits to homeowners, are administered by HUD,

2. For example, much of Montgomery County, Maryland, including areas near the District of Columbia, is unincorporated and hence covered by FmHA programs. In fact, however, only nineteen FmHA loans had been given in Montgomery County as of 1970.

3. Nonrural borrowers are eligible if they live in any place with a population of 10,000–50,000, in certain nonrural subdivisions, or in certain resort areas.

4. One minor outcropping of FmHA authority stretches the meaning of "farmer" and "home" to the point of absurdity: oyster beds are eligible for emergency loans. See Public Law 87-128, Aug. 8, 1961, which stipulates that loans may be made for "financing land and water development, rice, and conservation" (75 Stat. 310).

5. Clay L. Cochran of the National Rural Housing Coalition alleged that the Federal Housing Administration is unable to operate effectively in nonmetropolitan areas and in towns of less than 25,000 (*Housing and Urban Development Legislation of 1970*, Hearings before the Subcommittee on Housing and Urban Affairs of the Senate Committee on Banking and Currency, 91 Cong. 2 sess. [1970], Pt. 1, p. 465).

however. It is charged with developing federal housing policies, and any dilution of its power may lead to inconsistent or unbalanced programs. Without such dilution, the problems of rural areas may be neglected. The question is further complicated by the interests of the congressional committees and subcommittees that oversee these programs.

In practice, FHA and FmHA are accustomed to cooperating: FmHA administers HUD's homeownership assistance program in rural areas; FHA is encouraging rural financial institutions to make loans eligible for FHA insurance. Since the difficulty that residents in thinly settled areas face in getting credit is likely to persist, the theoretical case for FmHA operations in rural areas will remain strong for some time; the political case may last even longer.

Farmers Home Administration

Farmers Home Administration is a misnomer. In the years before 1961, the expansion of agricultural output rather than the improvement of housing quality claimed most of the agency's loans and grants. Since then, housing programs have come to dominate FmHA activities, but fewer than 10 percent of housing loans are made to farmers.[6]

Many FmHA programs originated with the Farm Security Administration (FSA), an ill-starred agency doomed by repeated allegations of utopian political radicalism.[7] The FSA, born in 1937 and superseded by FmHA in 1946, helped tenant farmers buy their own farms, made rural rehabilitation loans and grants, and established cooperatives.[8] Among its other programs, perhaps the most prominent was for migratory farm laborers. Widespread political opposition to FSA's allegedly "socialistic" and "impractical"

---

6. In fiscal year 1969, farmers received 6.9 percent and in 1968, 8.8 percent of the direct and insured loans made under FmHA's major housing program.

7. See Baldwin, *Poverty and Politics.*

8. Ibid., p. 317. At least one FSA activity, the promotion of neighborhood action, has a curiously contemporary ring. The FSA encouraged groups of six to eight families to meet, to discuss mutual problems, and to take collective action. The problems and political consequences of this program also sound oddly familiar. "Difficulties in implementation were plentiful—subjective fears and embarrassments among participating families, lack of training and understanding among supervisory personnel of the FSA, the tendency for supervisors to dominate the discussions, and difficulties in launching and maintaining a regular schedule of meetings. . . . These groups were viewed by some suspicious critics of the FSA as particularly subversive of the *status quo.* Who could tell what might emerge from such 'clandestine' activity?" Ibid., p. 208.

farming projects, its promotion of "pressure groups," and its attempts to "regiment" clients and "destroy their individualism, initiative, and self-respect" led to its replacement.[9]

By contrast, the Farmers Home Administration has enjoyed consistent support from Congress and, in particular, from appropriation subcommittees on which the very southern states whose representatives destroyed FSA are heavily represented.[10]

The farm ownership and operating loan programs that were FmHA's principal activities in its first twenty-five years both evolved from earlier programs of the FSA to encourage farm ownership by tenants and to aid farmers with production and subsistence loans.[11] The present activities of FmHA differ from those of FSA because the nature of the farm problem and the national perception of that problem have changed. The depression-related rural poverty that FSA fought was a stubborn but temporary problem. Farm poverty today is regarded as a consequence of technological change that has reduced the demand for farm labor. The crucial dilemma in designing farm policy today is how to ameliorate the conditions of poverty without unduly muting the incentives that induce workers to move from low-paying farm work to high-paying activities in towns, small cities, and metropolitan areas. The income differential between farming and other industries has remained so large that farm population has in fact declined rapidly both in relation to nonfarm population and absolutely.

Housing Loans

Large-scale housing assistance for farmers began with the Housing Act of 1949. In 1961 the nonfarmer became eligible for FmHA housing assistance if he owned real estate in a "rural" area, lacked sufficient resources "to provide the necessary housing and buildings on his own account," and was unable to obtain credit "from other sources upon terms and conditions

9. Summarized from the report of the Joint Committee on Reduction of Nonessential Federal Expenditures, headed by Senator Harry F. Byrd, Sr. (Democrat, Virginia), which was highly critical of the FSA. Ibid., p. 352.

10. In 1970 the chairman and four of six Democratic members (including the two ranking members) of the Senate Subcommittee on Appropriations concerned with the FmHA budget were from the South. In the House of Representatives the corresponding subcommittee membership included southerners as chairman and two of four Democratic members (including the ranking member).

11. A smaller program of loans for farm labor housing also has antecedents in FSA.

Table 9-1. Distribution of Borrowers under FmHA Loan Program, by Income and Other Characteristics, 1969

In percent

Characteristic	Distribution	Characteristic	Distribution
Income (dollars)		Net worth (dollars)	
Under 3,000	5.8	Under 5,000	82.9
3,000–3,999	8.0	5,000–9,999	12.0
4,000–4,999	12.7	10,000–14,999	2.3
5,000–5,999	20.4	15,000–49,999	2.1
6,000–6,999	24.7	50,000–74,999	0.6
7,000–7,999	17.2	75,000 and over	0.0
8,000–8,999	5.2	Region[a]	
9,000–9,999	2.4	Southeast	56.4
10,000 and over	3.6	Northeast	15.4
Residence		West	7.4
Farm	6.6	Central	20.8
Open country	48.4	Age of family head	
Place under 1,000 population	16.6	Under 30	39.3
Place of 1,000–2,499		30–39	29.2
population	15.2	40–49	17.0
Place of 2,500–5,500		50–59	8.7
population	13.2	60 and over	5.8

Source: U.S. Department of Agriculture (USDA), Farmers Home Administration (FmHA), tabulations, April 1970. The program coverage of the tabulations varies slightly among the characteristics presented.
a. Distribution is for 1968.

which he could reasonably be expected to fulfill."[12] These criteria are vague enough so that it is not clear who is excluded from receiving FmHA loans, aside from inhabitants of densely populated areas. Some owners of properties within standard metropolitan statistical areas and some wealthy and high-income families have received loans. The great majority of loans, however, have been made to households in small towns or open country and with modest incomes and wealth. The median income of recipients was $6,300 in 1967 and $6,100 in 1968 and 1969. Relatively few households with very low incomes have recieved loans. Fewer than one loan in ten has gone to a farmer (see Table 9-1). FmHA is a "lender of last resort," since applicants must show that they cannot obtain credit elsewhere at fair terms. The FmHA loan officer retains significant discretion since FmHA charges less than market rates and lacks sufficient funds to satisfy all rural credit demands.

Under section 502 of the Housing Act of 1949 FmHA administers several

12. Housing Act of 1949, Title V, Sec. 501(c), as amended.

related housing programs differentiated on the basis of the income of borrowers; whether FmHA retains the loan in its portfolio or sells it; whether the loan is for senior citizens, for repair of damages caused by natural disasters, for mutual self-help housing, or for certain other specified purposes; and whether the loan is "initial" or "subsequent." The largest segment consists of initial loans, for nonelderly households with low to moderate incomes, which FmHA sells to private investors.[13]

Borrowers' Income

Borrowers are classified as either low to moderate income or above moderate income. The income limits of the two groups overlap,[14] probably because of variations in family size and in living costs.

The practical distinction between the two groups is clear; low to moderate income borrowers have paid interest rates 1.5 to 2.75 percentage points below those charged above moderate income households.[15] Loans to the former have gone increasingly to households with incomes of less than $8,000. Loans to the latter constituted well under 10 percent of FmHA's loans between 1967 and 1970, when they were terminated. Loans are restricted to amounts adequate to finance construction, purchase, or repair of modest single-family units and have averaged less than $10,000 each.[16]

13. Loans were made to above moderate income families until 1970. Farmers whose homes are destroyed or damaged may obtain 3 percent disaster loans. Members of groups of low income families can borrow for self-help housing; FmHA provides technical assistance and training and aids in site preparation. Very poor, mostly aged, homeowners can borrow up to $2,500 at 1 percent interest for minor housing repairs necessary to bring units up to minimum standards. FmHA also administers small programs of loans for multifamily housing.

14. In fiscal year 1967, for example, 6 percent of above moderate income borrowers had incomes of less than $7,000 per year while over 25 percent of low to moderate income families had incomes of more than $7,000 per year. In fact, more borrowers with incomes above $10,000 per year were classified as low to moderate than as above moderate income (1,720 versus 1,362). In later years, the overlap persisted although not to quite the same degree.

15. In 1970, for example, above moderate income households paid 8.5 percent interest plus a 0.5 percent insurance premium, while low to moderate income households paid 6.25 percent interest and no insurance premium.

16. Neither legislation nor regulation imposes an absolute limit on the size of loan that can be made. "Modest" housing is interpreted to mean units of not more than about 1,400 square feet and in 1969, 96.7 and 75.0 percent, respectively, of all low to moderate and above moderate income loans were on houses of less than 1,400 square feet.

Insured and Direct Loans

After it makes a loan, FmHA may either retain the loan in its portfolio or sell it to a private lender, guaranteeing payment of principle and interest. The former is a "direct" loan, the latter an "insured" loan. Whether or not FmHA insures and sells a loan does not affect the borrower in the slightest. The amount he can borrow, his repayment period, and his interest rate are all decided beforehand. Most direct loans carry very low interest rates, are for very small amounts, and are made to very low income families for repair or improvement purposes. The economic impact of direct and insured loans is identical.

The impact of the two on the federal budget differs markedly, however. Proceeds from the sale of insured loans are deducted from net new loans in computing budget outlays. Generally they have earned less than market interest rates in recent years. FmHA has faced two options in marketing these loans. It could sell them at a discount so that purchasers could earn as much as they earn on other assets (at interest rates prevailing in late 1970, the required discount would be about 20 percent on loans to low to moderate income households). The agency has chosen instead to pay purchasers an interest subsidy adequate to induce them to pay face value for the bonds.[17] Though FmHA reportedly does this "for administrative reasons,"[18] a more likely explanation is that payment of an interest subsidy

17. In 1968, Senator Spessard L. Holland of Florida remarked on the implicit subsidy in FmHA policies: "Generally, you speak of an insured loan as a loan where the lender pays to the insuring agency for the assurance that he will collect and receive his full loan with interest. Here now you have the reverse. The Government is paying the lender to make the insured loan and is, in addition, assuring the collection of it, principal and interest. This is the first time I ever heard of an arrangement of this sort. I will be interested in seeing the legal opinions on this point. In other words, instead of the maker of the loan paying something to have his loan insured, to the contrary he is being paid a subsidy for making the loan and also is getting the assurance. That is the most unusual thing I ever heard of. . . . There is no way to construe this operation except as a subsidy that I can see and it is a subsidy and you are paying the lender to assume for the Government and for the poor borrower the obligation of lending and in addition you are assuring him that he can count on collection of the principal and interest of his loan or else the Government will pay it." *Department of Agriculture and Related Agencies Appropriations for Fiscal Year 1969*, Hearings before the Subcommittee of the Senate Committee on Appropriations, 90 Cong. 2 sess. (1968), Pt. 1, p. 1000.

18. The general counsel of the Department of Agriculture stated in an opinion (No. 118, Nov. 15, 1963) to the FmHA administrator: "We are informed that for administrative reasons, *which need not be discussed here*, it is preferable to sell the notes at a higher yield to the lender in lieu of sale at a discount. It seems that sale by either of these methods would have the same results, that is, the loss which would be borne by the fund would be the same." *Department of Agriculture and Related Agencies Appropriations for Fiscal Year 1969*, Senate Hearings, Pt. 1, p. 981. Emphasis added.

results in a much smaller current budget expenditure than does selling loans at a discount. For example, on a thirty-three-year loan, if the face interest rate were 7.25 percent and the current yield on equivalent assets were 9.5 percent, the first-year net budget cost from $1 million of insured loans would be $195,025 if the bond were discounted and only $19,503 if the interest subsidy were employed. The long-run cost of both alternatives is indeed the same *if outlays are discounted to present value at the market rate of interest*, but the timing is radically different.[19]

The interest subsidy is similar to that provided purchasers of participation certificates, which are securities representing an interest in a pool of government-owned assets. Until 1968, proceeds from sale of participation certificates were subtracted from government expenditures; since then they have been treated, like Treasury borrowing, as a source of finance and have been abandoned because they do not reduce the apparent size of federal spending or deficit.[20]

In 1969, Senator Spessard Holland, in a discussion with Charles L. Grant, director of finance for the Department of Agriculture, pointed up the parallels between participation sales and the sale of insured loans. The senator asked if the sale of insured loans were made through participation certificates:

MR. GRANT: It is very similar in effect to participation certificates, Mr. Chairman, but the procedure is a little different. . . . These are individual loans, not certificates of interest. . . .

SENATOR HOLLAND: Do you have to sell below par?

MR. GRANT: No, we do not. We sell at whatever interest rate is necessary to attract the money. . . .

SENATOR HOLLAND: Does this mean that you have to pay an interest rate sizably more than that carried by your paper?

MR. GRANT: Yes, sir, and the difference will come out of the insurance funds. . . . But this is one of the ways in which the Treasury and the Government is meeting the expenditure limitation with which we must live.

SENATOR HOLLAND: I agree with you. I see little difference between this and the participation——

MR. GRANT: The only difference is one of mechanics. The end result is the same.[21]

19. This example ignores the value to purchasers of FmHA's promise to repurchase the loans at face value if interest rates increase.

20. For a discussion of these issues, see Wilfred Lewis, Jr., *Budget Concepts for Economic Analysis* (Brookings Institution, 1968).

21. *Department of Agriculture and Related Agencies Appropriations for Fiscal Year 1970*, Hearings before the Subcommittee of the Senate Committee on Appropriations, 91 Cong. 1 sess. (1969), Pt. 1, p. 445.

One consequence of FmHA accounting practices is that program activity—placement of new loans—may have no relation to budget expenditures. The 1971 budget, for example, called for an increase in loans of $633 million and a decrease in expenditures of $969 million. This extraordinary discrepancy was possible because FmHA had repurchased large quantities of loans during fiscal years 1969 and 1970 that it intended to sell during 1971. This kind of budgeting causes lending activity to expand in some years and contract in others because of adventitious events in financial markets rather than as a reflection of program objectives.

Interest Credit Loans

Low to moderate income families who are eligible for FmHA loans may obtain interest credit assistance similar to that provided under the Federal Housing Administration's homeownership and rental assistance programs.[22] Recipients must have incomes of less than $7,000 and net worth of less than $5,000 excluding household goods.[23] Benefits for homeowners reduce the sum of mortgage payments, property taxes, and insurance to 20 percent of income or to the amount that would have been due had the mortgage been amortized at 1 percent, whichever is more. On a thirty-three-year loan, amortization at 1 percent rather than 7.25 percent would reduce annual payments from $80.50 per $1,000 borrowed to $35.73, a 55.6 percent subsidy. Most households, of course, will receive somewhat smaller subsidies. In the first half of fiscal year 1970, 18 percent of households receiving FmHA loans also received interest credits;[24] the fraction rose to one-third during the first ten months of fiscal year 1971 and was still going up.

FmHA also offers two forms of rental assistance similar to that provided under the Federal Housing Administration's programs. Under one, nonprofit organizations and cooperatives can obtain 3 percent loans on buildings intended for tenants with incomes below specified levels. Under the other, eligible organizations may obtain loans at subsidized interest rates— 7.25 percent in fiscal year 1971—as well as subsidies equal to the difference between 25 percent of adjusted tenant income and a basic rent necessary to

22. FmHA also administers FHA's homeownership assistance program in rural areas; it placed 2,382 such loans in fiscal year 1970.

23. U.S. Department of Agriculture, Farmers Home Administration, "Section 502 Rural Housing Loan Policies, Procedures, and Authorizations," FHA Instruction 444.1 (FHA, Sept. 29, 1969; processed), Section VII, N 1, a.

24. Unpublished FmHA tabulation, dated March 1970.

cover amortization over fifty years at 7.25 percent and other costs. As with FHA's rental assistance program, tenants must pay enough rent to amortize the project's debt at an interest rate of 1 percent.

Administration

As with most government activities, the way FmHA administers its housing programs determines who benefits from them and how the public will regard them. Field offices serving one or a few counties administer the programs of the Farmers Home Administration. The local office is a sort of credit supermarket that administers not only housing programs, but also farm ownership and operating loans and other FmHA programs. Traditionally, FmHA has offered advice and technical assistance to farmers, along with credit. Since these services are less important for most mortgagors (particularly nonfarmers), administrative costs should rise less rapidly than loan activity as mortgage lending represents an increasing fraction of FmHA's growing activities. In fact, wages have risen so much faster than administrative appropriations that the number of FmHA employees has risen less than 10 percent since 1967, the very period of rapid increase in home loan activity; this fact may explain in part why fewer home loans have been made than anticipated in recent budgets. Personnel shortages could have hindered efforts to direct more credit to the poor: it is time consuming to make small loans to families who can't fill out forms or who live in remote places; it is much easier to serve well-situated, better-educated applicants who take less time and probably have more income.

Level and Distribution of Benefits

The typical FmHA home borrower is a southerner under the age of forty. He has an income of between $5,000 and $8,000 per year and less than $5,000 in assets. He is not a farmer, but he lives in a small town or open country (see Table 9-1).

Borrowers receive two kinds of benefits from FmHA's home mortgage programs. First, FmHA provides home mortgage credit in communities where private lenders either do not operate or lend on stringent terms reminiscent of the past. Without FmHA some borrowers, low and high risk alike, could not obtain credit even at conventional interest rates. The availability of FmHA credit facilitates residential construction and thereby increases population and residential construction and provides other benefits in such "credit deserts." The value of the benefits is the amount of money that would just compensate FmHA borrowers for the loss of credit at unsubsidized rates.

Second, FmHA borrowers receive a subsidy when they get a loan. On insured and direct loans to low to moderate income households, borrowers paid 5 percent interest in fiscal years 1967 and 1968, 5.13 percent in most of 1969, 6.25 percent during 1970, and 7.25 percent during 1971. These loans accounted for roughly 90 percent of those made to the borrowers described in Table 9-1. Rates on disaster loans were 3 percent throughout this period. Rates on loans to those with very low incomes were 4 percent until 1969, when they were cut to 1 percent.

If commercial lenders operated in these areas, they would charge FmHA borrowers interest rates at least as high as those charged conventional borrowers in other parts of the country and probably higher to offset the extra costs of operating in rural areas and of making small loans to risky borrowers. Most of FmHA's insured loans are under $10,000 and nearly all of its direct housing loans are under $2,000.[25] FmHA borrowers typically have moderate to low incomes and few assets, characteristics normally associated with high default risk.

Despite the fact that FmHA will make 100 percent loans on new and existing homes if the structure conforms with FmHA's model of what a simple home should be, its default rates have not been high. Foreclosures have been minuscule—less than 0.1 percent of all loans made (default rates for specific periods are not available).[26] The foreclosure rate of FmHA is far below that of either FHA or VA, a fact much advertised in appropriation hearings; even allowing for the different bases for computing rates, it is a small fraction of the FHA and VA default rates.[27] Foreclosure is only the final step in the chain of delinquency, however. FmHA is reputed to be quite patient with borrowers who are in arrears, delaying foreclosure

25. During fiscal year 1968, 23,659 out of 43,521 initial nonfarm housing loans were under $10,000 (unpublished FmHA tabulations) and 4,479 out of 5,013 direct loans were made for repairs under a program where loans average $1,000. *Department of Agriculture and Related Agencies Appropriations for Fiscal Year 1970*, Hearings, p. 425.

26. *Department of Agriculture Appropriations for 1970*, Hearings before a Subcommittee of the House Committee on Appropriations, 91 Cong. 1 sess. (1969), Pt. 3, p. 406.

27. Ibid., pp. 406–7. The comparison is distorted since the FmHA foreclosure rate is the ratio of foreclosures in the current year to the cumulative number of borrowers while FHA and VA default rates are the ratio of defaults in the current year to the number of currently mortgaged homes.

for many months if necessary. As of January 1, 1969, payments on 11 percent of all direct and insured housing loans were behind schedule, up from 6 percent in 1964.[28] By comparison, payments on 1.75 percent of conventional mortgages, 3.15 percent of VA guaranteed loans, and 3.75 percent of FHA insured loans were in arrears on December 31, 1969.[29] Such delays entail costs in additional interest charges and administrative expenses.

Private lenders almost certainly would have charged FmHA borrowers more than they charged conventional mortgagors, much more if credit would be unavailable at reasonable rates, as FmHA claims. The estimates of benefits to FmHA borrowers are shown in Table 9-2; they rest on the presumption that those households could have obtained credit from private sources at the yield of FHA mortgages. This assumption almost certainly understates benefits to FmHA borrowers. The first year benefits under insured loans to households who secured loans totaled $10.8 million in 1969 and $7.4 million in 1968. The present value of interest savings to FmHA borrowers over the life of their loans was far larger—$123 million and $92 million, respectively. Seventy percent of this subsidy accrued to households with incomes of $5,000 to $8,000 per year. The subsidy grew from 22 percent to 28 percent of the face value of loans between 1968 and 1969 as interest rates in the economy as a whole grew faster than those charged FmHA borrowers. For fiscal year 1970 the present value of benefits rose to $188 million (on $729 million in loans, with a yield on FHA mortgages of 9.20 percent, including 0.5 percent insurance premium, and an FmHA interest charge of 6.25 percent). Subsidy costs are likely to rise still further, even though the gap between FmHA and FHA interest rates is likely to narrow. The 1972 budget called for $1.6 billion in loans to low to moderate income families. The present value of subsidies in this program may thus approach $300 million in 1972 and low income households may receive a somewhat larger fraction of benefits than in the past.

28. Of insured loans, 14,409 out of 128,636 loans with unpaid balances were in arrears. The proportion of direct loans on which payments were behind schedule was about the same. U.S. Department of Agriculture, Farmers Home Administration, "Annual Report: Status of Rural Housing, Labor Housing and Rental Housing Loan Accounts, January 1, 1969," Tables 3 and 4.

29. Mortgage Bankers Association of America, "MBA's National Delinquency Survey, December 31, 1969" (processed). The proportions in two regions in the southeastern quadrant of the United States, where FmHA carries out most of its lending activity, were only 1.04 and 0.95 percent for conventional loans, 2.66 and 1.93 percent for VA guaranteed loans, and 2.63 and 2.71 percent for FHA insured mortgages.

Table 9-2. Distribution of Benefits from FmHA Rural Housing Loans to
Low to Moderate Income Households, by Income Bracket, 1968 and 1969

Income bracket (dollars)	Amount of benefits (thousands of dollars)		Percent of total benefits	
	1968[a]	1969[b]	1968[a]	1969[b]
Under 2,000	202	\440	2.7	\4.1
2,000–2,999	226		3.1	
3,000–3,999	440	709	5.9	6.6
4,000–4,999	885	1,254	11.9	11.6
5,000–5,999	1,641	2,278	22.2	21.1
6,000–6,999	2,158	3,114	29.1	28.8
7,000–7,999	1,373	2,256	18.5	20.8
8,000–8,999	346	508	4.7	4.7
9,000–9,999	84	114	1.1	1.1
10,000 and over	50	146	0.7	1.4
First year benefits	7,406	10,819	100.0	100.0
Present value of total benefits over life of loan	92,389	122,980	...	...
Total loans	419,000	441,000	...	...

Sources: USDA, FmHA, tabulations, April 1970; *The Budget of the United States Government, 1970—Appendix*, and *The Budget of the United States Government, 1971—Appendix*. Figures are rounded and may not add to totals.

a. FHA borrowers paid 7.21 percent (6.71 percent interest plus 0.5 percent insurance premium); FmHA borrowers paid 5 percent. Figures include nonfarm direct and insured initial loans, made under section 502 of the Housing Act of 1949; farm loans accounted for 8.78 percent of all loans.

b. FHA borrowers paid 8.13 percent (7.63 percent interest plus 0.5 percent insurance premium); FmHA borrowers paid 5.13 percent. Figures are based on a sample of direct and insured farm and nonfarm loans made under section 502 for the purchase of existing units that did not require rehabilitation; amount of benefits by income class is blown up by global weights.

Borrowers under other FmHA programs also receive implicit subsidies. In 1969, above moderate income families borrowed $40 million and in 1970, $22 million at an interest rate equal to the FHA ceiling. FmHA expects to make loans under other programs totaling $69 million in 1971 and $60 million in 1972.[30]

None of these subsidies appears consistently or completely as a budget expenditure since FmHA budgeting is dominated by net sales or purchases of loans. It is impossible, therefore, to discover any budget outlay statistics that reflect the real subsidies involved.

30. These programs include some low to moderate income direct loans, very low income housing repair direct loans, rural rental housing direct loans, rural housing site insured loans, farm labor housing insured loans, and rural rental housing insured loans.

Summary

The Farmers Home Administration manages a major federal housing program that is intended (under the 1972 budget) to double between 1970 and 1972. FmHA activities, however, receive considerably less attention than many smaller programs. Their relative obscurity may be explained in part by the location of FmHA program activities outside of large urban areas, in part by the relative paucity of statistical and other information about the programs, and in part by budget conventions that obscure the subsidy element in FmHA's lending activity. These subsidies reached $123 million in 1969 and may reach $300 million by 1972. The benefits accrue mostly to families with incomes of $5,000 to $8,000 per year, a range that would lie somewhat below the median family income for the nation as a whole but probably straddles median income in the areas FmHA serves.

chapter ten **Home Delivery:**
How
and
for Whom?

Should the federal government continue its present
housing policies? If not, how should it deal with America's housing problems? Answers to these questions require a knowledge of the way housing
markets work or fail to work, an understanding of how existing policies
affect housing markets and whom they benefit, and judgments about which
problems are most important.

Among the basic questions every country faces in designing a housing
policy are whether the government should concern itself with new or existing housing, or both; what kind of standards—if any—it should set for the
quality of housing; whether policies should be directed at demand or supply, or both; whether subsidies should be channeled directly to the poor or
to other income groups in the expectation that filtering will carry benefits
to the poor; whether policies should be operated within the competitive
housing market or independently of it; whether they should be designed to
improve competition in housing markets; and whether they should be designed to affect housing services alone or the full range of residential services collectively.

The answers a country gives to such questions represent its housing
strategy. Its strategy helps determine the cost of its housing policy, the
distribution of income, the cleanliness, safety, and design of cities, the
importance of markets, and other important political and economic conditions. Its answers will be affected by the level, distribution, and rate of
growth of per capita income; the rate of population growth; migration;
and construction costs. Rich countries can choose high mandatory housing
standards and large subsidies that poor countries could not afford. How

159

income is distributed affects the character of housing and the dispersion of political power. A rapidly growing or migrating population must make a considerable investment in new housing just to maintain standards and prevent overcrowding.

Even after a housing strategy has been adopted, many important tactical issues will remain. For example, should subsidies be provided directly to occupants or indirectly through construction subsidies, tax incentives, or various credit market devices? Should reliance be placed on statutory prohibitions and requirements or on incentives? Although the selection of a housing strategy does not settle such tactical questions, it is the basic decision, the expression of the goals a nation sets for itself.

Among the housing strategies the United States might plausibly adopt are three sketched by Anthony Downs:

Filtering strategies involve strict enforcement of high or moderate quality standards for all new construction, and either (a) no public housing subsidies at all or (b) public subsidies focused mainly on middle-income or high-income households. Thus, nearly all new housing units are occupied by non-poor households. Poor households receive decent units through filtering down of older units from higher income households.

Low-income subsidy strategies also involve strict enforcement of high or moderate quality standards (usually the latter) for all new construction, but include large scale public housing subsidies allocated directly to low-income households. High standard versions require either larger total public subsidies or reach fewer poor households than moderate standard versions. The latter are better able to use the economies of mass produced or industrialized housing.

Minimal standard strategies involve only partial enforcement of any housing quality standards in urban areas, primarily in existing good quality neighborhoods. A great deal of the new construction under such strategies consists of zero standard units built by their occupants. Any housing subsidies employed can be either concentrated on the poor or spread over all income groups.[1]

A country's choice of strategy should reflect the rationale of its housing policy.[2] If that rationale favors a weak and vague housing policy—no more perhaps than removal of discriminatory and monopolistic practices—the "minimal standards" strategy is appropriate. Under such a position bad housing would be seen as a problem of low income; low income, but not bad housing, might be a matter of collective concern. No construction

1. "Housing the Urban Poor: The Economics of Various Strategies," *American Economic Review*, Vol. 59 (September 1969), p. 649.

2. Chapter 1 examined various reasons for adopting policies that interfere with the free operation of the housing market. In regrettably few areas does hard evidence suggest specific remedies, but in a disquietingly large number a widespread consensus supports collective action.

standards should be imposed, for the market should generate the kinds and amounts of housing people demand. The zero standards approach assumes that in a country as rich as the United States few shacks or hovels would be built and few would persist because nearly everyone would demand housing consistent with his income and taste and would get it. Some construction might be far below standards now permitted, but it would satisfy the demand for housing by consumers who feel such housing best satisfies their needs. A few hovels and shacks might continue to exist for the destitute few who could not afford anything better.

The "minimal standards" position is not inconsistent with radical income redistribution to aid the poor, and even with complete income equality. It presumes that the market reliably reflects individual tastes and it downgrades the importance of nonmarket social and economic interaction, but it does not necessarily involve passive acceptance of poverty. An advocate of both zero housing standards and major income redistribution might rationally forsake zero housing standards if the prospects for direct redistribution of income were poorer than for indirect redistribution through housing policy.

The choice on economic grounds between filtering and low income subsidy strategies hinges on which of the various reasons for government actions in the housing market seem most compelling. If market imperfections, social costs of bad housing, racial discrimination, and other types of market failures are most often associated with housing inhabited by the poor, a low income subsidy strategy would be indicated. If such imperfections occur throughout the housing market, a filtering strategy, or some hybrid filtering–low income subsidy strategy, would be called for.

The simple laws of division decree that with a given sum of money, more families can be helped under a filtering strategy than under a low income subsidy strategy.

The amount of subsidy per household needed to close the gap between a household's own ability to pay and the cost of a new decent unit is larger, the lower the household's income. Therefore, any given sized public housing subsidy can generate more new production of decent units if concentrated upon middle-income and upper-income groups than if concentrated upon the poorest groups. True, the frictions of the housing market mean that the immediate impact of such larger outputs upon the poorest households will be far less than a lower total output directly distributed to them. Yet focusing housing subsidies upon middle-income groups ... enables the government to assist more households per million dollars of subsidy, and therefore may be considered *politically* more efficient than direct housing aid to the poor.[3]

3. Downs, "Housing the Urban Poor," pp. 647–48. Emphasis added.

Table 10-1. Distribution of Benefits from Federal Housing Policies

Millions of dollars

Income bracket (dollars)[a]	Income tax laws, 1966[b]	FHA and VA programs, 1966[b]	Public housing, 1966[b]	Below-market-interest-rate loans, 1970[c]	Subsidy provided by			
					Home-ownership assistance, 1972[d]	Rental assistance, 1972[d]	Rent supplements, 1972[d]	Rural housing loans, 1969[e]
Under 1,000	253 }		27	*	...	...	...	* }
1,000–2,000		5 }	138	1	...	...	...	
2,000–3,000			128	1	...	...	...	
3,000–4,000	328 }	22	91	3	...	...	...	1
4,000–5,000		36	57	5	...	...	...	1
5,000–6,000	544 }	34	38	6	...	...	...	2
6,000–7,000		24	30 }	6	...	...	...	3
7,000–8,000	1,359 }	14		4	...	...	...	2
8,000–9,000				2	...	...	...	1
9,000–10,000	1,986	5 }		1	...	...	...	*
10,000–15,000	1,256		2 }	* }	...	...	...	* }
15,000–25,000	770				...	...	...	
25,000–50,000	318	5 }			...	...	...	
50,000–100,000	169				...	...	...	
Over 100,000					...	...	...	
Total, annual benefits	6,982	f	510	28	299	151	91	11
Present value of benefits	*f*	*141*	*f*	*94*	*2,078[g]*	*1,172[g]*	*1,185[g]*	*123*

* Less than $500,000.
a. Definitions of income vary slightly from one program to another.
b. Median family income was $7,500 (U.S. Bureau of the Census, *Current Population Reports*, Series P-60, No. 75, "Income in 1969 of Families and Persons in the United States" [1970]).
c. Median family income was $8,632 (Ibid.).
d. Benefits by income brackets were not estimated; total benefits indicated are estimated federal program costs as reported in *The Budget of the United States Government, 1972: Appendix*, p. 521.
e. Median family income outside metropolitan areas was $7,982 (Ibid.).
f. Not estimated.
g. Calculated from requested budget authority for 1972 (see note *d*) and data in Table 8-3.

The crucial question is how serious the frictions are that defer the benefits of filtering for the poorest households. If filtering proceeds smoothly and quickly, the costs of delay may pale before the political gain of securing support from other income groups. If filtering works sluggishly, or if certain segments of the housing market remain largely unaffected, then a dilemma may exist between politically feasible programs that help least those who need help most and programs of direct aid for the poor around which no consensus can be formed.

The American Filtering Strategy

At no time has Congress or the President publicly attempted to develop a housing strategy. Instead, legislation has been proposed, debated, amended, and enacted piece by piece. Despite this lack of neatness, the record indicates that the United States rather consistently has pursued a filtering strategy.

High construction standards prevail in virtually all large cities and suburbs and in most towns of moderate size. The requirement of workable programs for community improvement as a condition for participation in various federal programs has encouraged adoption of local building and housing codes. These codes impose construction standards typical of middle and upper class housing and property maintenance standards acceptable in middle class housing.

The chief element of the filtering strategy is the subsidy policy. The subsidy policy in the United States is clearly focused on the middle and upper middle brackets (see Table 10-1). Overwhelmingly the largest housing subsidy is favorable tax treatment of homeowners which, in 1966, left them with at least $7 billion more in disposable income than they would have retained if they were taxed as are other investors. The estimate would be larger if it included tax savings arising from accelerated depreciation on rented housing and other items. Only 8 percent of this subsidy accrues to taxpayers with incomes of less than $5,000. Taxpayers with incomes of more than $50,000 per year saved $487 million, slightly less than the total value of low rent public housing subsidies. Such inequitable subsidies are defensible as instruments for improving housing quality only if the national goal is to encourage the relatively well-to-do to buy even better housing than they would buy without a subsidy. Despite the high cost, inequity, and inefficiency of this accident of tax history, there is little prospect for reform in this part of the tax code.

The protection provided lenders against default by borrowers offered by the Federal Housing Administration (FHA) and the Veterans Administration (VA) produced subsidies in 1966 with a present value of about $141 million. The savings in cost of default protection that the agencies provide is a modest subsidy that accrues primarily to lower middle income families.

A much more significant contribution of the FHA and VA regulations is the relaxation of terms on home mortgages by lenders in general. Even a small part of the benefits of this relaxation would dwarf those from the provision of default protection below actuarial costs. By making home-ownership more accessible, FHA and VA open up tax benefits to many families. Improvements in the operation of the home mortgage market enable families who prefer homeownership (and would do so without tax benefits) to secure unsubsidized mortgages on attractive terms. These subsidiary benefits of the FHA and VA participation in home financing are almost certainly vastly larger than the amounts shown in Table 10-1.

Other agencies—the Federal National Mortgage Association (FNMA), the Government National Mortgage Association (GNMA), and the Federal Home Loan Banks (FHLBs)—have also affected mortgage lending operations. By purchasing and selling mortgages (FNMA and GNMA) or by lending to financial intermediaries (FHLBs), they have influenced the size and timing of the flow of mortgage credit. In addition, FNMA has created a secondary market in which mortgagees can sell mortgages if their holdings become excessive. This option may have encouraged banks and other lending institutions to increase their mortgage holdings. The benefits of these programs are not reflected in the estimates in Table 10-1.

Low rent public housing is the major exception to the filtering strategy. More than 86 percent of the $510 million in benefits in 1966 from that program accrued to families with incomes under $5,000. (This amount is about one-third of the value of income tax benefits to households with $25,000 or more in income.) For most of its history, public housing has been unique among federally supported housing programs in that governmental agencies have been prominent in planning, contracting, and management. The program has expanded greatly since 1966, and the national housing goal projects substantial additional growth. Low income households are also the primary beneficiaries of the newer rent supplement program. Total rent supplement payments, projected at $91 million in 1972, are expected to rise continuously thereafter but to remain much smaller than the benefits from low rent public housing.

Four of the federal government's subsidy programs are designed for lower middle income households. The below-market-interest-rate loans insured by FHA generated approximately $28 million in benefits in 1970, mostly for relatively small households with incomes of $4,000–$7,000 per year. Because of changes in federal budgeting practices, a new program of rental assistance was added in 1968 to serve the same income category; it is expected to provide $151 million in benefits in 1972. Congress enacted a companion program of homeownership assistance at the same time; its benefits are expected to reach $299 million in 1972. The national housing goal projects the construction of 2.7 million units under homeownership and rental assistance. The Farmers Home Administration (FmHA) subsidizes loans for households in the $5,000–$8,000 income range. It provided approximately $11 million in benefits in 1969, and the President has requested authority for expanded lending activity by FmHA.

Until 1970, United States housing subsidies added up unambiguously to a filtering strategy. If rent supplements, rental and homeownership assistance, and public housing grow as projected—a distinctly bullish assumption in light of past failures to follow growth projections in housing programs and of administrative problems now arising—they will cloud the purity of this strategy with elements of a lower middle income subsidy strategy.

Shortcomings of the Filtering Strategy

Some of the shortcomings of federal housing policy are specific to individual programs; others are endemic weaknesses in the filtering strategy the United States has pursued; still others grow out of a dubious conception of the nature of America's housing problem.

On equity grounds the rationale for existing housing programs is extremely weak. The largest program, income tax benefits for homeowners, has indefensible distributional consequences. All programs reach only a small proportion of households potentially eligible on the basis of income alone. A majority of poor households receive no direct housing assistance, though many may enjoy some improvement in housing through filtering.

Given expenditure limitations on housing subsidy programs and benefits per recipient, there is just not enough money to provide assistance for all who are eligible on the basis of income. Unfortunately, it is not possible simply to increase expenditure limitations and accommodate all eligible families within a set number of years. As a practical matter, assistance linked to new construction cannot be extended much beyond currently projected levels. In developing the ten-year housing goal, the Department of Housing and Urban Development found that construction of 6 million assisted units in five rather than ten years was not feasible. Either residential construction activity have ballooned to unsustainable levels or unassisted construction would have been squeezed to intolerably low levels during a period of broad excess demand.

The linkage between most overt subsidies and new housing units creates another equity issue. Households above the eligibility levels for subsidies may have poorer neighbors living in better, subsidized housing than they can afford. Such situations create resentment and political resistance to housing assistance.

Because most subsidies apply to new construction, the cost of housing assistance is higher than the cost of a program utilizing socially acceptable existing housing. Under the new homeownership and rental assistance programs, costs have run at about $1,000 per household per year. In addition, households must pay 20–25 percent of their income toward housing. The median housing cost under homeownership assistance of $1,608 in 1969 contrasts sharply with the Bureau of Labor Statistics' low cost budget item for shelter for a family of four in 1967 of $1,013.[4] Clearly, the government pays a premium to house assisted families predominantly in new units.

One reason that housing subsidies have been linked to new construction is the fear that subsidies alone would drive up the price of housing available to the poor. It is assumed that subsidy recipients are unable to choose new neighborhoods or different residences, that landlords can jack up rents with impunity, and that little effective competition exists in the housing market. Policy makers also fear the responses of those displaced should the poor succeed in acquiring housing outside their old neighborhoods.

By making housing subsidies applicable to new construction, policy makers hoped to provide improved housing for some groups without causing other groups to be housed less well. Increased demand would be met by new units, not by units captured from other households. Most evidence, however, suggests that the housing stock a nation will support is determined by such factors as the number of households, income, and the price of housing relative to other goods; residential construction, in turn, de-

---

4. U.S. Bureau of Labor Statistics, *Three Standards of Living for an Urban Family of Four Persons, Spring 1967*, Bulletin 1570-5 (1969), p. 15. The median subsidy in 1969 was $54 per month and the median payment by mortgagor $80, or an annual cost of $1,608.

pends on household formation, changes in income, changes in the relative price of housing, and credit market conditions. Federal subsidies may cause a temporary increase in residential construction or influence the kind of units built, but there is no evidence that linking subsidies to new construction results permanently in a larger housing stock than unrestricted subsidies would provide. Federal subsidies reduce the amount of bad housing since they increase the income of households too poor to demand adequate housing. This objective could be more easily achieved if existing rather than new housing were used.

An Alternative Strategy: The Housing Assistance Plan

Recognition of the inequities and excessive cost of subsidy programs has led many analysts to recommend a general subsidy payable to all (or nearly all) households with incomes below stipulated levels.[5] Although housing allowance plans differ in major respects, all would provide eligible households with cash or special certificates to defray part of the cost of new or existing housing selected by the recipients. The Department of Housing and Urban Development has announced plans to support a variety of experimental housing allowance plans.[6]

Answers to a number of policy questions would shape the precise character of the Housing Assistance Plan.[7]

Should benefits be paid in cash or rent certificates? Recipients would be free to spend cash benefits on goods other than housing, and the assistance might add no more to housing expenditures than would general cash assistance. Administrative costs, however, would be minimized since there would be no need to verify the uses to which the benefits were put. Payments tied to actual housing outlays—in the form of rent certificates or

5. See Edwin Kuh, "A Basis for Welfare Reform," *Public Interest*, No. 15 (Spring 1969), pp. 112–17; William D. Nordhaus, "Tax Incentives for Low Income Housing," in National Tax Association, *Proceedings of the Sixty-First Annual Conference on Taxation* (1968), pp. 396–414; Eugene Smolensky, "Public Housing or Income Supplements—The Economics of Housing for the Poor," *Journal of the American Institute of Planners*, Vol. 34 (March 1968), pp. 94–101; Frank de Leeuw, Sam H. Leaman, and Helen Blank, "The Design of a Housing Allowance," Working Paper 112-25 (Urban Institute, Oct. 6, 1970; processed).

6. See Jack Rosenthal, "HUD To Give Poor Funds for Homes," *New York Times*, Dec. 19, 1971.

7. This discussion leans heavily on de Leeuw, Leaman, and Blank, "The Design of a Housing Allowance."

mortgage payment coupons, or as the exact difference between housing costs and some fraction of income—would encourage households to spend more on housing than they would if benefits were unrestricted. Efforts to tie payments to housing expenditures would raise administrative costs since it would be necessary to verify rents paid (a difficult task since tenants and landlords would have incentives to collude) or to make sure that a black market for certificates or coupons did not arise.[8] Moreover, introduction of large tied housing subsidies might drive up the price of housing without improving quality commensurately; coupons or certificates would be "funny money," applicable to housing but nothing else. If the housing market were competitive, property owners would bid for tenants (or buyers) by improving housing quality.

Should housing benefits be combined with requirements that private landlords or homeowners upgrade low quality housing? The government could undertake a vigorous program of code enforcement. Or benefits could be withheld from households residing in units that do not meet minimum standards. Deficient units would either become vacant or their owners would be subject to fines. Presumably, standards would be set at a level that could be supported and maintained from housing allowance payments. Direct efforts to control housing quality are especially attractive to those who fear that landlords would simply raise rents if large tied housing subsidies were paid. Past governmental efforts effectively and honestly to administer a program of code enforcement or some other measure to upgrade housing quality by fiat have failed repeatedly, perhaps because tenants were not able to pay enough to support housing at code standards.[9]

Who should be eligible for benefits? The plan might be limited to renters, on the assumption that homeowners must be less needy since they could amass a downpayment and undertake a commitment to monthly mortgage payments. The plan might include homeowners, but only if they are making monthly mortgage payments. Households who owned their residence free-and-clear might be excluded on the theory that any benefits to them would

8. See Gordon Tullock, "Subsidized Housing in a Competitive Market: Comment," and Edgar O. Olsen, "Subsidized Housing in a Competitive Market: Reply," *American Economic Review*, Vol. 61 (March 1971), pp. 218–19 and 220–28.

9. There is no doubt that some slumlords exploit tenants and earn unconscionable profits. This behavior cannot explain the large and increasing number of abandoned units in major cities. See Michael A. Stegman, "Slum Housing: Cash Flow, Maintenance and Management," in Stephen D. Messner (ed.), *Proceedings, American Real Estate and Urban Economics Association, 1969*, Vol. 4 (1970), pp. 231–52; and George Sternlieb, *The Tenement Landlord* (Rutgers University Press, 1969).

Table 10-2. Projected Annual Cost and Number of Beneficiaries under Housing Assistance Plan, by Coverage and Housing Costs, 1967

Coverage	Cost of plan (billions of dollars)		Number of beneficiaries (millions of households)	
	Stable housing costs	Housing costs rise 10 percent	Stable housing costs	Housing costs rise 10 percent
Universal	4.9	6.2	12.3	14.1
All families and all persons 65 and over	3.7	4.8	8.2	9.7
Families with children and all persons 65 and over	3.2	4.1	6.8	8.0
All families and all persons 65 and over, except homeowners without mortgages	3.2	4.1	6.9	8.0

Source: See Appendix C.

necessarily support consumption of goods other than housing. Single persons or couples under sixty-five years old might be excluded on the grounds that resources should be concentrated on the aged and families with children. While limitations based on other criteria than measurable need dilute equity, limited resources might compel policy makers to curtail eligibility. Ideally such limitations should not be based on criteria subject to control by potential beneficiaries; for example, a household that owned its residence free-and-clear could easily mortgage its house if the making of mortgage payments were a condition for benefits.

Cost Estimates

Tables 10-2 and 10-3 contain estimates of the costs of several variations of the Housing Assistance Plan, an illustrative housing allowance system. Each household is presumed to spend one-fourth of adjusted income (the sum of income from all sources and one-fifth of net worth) on housing. Housing costs are set equal to shelter costs reported in the low cost budget for a family of four estimated by the Bureau of Labor Statistics for spring 1967. Benefits are equal to the difference between these two amounts.[10] Since BLS estimates of housing costs vary from one region to another, the amount of the subsidy would also vary. For example, in San Francisco the

10. Estimates are based on income including public assistance and other welfare programs reported for 1967. Welfare reform would substantially reduce these estimates. For a description of the way the estimates were made see Appendix C.

Table 10-3. Projected Distribution of Annual Benefits and of Beneficiaries under a Universal Housing Assistance Plan, by Income Bracket, Region, and Residence, 1967

Income bracket (dollars)	Total	Census region				Residence				Incidence
						Standard metropolitan statistical area				
		Northeast	North Central	South	West	Central city	Outside central city	Other urban	Rural	Average annual benefit (dollars)
						Benefits (millions of dollars)				
Under 1,000	1,459	279	367	561	252	532	256	208	462	550
1,000–1,999	1,388	232	347	602	208	555	247	185	402	381
2,000–2,999	863	130	215	385	133	339	159	100	266	373
3,000–3,999	621	95	168	229	130	251	148	64	159	408
4,000–4,999	339	59	94	116	70	138	89	39	74	304
5,000–7,499	209	27	75	57	49	97	58	26	28	202
Total	4,880	822	1,266	1,949	842	1,911	955	622	1,391	397
						Beneficiaries (millions of households)				Percent of population receiving benefits
Under 1,000	2.7	0.5	0.7	1.1	0.4	1.0	0.4	0.4	0.8	82.3
1,000–1,999	3.6	0.8	0.9	1.4	0.6	1.5	0.6	0.6	1.0	67.8
2,000–2,999	2.3	0.4	0.5	0.9	0.4	0.9	0.4	0.4	0.6	47.2
3,000–3,999	1.5	0.3	0.3	0.6	0.3	0.6	0.4	0.2	0.4	32.2
4,000–4,999	1.1	0.2	0.3	0.4	0.2	0.4	0.3	0.1	0.3	24.7
5,000–7,499	1.0	0.2	0.3	0.3	0.2	0.4	0.3	0.1	0.2	8.1
Total	12.3	2.4	3.1	4.7	2.1	4.7	2.4	1.8	3.3	19.9
						Percent of population receiving benefits				
	19.9	15.5	17.4	26.3	19.7	23.3	11.9	21.2	26.4	

Source: Derived by author. See Appendix C for method.

BLS rental was set at $1,519 for a family of four, and in Austin, Texas, at $1,056;[11] a family with an income of $3,000 and no net worth would receive $769 per year in San Francisco and $306 in Austin. Table 10-2 presents estimates of the costs of benefits (exclusive of administrative costs) under a universal coverage plan and three limited coverage plans. Because the cost of a Housing Assistance Plan and the number of households it reaches are quite sensitive to the behavior of housing costs, one set of estimates is based on rental costs unaffected by benefits and another on a 10 percent rise in rents. If housing allowances raise rental costs 10 percent, payments to recipients rise roughly 25 percent and the number of households eligible for assistance 15 percent. Exclusion of single people under age sixty-five from the benefits reduces the cost by about one-fourth and the number of eligible households by almost one-third. Restricting eligibility further, by excluding either childless couples under age sixty-five or homeowners without mortgages, reduces the size of benefits and the number of beneficiaries modestly. Other changes in the Housing Assistance Plan would increase costs. For example, if households were presumed to spend less than one-fourth of adjusted income or if a small amount of net worth were disregarded in computing adjusted income, the number of beneficiaries and their payments would go up.

The distribution of benefits and beneficiaries by region and income bracket for a universal plan under which housing costs remain stable is shown in Table 10-3. The South receives benefits for a larger percentage of households and in a larger total amount than any other region. The fact that incomes in the South are lower than in other regions explains both results. Most payments go to households living in central cities or in rural areas. Roughly one-fourth of households in these areas would receive housing allowances. Exclusion of households only eligible for small benefits, say, under $100 per year, would lower the number of beneficiaries by 1.8 million but would cut benefits only $89 million. Such a limitation might be justified on administrative grounds.

The administrative costs of a loosely administered Housing Assistance Plan—spot income verification and untied benefits, for example—might be as low as $15–$20 per household, the cost of administering veterans' benefits, or $70–$95 million in the aggregate.[12] For a tightly administered

11. Bureau of Labor Statistics, *Three Standards of Living*, p. 25.
12. Sam H. Leaman, "Estimated Administrative Cost of a National Housing Allowance," Working Paper 112-17 (Urban Institue, May 13, 1970; revised, May 22, 1970; processed), pp. 4–5.

plan—detailed applications, universal income checks, and tied benefits, for example—annual administrative costs might run as high as $100–$130 per household, the administrative cost per case under public assistance, or $500–$600 million in the aggregate. Tight administration would reduce benefits by uncovering some cheating and by discouraging applications from some eligible applicants who dislike obtrusive investigations. Besides administrative outlays, program costs should include the costs of code enforcement or of other direct efforts to raise housing quality.

Initially, benefits probably should not be tied to housing outlays. To do so would run the risk that benefits would be eroded by increased housing costs. Such risks might be reduced if benefits were gradually tied to housing expenditures,[13] and particularly if independent actions to upgrade housing quality were undertaken.

The Housing Assistance Plan is a possible substitute for direct subsidy programs such as homeownership and rental assistance, rent supplements, low rent public housing, below-market-interest-rate loans, and Farmers Home Administration loans to low to moderate income households. It is not a substitute for programs such as mortgage insurance and loan guarantees, secondary market operations, or Federal Home Loan Bank advances to members that influence the markets for mortgage credit. Nor is it designed to satisfy those who feel that the supply of housing for the poor is unresponsive to market forces and that governmental efforts to raise the supply of such housing are required to prevent subsidies from raising costs rather than quality. Housing markets seem to contain certain rigidities, notably those based on racial discrimination, that are not present in other markets; however, housing quality, in the narrow sense of better structures, has improved as income and wealth have increased. If the poor had adequate income to demand acceptable housing, if monetary conditions assured a plentiful supply of housing in the aggregate, and if laws against discrimination were vigorously enforced, the market for housing would probably respond by providing adequate housing for all. These conditions have never been fully satisfied. In their absence, special measures to channel adequate units to recipients of subsidies may be necessary.

13. For example, a household with a $1,600 income per year and basic housing costs of $1,200 per year would be expected to spend $400 of its own resources on housing and would be eligible for $800 in benefits. During the first year the household might receive $800 in cash, during the second year $500 in cash and $300 in housing certificates, and during the third year $200 in cash and $600 in certificates; during the fourth year it might receive $900 in certificates for which it would pay $100, and during the fifth year $1,200 in certificates for which it would pay $400 in cash.

The Housing Assistance Plan would complement a more comprehensive system of income supplements to poor households. Living costs vary from one region to another principally because of variations in housing costs. Yet no national system of income supplements has provided for variations in support levels based on living costs because Congress, it is thought, would not accept such a plan. Housing benefits paid in addition to a general system of income support would meet this problem by removing housing from the needs the basic system would have to support.

Limits of the Plan

The Housing Assistance Plan, like the less equitable programs it might replace, does not squarely meet the "bad housing" problem. It enables all households with incomes below stipulated levels to demand a larger quantity of housing services than they can now afford. If housing markets are even sluggishly responsive to demand, the quality of housing services for assisted households will improve as low quality units are upgraded or removed from the housing stock and as units presently occupied by non-recipients filter to beneficiaries of the program. But housing services are only one element of residential services, and inadequate housing services are only one element of the "bad housing" problem. Housing subsidies alone can do nothing, of course, to improve schools, to reduce crime rates, to make neighborhoods cleaner, or to improve transportation. These residential services depend on private behavior or on other public programs, largely under the control of state and local governments. Good schools and safe and convenient neighborhoods will always command a premium.

Since the essence of an equitable program of housing assistance lies precisely in the fact that all poor households are assisted *but not made better off than unassisted households*, recipients of housing benefits will continue to be least able to pay the premium for residential services. Even an equitable housing assistance plan will leave most aspects of the "bad housing" problem untouched. Though the Housing Assistance Plan may lead to better housing structures, it is very far from a panacea for squalid neighborhoods.

appendix A **Data on Selected**
Federal Housing Programs,
Early 1970s

prepared with the assistance of
Elizabeth Morley Knoll and Evelyn P. Fisher

Authority and type of program	Year estab-lished[a]	Admin-istering agency	Purposes	Coverage	Maximum terms[b]
UNSUBSIDIZED PROGRAMS (LOW RISK)					
Single-family housing					
NHA, sec. 203(b): basic home owner-ship	1934	FHA	To insure loans made to families certified as re-sponsible and able to ser-vice mortgage properly	Purchase of new or ex-isting dwelling with 1–4 units	$33,000 for 1 unit, $35,750 for 2 or 3, $41,250 for 4 (85% of foregoing for non-occupant); 97% of $15,000 sliding to 80% above $25,000 of FHA value and closing costs (slightly more for veterans); 35 years
NHA, sec. 203(h): disaster housing	1954	FHA	To insure loans made to victims of major disas-ters, riots, or civil disor-ders	Purchase of new or ex-isting single-family residence	$14,400; 100% of FHA value and closing costs; 35 years
NHA, sec. 203(k): major home im-provements	1961	FHA	To insure home improve-ment loans primarily, but not necessarily, outside urban renewal areas	Alteration, repair, or improvement of exist-ing dwelling with 1–4 units	$12,000 per unit (more in high cost area); loan plus existing debt not to exceed value limits for sec. 203(b); 20 years
NHA, sec. 213: cooperative housing	1950	FHA	To insure loans made to families purchasing units constructed under sec. 213 sales-type cooperative program	Purchase of single-family cooperative unit	Unit share of unpaid bal-ance of project mortgage; 30 years (35 in special cases)
NHA, sec. 220: urban renewal housing	1954	FHA	To insure loans made in urban renewal and code enforcement areas	Construction or reha-bilitation of dwelling with 1–11 units	For occupant mortgagor, $33,000 for 1 unit, $35,750 for 2 or 3, $41,250 for 4 plus $7,700 for each unit over 4; 97% of $15,000 sliding to 80% above $25,000 of estimated re-placement or rehabilita-tion cost (slightly more for veterans); 30 years (35 in special cases); more strin-gent terms for nonoccu-pant
NHA, sec. 220(h): home improvements in urban renewal areas	1961	FHA	To insure home improve-ment loans in urban re-newal, urban disaster, and code enforcement areas	Alteration, repair, im-provement of existing dwelling with 1–11 units	Lesser of cost of improve-ment or $12,000 per unit (more in high cost areas); loan plus existing debt not to exceed value limits for sec. 220; 20 years
NHA, sec. 234(c): condominiums	1961	FHA	To insure loans for indi-vidual units in condomin-ium projects	Purchase of unit in condominium project of 4 or more units	$33,000 to occupant mort-gagor, $28,050 to nonoc-cupant; 97% of $15,000 sliding to 80% above $25,000 of FHA value; 35 years
Multifamily housing					
NHA, sec. 207: basic rental housing	1934	FHA	To insure loans for apart-ment buildings with units of reasonable rent empha-sizing provisions for fami-lies with children	Construction or reha-bilitation of 8 or more rental units	$20 million to private mortgagor, $50 million to public, with limits of $9,900 for no-bedroom unit, $13,750 for 1-bed-

Abbreviations and notes are at end of table.

Subsidy	Number of units assisted[c] (thousands)				Estimated volume of insurance, June 30, 1971		
	Before 1960	1960–1964	1965–1970	Total	Total written (millions of dollars)	In force	
						Amount (millions of dollars)	Number of insurance contracts
None	4,490	1,842 Includes sec. 203(h)	2,288	8,620	95,468	51,200 Includes sec. 203(h) and sec. 203(i) unsubsidized high risk program	4,283,748
None		Included in sec. 203(b)				Included in sec. 203(b)	
None	...	2	1	3	16	9	2,000
None	25	8	1	34	425	188	17,456
None	1	2	3	7	80	60	4,759
None	...	*	*	*	**	**	3
None	...	*	6	6	136	132	8,118
None	111	108	31	265	3,234 Includes sec. 207 mobile home units and sec. 207 housing for elderly	2,081	1,385

Authority and type of program	Year established[a]	Administering agency	Purposes	Coverage	Maximum terms[b]
Multifamily housing (continued)					
					room, $16,500 for 2, $20,350 for 3, $23,100 for 4 or more (more in high cost areas or elevator buildings); 90% of estimated value for proposed construction, 90% of appraised value after rehabilitation (subject to limitations); 40 years
NHA, sec. 207: mobile home courts	1955	FHA	To insure loans for mobile home courts with units of reasonable rent emphasizing provisions for families with children	Construction or rehabilitation of mobile home courts	$1 million with limits of $2,500 per space (more in high cost areas); 90% of estimated value after completion or rehabilitation (subject to limitations); 40 years
NHA, sec. 213: management-type cooperatives	1950	FHA	To insure loans for nonprofit, management-type cooperatives	Construction, purchase, or rehabilitation of 5 or more units	Per unit limits same as for sec. 207 apartment units; total limits $20 million to private mortgagor, $25 million to public; 97% of estimated replacement cost for proposed units, of appraised value for existing, of estimated value after rehabilitation; 40 years
NHA, sec. 213: supplementary cooperative loans	1961	FHA	To insure supplementary loans for sec. 213 management-type cooperatives or related community facilities	Repair or improvement of housing, construction of community facilities, and refinancing for resale of cooperative memberships	Estimated cost of repairs plus debt not to exceed original mortgage; 97% of value of improvements or new facilities, provided total debt does not exceed original sec. 213 limits; remaining years of mortgage
NHA, sec. 213: sales-type cooperatives	1950	FHA	To insure loans for units to be individually sold to members of nonprofit cooperatives	Construction of 5 or more units	$33,000 per unit; $12.5 million per project; 40 years
NHA, sec. 220: urban renewal housing	1954	FHA	To insure loans in urban renewal, code enforcement, and natural disaster areas	Construction, rehabilitation, or purchase of rehabilitated dwellings with 2 or more rental units	Per unit limits same as for sec. 207 apartment units (more in high cost areas or elevator buildings); $50 million per project; percent of value limits same as for sec. 207 apartment units; 40 years
NHA, sec. 220(h): rental housing improvements for urban renewal projects	1961	FHA	To insure loans for rental housing in urban renewal, code enforcement, and natural disaster areas	Conversion, rehabilitation, repair, or improvement of existing dwelling with 5 or more units	Lesser of $12,000 per unit or estimated cost of improvement (more in high cost areas); loan plus existing debt not to exceed value limits for sec. 220; 20 years

Abbreviations and notes are at end of table.

	Number of units assisted⁰ (thousands)				Total written (millions of dollars)	Estimated volume of insurance, June 30, 1971 In force	
Subsidy	Before 1960	1960– 1964	1965– 1970	Total		Amount (millions of dollars)	Number of insurance contracts
None	*	3	17	20	Included in sec. 207 basic rental housing		
None	31	33	16	81	1,576	848	516
	Includes sec. 213 supplementary loans				Includes sec. 213 supplementary loans and sec. 213 sales-type loans		
None	Included in sec. 213 management-type loans				Included in sec. 213 management-type loans		
None	25	9	1	35	Included in sec. 213 management-type loans		
None	16	30	15	62	1,150	934	290
None	…	…	*	*	**	**	1

Authority and type of program	Year estab-lished[a]	Admin-istering agency	Purposes	Coverage	Maximum terms[b]

Multifamily housing (continued)

Authority and type of program	Year estab-lished[a]	Admin-istering agency	Purposes	Coverage	Maximum terms[b]
NHA, sec. 221(d)(3): low and moderate income projects (market rate)	1954	FHA	To insure loans for units to be occupied primarily by elderly, handicapped, or displaced low to moderate income families	Construction or rehabilitation of rental or cooperative units	$9,200 for no-bedroom unit, $12,937 for 1-bedroom, $15,525 for 2, $19,550 for 3, $22,137 for 4 or more (more in high cost areas or elevator buildings); $12.5 million per project; for public body, nonprofit corporation, cooperative, builder-seller, or investor-sponsor, 100% of estimated replacement cost for construction, or of estimated rehabilitation cost plus value of property before repair; for other mortgagors, 90% of above stipulations (subject to limitations); 40 years
NHA, sec. 221(d)(4): low and moderate income projects, especially for displaced families	1959	FHA	To insure loans for rental projects for low and moderate income families, with priority to families displaced by urban renewal or other federal action	Construction or rehabilitation of dwelling with 5 or more units	Per unit and total limits same as for sec. 221(d)(3) unsubsidized units; percent of value limits same as for "other" mortgagors under sec. 221(d)(3) unsubsidized; 40 years
NHA, sec. 234(d): condominiums	1964	FHA	To insure loans for housing to be sold as individual condominium units	Construction or rehabilitation of condominium with 4 or more units	$9,900 for no-bedroom unit, $13,750 for 1-bedroom, $16,500 for 2, $20,350 for 3, $23,100 for 4 or more (more in high cost areas or elevator buildings); $20 million per project to private mortgagor, $25 million to public; lesser of 90% of replacement cost or sum of unit mortgage amounts (limit of $33,000 per unit) for proposed construction; 90% of estimated rehabilitation cost plus estimated value before rehabilitation, or sum of unit mortgage amounts (subject to limitations); 40 years
NHA, sec. 241: supplemental loans	1968	FHA	To insure supplemental loans for projects already insured by FHA	Alteration, repair, additions, improvement of 2 or more units	Cost plus existing debt not to exceed limits on original mortgage; 90% of estimated value of improvement; remaining years of mortgage

Abbreviations and notes are at end of table.

Subsidy	Number of units assisted^c (thousands)				Estimated volume of insurance, June 30, 1971		
	Before 1960	1960–1964	1965–1970	Total	Total written (millions of dollars)	In force	
						Amount (millions of dollars)	Number of insurance contracts
None^d	n.a.	n.a.	n.a.	70	1,795	1,684	1,347
					Includes sec. 221(d)(4)		
None^d	n.a.	n.a.	n.a.	45	Included in sec. 221(d)(3) unsubsidized		
None	...	...	7	7	84	36	43
None	...	...	...	...	3	3	17
					Includes sec. 241 loans for nursing homes		

Authority and type of program	Year established[a]	Administering agency	Purposes	Coverage	Maximum terms[b]
Property improvement					
NHA, sec. 2: property improvement	1934	FHA	To insure loans (primarily personal unsecured) for property improvement	Construction, improvement, repair, or alteration of single or multifamily dwellings	$5,000 for single dwelling, $15,000 for multifamily; 7 years and 32 days
UNSUBSIDIZED PROGRAMS (HIGH RISK)					
NHA, sec. 203(i): low cost housing for outlying areas	1954	FHA	To insure loans for farm and nonfarm families, with emphasis on outlying areas	Purchase or construction of single-family housing	$16,000; 97% of FHA value; 30 years for occupant mortgagor (less for nonoccupant)
NHA, sec. 221(d)(2): housing for low and moderate income and displaced families	1954	FHA	To insure loans for low and moderate income families displaced by urban renewal or code enforcement (in 1961 broadened to include other low and moderate income families)	Construction, purchase, or rehabilitation of dwelling with 1–4 units	$18,000 for 1 unit, $24,000 for 2, $32,400 for 3, $39,600 for 4 (more in high cost areas or for 1 unit if family includes 5 or more); for displaced families, lesser of the FHA value plus closing costs or the above plus prepaid expenses minus $200 per unit; for others, lesser of FHA value plus closing costs or 97% of above plus prepaid expenses (subject to limitations); ratios lower for operative builders and on units to be rehabilitated; 30 years (35 or 40 in special cases)
NHA, sec. 223(e): declining urban area housing	1968	FHA	To insure loans for low and moderate income families in older, declining urban areas	Construction, repair, rehabilitation, or purchase of single or multifamily housing	Terms same as those for program under which borrower would qualify if location did not disqualify him
NHA, sec. 237: credit assistance	1968	FHA	To insure loans for persons with poor credit histories who otherwise would qualify under various FHA programs	Construction, rehabilitation, or purchase of single-family residences	$18,000 (more in high cost areas); other terms same as for program under which borrower would qualify if his credit were good
SUBSIDIZED PROGRAMS					
Single-family housing					
SRA, sec. 501: GI loans	1944	VA	To guarantee loans to veterans	Purchase or construction of residence	Lesser of 60 percent of outstanding loan principal or $12,500; 100% excluding closing costs; 30 years
SRA, sec. 512: direct loans to veterans	1950	VA	To make loans to veterans in small communities where private credit is unavailable	Purchase, construction, or repair of residence	$21,000 (more in high cost areas); 100%; 30 years
PL 2 (1933), sec. 1: specially adapted housing	1948	VA	To make grants to disabled veterans	Construction, purchase, or modification of specially adapted home for disabled veteran	$12,500

Abbreviations and notes are at end of table.

Subsidy	Number of units assisted[c] (thousands)				Estimated volume of insurance, June 30, 1971		
					Total written (millions of dollars)	In force	
	Before 1960	1960– 1964	1965– 1970	Total		Amount (millions of dollars)	Number of insurance contracts
None	23,357	3,967	2,574	29,898	20,743	1,332	1,401,584[e]
None	51	23	4	79	Included in sec. 203(b) single-family housing		
None[d]	13	112	342	467	5,439	4,445	382,333
None[d]	...	...	101	101	1,133 Includes sec. 223(d) (insurance on loan when expense of multi-family project exceeds income)	1,063	80,400
None	...	...	2	2	21	20	1,387
Little or no charge for default loss protection	4,961	829	1,109	6,898	81,445[f]	37,598[f]	3,597,757[f]
Roughly market rates on loans private lenders consider unprofitable	147[g]	106[g]	57[g]	310[g]	3,003	1,249	167,109
Grant	6[h]	2[h]	3[h]	11[h]	113[i]	...	...

Authority and type of program	Year established[a]	Administering agency	Purposes	Coverage	Maximum terms[b]
Single-family housing (continued)					
HA of 1949, sec. 502: basic housing for rural land owners	1949	FmHA	To make and insure loans for owners of farms and other rural real estate who are unable to secure credit under terms they could fulfill	Construction, purchase, improvement, repair, or refinancing for house of modest design and other farm buildings to provide decent, safe, and sanitary living	Normal value, with exceptions; 33 years
HA of 1949, sec. 502: rural senior citizen housing	1962	FmHA	To make and insure loans for rental housing for rural elderly	Same as for sec. 502 basic program	Same as for sec. 502 basic program
HA of 1949, sec. 502: rural disaster housing	1961	FmHA	To make loans for rural victims of natural disasters	Repair or replacement of rural dwelling and related facilities	Value of house before disaster; 33 years
HA of 1949, sec. 502: special loans	1967	FmHA	To make and insure special loans for rural, low income families who cannot qualify for sec. 502 basic program	Improvement, enlargement, or completion of structurally sound borrower-occupied dwelling and related facilities, including fees and expenses	$3,500 including previous improvement loans, but not in excess of appraised value; 33 years
HA of 1949, sec. 503: housing for very low income families	1949	FmHA	To make loans and give credits to families with income too low to make repayments under sec. 502 basic program but with prospects for qualifying within 5 years	Provision of adequate farm dwelling and buildings	Normal value, with exceptions; 33 years
HA of 1949, sec. 504: shelter-type housing	1949	FmHA	To make loans or combination loans and grants to very poor rural residents who cannot qualify under sec. 502 or sec. 503	Repair or improvement of dwelling or farm buildings and facilities that are unsafe or hazardous to health	$2,500 ($3,500 for major improvements involving water supply or plumbing); 10 years
HA of 1949, sec. 523: mutual and self-help housing	1968	FmHA	To make and insure loans to rural families for mutual or self-help housing, and to make grants to local public agencies or nonprofit organizations to develop self-help plans; followed experimental program begun in 1965	Construction for groups of families building own homes by mutually exchanging labor	Normal value, with exceptions; 33 years
NHA, sec. 221(h): below-market-rate sales housing	1966	FHA	To insure loans for families with incomes below public housing admission levels	Purchase of single-family unit rehabilitated under sec. 221(h) multifamily housing program	100% of unpaid balance of unit share of project mortgage; remaining years of mortgage

Abbreviations and notes are at end of table.

| Subsidy | Number of units assisted[o] (thousands) | | | | Estimated volume of insurance, June 30, 1971 | | |
| | Before 1960 | 1960–1964 | 1965–1970 | Total | Total written (millions of dollars) | In force | |
						Amount (millions of dollars)	Number of insurance contracts
Below-market-interest rate on loans (as low as 1 %); interest credits also available to some borrowers	34	54	225	313	3,484ʲ	n.a.	n.a.
		Includes sec. 502 special loans				Includes sec. 502 special loans	
Same as for sec. 502 basic program	...	2	14	15	94ʲ	n.a.	n.a.
Below-market-interest rate (5 % in 1971); deferment of payment of interest and principal up to 5 years for borrowers with income loss or debt increase because of the disaster	...	*	1	1	...	...	...
Same as for sec. 502 basic program	Included in sec. 502 basic program				Included in sec. 502 basic program		
Below-market-interest rate and credits on debt for 5 years	1	*	*	1	...	...	...
Below-market-interest rate on loans (1 % in 1971); grants	1	7	22	31	...	...	...
Below-market-interest rate on loans (3 % in 1971); grant	...	...	*	*	n.a.	n.a.	n.a.
		Includes sec. 524 units					
Waiver of insurance premium; below-market-interest rate as low as 1 %	...	...	2	2	18	17	1,454

Authority and type of program	Year estab-lished[a]	Admin-istering agency	Purposes	Coverage	Maximum terms[b]
Single-family housing (continued)					
NHA, sec. 221(i): condominiums	1968	FHA	To insure loans for low and moderate income families	Purchase of condo-minium unit in project financed under sec. 221(d)(3) subsidized multifamily housing program	100% of appraised value including unit share of common facilities; 3% downpayment (may be applied to closing costs); 40 years
NHA, sec. 235(i): lower income homeownership	1968	FHA	To insure loans for fami-lies with incomes up to 135% of public housing admission level (20% of appropriations may be used for families with higher incomes that do not exceed 90% of limit for sec. 221[d][3] subsi-dized multifamily pro-gram)	Construction or reha-bilitation of dwelling with 1–2 units	$18,000 for 1 unit, $24,000 for 2 (more in high cost areas and for families of 5 or more); 100% of FHA value (less for high income mortgagor), $200 down-payment; 30 years (40 in special cases)
NHA, sec. 235(j): home ownership rehabilitation	1968	FHA	To insure loans for low income families	Purchase of dwelling with 1–2 units, rehabil-itated under sec. 235(j) multifamily housing program	$18,000 for 1 unit, $24,000 for 2 (more in high cost areas and for families of 5 or more); 100% of unpaid balance of unit share of project mortgage, $200 downpayment; 35 years (40 in special cases)
HA of 1964, sec. 312: urban renewal rehabilitation loans	1964	ASCD	To make loans in urban renewal or code enforce-ment areas to families who cannot borrow else-where (preference to fami-lies with incomes below limits for sec. 221[d][3] subsidized multifamily program)	Rehabilitation of own-er-occupied or rental properties to bring units up to local stan-dards	Same as for sec. 220(h) un-subsidized single-family program
HA of 1949, sec. 115: urban renewal rehabilitation grants	1965	ASCD	To make grants to fami-lies with incomes under $3,000 in urban renewal areas and other areas that are being upgraded and to owner-occupants of unin-surable property	Rehabilitation of dwelling and real property	$3,500 (less to families with income over $3,000)
HA of 1949, secs. 115, 312: combination of urban renewal rehabilitation grants and loan	1965	ASCD	To make combination grant and loan under secs. 115 and 312 to families who require financing in excess of sec. 115 limits	Same as secs. 115 and 312	For grant, same as sec. 115; for loan, same as sec. 312
Multifamily housing					
USHA, secs. 9, 10: low rent public housing	1937	FHA	To make loan commit-ments to local housing authorities, which provide security for bonds for low rent housing for families in the lowest income group, and to make rent	Construction, rehabil-itation, or purchase of existing dwelling units, and administration costs of project	$2,400 per room, $3,500 for elderly (more in high cost areas); 40 years

Abbreviations and notes are at end of table.

| Subsidy | Number of units assisted[c] (thousands) | | | | Estimated volume of insurance, June 30, 1971 | | |
| | Before 1960 | 1960– 1964 | 1965– 1970 | Total | Total written (millions of dollars) | In force | |
						Amount (millions of dollars)	Number of insurance contracts
Below-market-interest rate	...	...	n.a.	n.a.	**	**	1
Reduction of interest rate to as little as 1%, depending on income	...	...	131	131	3,324	3,257	191,788
	The Budget of the United States Government, 1973, projects 588,000 units under payment in fiscal year 1973				Includes sec. 235(j) single-family loans		
Same as for sec. 235(i)	...	...	*	*	Included in sec. 235(i)		
	The Budget projects 331,200 units under payment in fiscal year 1973						
Below-market-interest rate (3% in 1971)	...	...	21	21	...	...	...
Grant	...	...	23	23	...	...	...
Grant; below-market-interest rate (3% in 1971)	...	...	7	7	n.a.	n.a.	n.a.
Principal and interest on bonds; rent supplement; tax exemption of bond interest; construction loans	424	118	326	867	...	...	...

Authority and type of program	Year estab-lished[a]	Admin-istering agency	Purposes	Coverage	Maximum terms[b]
Multifamily housing *(continued)*			supplement payments to maintain low rents (tenant may purchase unit [HA of 1965])		
HA of 1949, sec. 514: loans to aid domestic farm labor	1961	FmHA	To insure loans for housing for domestic farm laborers	Construction, rehabil-itation, purchase of structures (including household furnishings) and related facilities	100% of estimated value; 33 years
HA of 1949, secs. 515, 521: housing for low or moderate income rural families	1962 1968	FmHA	To make and insure loans to provide housing for low and moderate income rural families, with em-phasis on elderly	Construction, pur-chase, or rehabilitation of rental or coopera-tive housing and re-lated facilities	$750,000 for insured loan; 100% of development cost or value of security for di-rect loan; 50 years
HA of 1949, sec. 516: grants to aid domestic farm labor	1964	FmHA	To make grants to state or local governments or to nonprofit organizations for provision of low rent housing for domestic farm laborers	Construction, rehabil-itation, purchase of structures (including household furnishings)	90% of development cost
HA of 1949, sec. 522: rural job trainee housing	1968	FmHA	To make loans and pro-vide financial and techni-cal assistance for housing for residents of rural areas receiving job train-ing under federally as-sisted programs	Land and construction for housing and related facilities, including mobile homes	100% of capital costs, plus interest; 33 years
NHA, sec. 221(d)(3): below-market-interest-rate loans to low and moder-ate income families	1961	FHA	To insure loans for rental or cooperative housing for elderly and handi-capped families with low and moderate incomes	Construction or reha-bilitation of dwelling with 5 or more units	Same as for sec. 221(d)(3) unsubsidized multifamily program
HUDA of 1965, sec. 101: rent supplements	1965	FHA	To subsidize rents for low income families who are displaced, elderly, physi-cally handicapped, occu-pying substandard housing or housing damaged by natural disaster, or whose head is in armed forces	New or substantially rehabilitated rental units built under FHA (principally sec. 221[d][3]) programs, in areas with workable program	Fair market value for gross rent; 40 years
NHA, sec. 221(h): below-market-rate rehabilitation sales housing	1966	FHA	To insure loans for homes to be resold to low in-come families under sec. 221(h) single-family housing program	Rehabilitation of 4 or more dwellings with 1–2 units each	$18,000 for 1 family unit, $24,000 for 2 (more in high cost areas); 100% of estimated rehabilitation cost plus appraised value before rehabilitation or purchase price; 40 years
NHA, sec. 235(j): rehabilitation sales housing	1968	FHA	To insure loans for homes to be sold to low income families under sec. 235(j) single-family housing pro-gram	Same as for sec. 221(h) multifamily housing program	Same as for sec. 221(h) multifamily housing pro-gram

Abbreviations and notes are at end of table.

| Subsidy | Number of units assisted[c] (thousands) | | | | Estimated volume of insurance, June 30, 1971 | | |
| | | | | | Total written (millions of dollars) | In force | |
	Before 1960	1960–1964	1965–1970	Total		Amount (millions of dollars)	Number of insurance contracts
Below-market-interest rate (1 % in 1971); tax incentives through rapid depreciation	...	1[k]	6[k]	7[k]	15	n.a.	n.a.
		Includes sec. 516 units					
Below-market-interest rate	...	*	8	8	86[j]	n.a.	n.a.
		Includes sec. 515 housing for elderly					
Grant		Included in sec. 514 units			...	...	...
Below-market-interest rate, as low as 1 %; technical assistance and nonrepayable financial assistance	n.a.	n.a.	n.a.	n.a.	...	...	...
Below-market-interest rate (3 % in 1971); tax incentives through rapid depreciation	...	27	154	182	2,723	2,349	1,376
Difference between gross rent and 25 % of tenant's income	...	...	42[l]	42[l]	...	...	...
Below-market-interest rate	...	...	3	3	30	15	182
Assistance payments that reduce interest rate to as little as 1 %	...	...	1	1	15	15	118

Authority and type of program	Year estab- lished[a]	Admin- istering agency	Purposes	Coverage	Maximum terms[b]
Multifamily housing (continued)					
NHA, sec. 236: rental and coop- erative housing assistance	1968	FHA	To insure loans in order to reduce rent for lower income, primarily elderly or handicapped, persons; priority to displaced persons	Construction or reha- bilitation of 5 or more cooperative units	Same as for sec. 221(d)(3) subsidized multifamily housing program
Housing-related aid					
HUDA of 1968, sec. 106: assistance to nonprofit sponsors	1968	FHA	To make loans and give aid to nonprofit sponsors of subsidized rental hous- ing for low and moderate income families	Preconstruction ex- penses on any feder- ally assisted program (some exceptions be- fore 1970)	80% of preconstruction costs; 2 years
HA of 1949, sec. 524: rural housing sites	1969	FmHA	To make loans to non- profit sponsors of subsi- dized housing under NHA, secs. 235, 236, and HA of 1949, sec. 521	Acquisition and devel- opment of land as building sites	Amounts and loan-to- value ratios as determined by FmHA; 2 years
HUDA of 1968, sec. 907: national housing partnerships	1968	HUD	To spread investment risks among investors in low and moderate income housing through joint ventures with private profit oriented investors	Mass scale construc- tion or rehabilitation of housing and related facilities	25% of initial equity in- vestment unless balance is not locally obtainable

PROGRAMS FOR SPECIAL GROUPS
Housing for elderly or handicapped

Authority and type of program	Year estab- lished[a]	Admin- istering agency	Purposes	Coverage	Maximum terms[b]
HA of 1959, sec. 202: rental or cooperative housing	1959	FHA	To make loans to non- profit or limited profit sponsors, consumer coop- eratives, and public agen- cies for housing for lower middle income elderly or handicapped persons (con- version of program to NHA, sec. 236, was begun in 1969)	Construction, rehabil- itation, or improve- ment of rental or co- operative housing	100% of development cost for nonprofit mortgagor, 90% for limited profit; 50 years
NHA, sec. 207: specially designed housing	1956	FHA	To insure loans for rental housing designed for el- derly (program reoriented toward families with children, 1959)	Same as for sec. 207 multifamily housing program	Same as for sec. 207 multi- family housing program
NHA, sec. 231: specially designed housing	1959	FHA	To insure loans for rental housing designed for el- derly and handicapped (replaced sec. 207 pro- gram for elderly)	Construction or reha- bilitation of dwelling with 8 or more units	$8,800 for no-bedroom unit, $12,375 for 1-bed- room, $14,850 for 2, $18,700 for 3, $21,175 for 4 (more in high cost areas or elevator buildings); $12.5 million per project for private mortgagor, $50 million for public; 100% of estimated replacement cost for nonprofit mort- gagor, 90% for profit (ratio varies for rehabili- tation); 40 years

Abbreviations and notes are at end of table.

| Subsidy | Number of units assisted[a] (thousands) | | | | Estimated volume of insurance, June 30, 1971 | | |
| | Before 1960 | 1960– 1964 | 1965– 1970 | Total | Total written (millions of dollars) | In force | |
						Amount (millions of dollars)	Number of insurance contracts
Interest reduction payments that reduce interest rate to as little as 1 %; tax incentives through rapid depreciation	...	...	124	124	2,661	2,640	1,456
	Includes sec. 236 housing for elderly				Includes sec. 236 housing for elderly		
Free technical assistance, advice, and information; interest-free loans	...	...	...	...	...	...	...
None	Included in sec. 523 units				...	...	...
Tax incentives through rapid depreciation	...	...	...	...	...	...	...
Below-market-interest rate (3 % in 1971); tax incentives through rapid depreciation	...	4	27	32	...	...	...
None	4	*	...	4	Included in sec. 207 multifamily housing		
None[d]	*	31	9	40	510	285	175

Authority and type of program	Year estab-lished[a]	Admin-istering agency	Purposes	Coverage	Maximum terms[b]
Housing for elderly or handicapped (continued)					
NHA, sec. 236: interest rate subsidy	1968	FHA	To insure loans (including refinancing of sec. 202 projects) and to make interest reduction payments for rental or cooperative housing for elderly, lower income families	Same as for sec. 236 multifamily housing program	Same as for sec. 236 multifamily housing program
HUDA of 1965, sec. 101: rent supplements	1965	FHA	To subsidize rents for low income elderly or handicapped	Same as for sec. 101 multifamily housing program	Same as for sec. 101 multifamily housing program
HA of 1949, sec. 515: housing for low or moderate income rural families	1962	FmHA	To make and insure loans for housing for low or moderate income elderly rural families	Same as for sec. 515 multifamily housing program	Same as for sec. 515 multifamily housing program
Hospitals and nursing homes					
NHA, sec. 232: nursing and intermediate care facilities	1959	FHA	To insure loans for nursing homes and intermediate care facilities	Construction or rehabilitation of facilities (including major equipment)	$12.5 million per project; 90% of estimated value of the project when completed; 20 years
NHA, sec. 241: supplemental loans for nursing homes	1968	FHA	To insure supplementary loans for nursing homes currently or previously insured under NHA programs	Alteration, repair, addition, or improvement of facility, and purchase of equipment for nursing homes	Estimated cost of repairs plus debt may not exceed original mortgage; 90% of estimated value of improvements; remaining years of mortgage
NHA, sec. 242: hospitals	1968	FHA	To insure loans to hospitals	Construction, rehabilitation, and equipment	$50 million; 90% of estimated replacement cost; term of years for complete amortization to be determined by FHA
Defense housing					
NHA, sec. 222: servicemen's housing	1954	FHA	To insure loans for servicemen	Purchase, construction, or rehabilitation of single-family dwelling or unit in condominium insured under any other section of NHA	Same loan amounts as for secs. 203(b), 234(c), 203(i), and 221(d)(2) programs; 97% of $15,000 sliding to 85% above $25,000 of FHA value plus closing costs (with exceptions); 30 years (more in special cases)
NHA, sec. 809: armed services (civilian) housing	1956	FHA	To insure loans for civilian employees of research or development installations of the armed services	Same as for sec. 203(b) single-family program	Same as for sec. 203(b) single-family housing program
NHA, sec. 810(f): armed services (impacted areas) rental housing	1959	FHA	To insure loans for rental housing for military or civilian employees of defense installations	Construction of housing with 8 or more units	$9,000 for no-bedroom unit, $12,500 for 1-bedroom, $15,000 for 2, $18,500 for 3 or more (more in high cost areas); $5 million per project; 90% of estimated value; 40 years

Abbreviations and notes are at end of table.

Subsidy	Number of units assisted[e] (thousands)				Estimated volume of insurance, June 30, 1971		
					Total written (millions of dollars)	In force	
	Before 1960	1960–1964	1965–1970	Total		Amount (millions of dollars)	Number of insurance contracts
Interest reduction payments that reduce interest to as little as 1%	Included in sec. 236 multifamily housing				Included in sec. 236 multifamily housing		
Difference between gross rent and 25% of tenant's income	...	...	3[1]	3[1]	...	...	...
Below-market-interest rate	Included in secs. 515 and 521 multifamily housing				Included in secs. 515 and 521 multifamily housing		
None	...	27[m]	49[m]	76[m]	637	533	693
None[d]	...	...	1	1	Included in sec. 241 multifamily housing		
None	...	...	1[m]	1[m]	258	258	26
DOD payment of FHA insurance premium	68	85	79	232	3,425	2,083	160,242
None	4	7	6	16	256	190	13,275
None	...	1	1	3	30	21	13
		Includes secs. 810(g), 810(h)				Includes secs. 810(g), 810(h)	

Authority and type of program	Year estab- lished[a]	Admin- istering agency	Purposes	Coverage	Maximum terms[b]
Defense housing (continued)					
NHA, sec. 810(g): armed services (impacted areas) rental and sales projects	1959	FHA	To insure loans for rental housing for eventual sale to civilian or military employees of defense installations	Construction of 8 or more single-family units	$5 million; 97% of $15,000 sliding to 80% above $25,000 of FHA value plus closing costs; 40 years (less in special cases)
NHA, sec. 810(h): armed services (impacted areas) acquisition loans	1959	FHA	To insure loans to military or civilian employees of defense installations for acquisition of housing	Purchase of single-family units built under sec. 810(g)	Unit share of unpaid balance of project mortgage; 30 years (more in special cases)
PL 554 (1962), secs. 502, 503: appropriated funds for military housing	1962	DOD	To provide housing at military locations for military families	Construction, acquisition, addition, alteration, operation, or maintenance of family housing built on military owned land and operated as public quarters	...
PL 968 (1956), secs. 411, 515: leased military housing	1956	DOD	To lease housing for military families when there is a lack at or near military installations	Acquisition by lease of family housing and community facilities, in U.S. and foreign countries	...
HUDA of 1965, sec. 107: defaulted mortgagor	1965	HUD and VA	To assume mortgage payments for unemployed servicemen or civilians released by closing of federal installation	Mortgage payments on owner-occupied dwelling for a defaulted loan	2 years; mortgagor must repay full payment cost plus reasonable interest
DCMDA, sec. 1013: closing of military bases	1966	DOD	To compensate for losses on homes by military and civilian employees who are unemployed or forced to relocate because of closing of a military base	Loss on 1- or 2-family owner-occupied dwellings that may be or have been sold at less than fair market value	Difference between 95% of fair market value prior to base closing and market value at time of sale, or 90% of prior fair market value, or amount of outstanding mortgage
Housing for educational institutions					
HA of 1950, sec. 401: college housing loans	1950	FHA	To make loans for housing and related facilities for students and faculties in educational institutions	Purchase, construction, or rehabilitation of dormitories, apartments, dwellings, and college-related facilities	100% of development cost; 50 years
HA of 1950, sec. 401: college housing grants	1968	FHA	To make grants for debt service for housing and related facilities for students and faculties in educational institutions that cannot reasonably finance the debt privately	Purchase, construction, rehabilitation of dormitories, apartments, dwellings, and college-related facilities	40 years
Housing in Alaska					
DCMDA, sec. 1004: Alaska housing	1966	HUD	To make loans and grants to Alaska residents otherwise unable to finance housing and related facilities under terms they can afford	Construction of individual dwelling units, using mutual and self-help when feasible	Cost may not exceed average of $10,875 per dwelling unit; grants limited to 75% of cost

Abbreviations and notes are at end of table.

| Subsidy | Number of units assisted[o] (thousands) | | | | Estimated volume of insurance, June 30, 1971 | | |
	Before 1960	1960–1964	1965–1970	Total	Total written (millions of dollars)	In force Amount (millions of dollars)	In force Number of insurance contracts
None	Included in sec. 810(f)				Included in sec. 810(f)		
None	Included in sec. 810(f)				Included in sec. 810(f)		
Cost of the housing program	...	12	33	45	...	...	...
Cost of leases	...	...	...	11ᵃ	...	...	...
None	...	...	n.a.	n.a.	...	...	...
Cash payment	...	...	3	3	...	...	...
Below-market-interest rate (3% in 1971)	233°	360° Includes sec. 401 grants	237°	830°	...	...	...
Difference between actual debt service payment and payment at 3% interest	Included in sec. 401 loans				...	...	...
Grant	...	...	•	•	...	...	...

Authority and type of program	Year established[a]	Administering agency	Purposes	Coverage	Maximum terms[b]
RESEARCH AND DEVELOPMENT PROGRAMS					
Technical					
HA of 1948, sec. 301: standardized home building	1948	HHFA	To develop and promote standardized building codes and materials for more uniform administration	Technical research and studies on acceptance and application of standardized building codes and standardized methods for assembly of home building materials and equipment	...
		FHA	To make technical studies	Research in housing and construction practices	...
NHA, sec. 233: experimental housing	1961	FHA	To lower housing costs and improve standards by insuring loans on single or multifamily dwellings involving testing of advanced technology (dwellings must meet certain specified requirements)	Housing design, materials, or construction, or neighborhood design	...
HA of 1961, sec. 207: demonstration programs	1961	HUD	To make grants for demonstration programs of new or improved means of providing housing for low income families, including handicapped	Research, development, demonstration	...
HUDA of 1968, sec. 108: experimental housing	1968	HUD	To provide sites and insure loans for public and private projects using new technologies for housing for lower income families	Large scale experimentation; mass production; environmental quality	...
DCMDA, sec. 1010: technological advancement	1966	HUD	To provide funds for reducing the cost and improving the quality of housing through advances in technology	Research, testing, demonstration; promotion of new techniques, materials, and methods	...
Announcement by Secretary of HUD: Operation Breakthrough	1969	HUD	To award contracts for experimental production, marketing, and management projects to improve the housing process	Development and testing of innovations in housing design, construction, land use, financing, management, and marketing for volume production	...
Announcement by DOD: family housing research	1967	DOD	To award contracts for experimental production of housing on military bases to find ways to reduce costs	Assembly line production	...
Nontechnical					
President's Conference on Home Building and Home Ownership (PCHB)	1931	PCHB	To recommend federal action to support housing market; reflected in federal savings and loan system legislation (1932) and mortgage insurance legislation (1934); also recommended programs stress-	...	...

Abbreviations and notes are at end of table.

| Subsidy | Number of units assisted^c (thousands) | | | | Estimated volume of insurance, June 30, 1971 | | |
	Before 1960	1960– 1964	1965– 1970	Total	Total written (millions of dollars)	In force Amount (millions of dollars)	Number of insurance contracts
Obligations of $5 million, fiscal years 1948–54	...	...	...	...	...	...	...
Obligations of $4 million, fiscal years 1957–69	...	...	...	...	...	...	...
...	...	...	...	...	...	...	...
Outlays of $6 million, fiscal years 1961–67	...	...	...	...	...	...	...
Outlays of $6 million, fiscal years 1968–71	...	...	...	...	...	...	...
Outlays of $49 million, fiscal years 1966–69; includes Operation Breakthrough	...	...	...	...	...	...	...
Included in DCMDA, sec. 1010	...	...	...	...	...	...	...
Appropriations of $6 million, fiscal years 1967–71	...	...	...	...	...	...	...
...	...	...	...	...	...	...	...

Authority and type of program	Year estab-lished[a]	Admin-istering agency	Purposes	Coverage	Maximum terms[b]
Nontechnical (continued)			ing single-family houses, improved planning, zoning, and technology, broadened home ownership, adequate system of home credit, elimination of slums and overcrowding, large scale housing operations		
Joint [Congressional] Committee on Housing (JCH)	1947	JCH	To recommend legislative action to alleviate housing shortage and reform public housing and slum clearance programs; reflected in Housing Act of 1949	...	...
President's Advisory Committee on Government Housing Policies and Programs (PAC)	1953	PAC	To recommend reforms; reflected in legislation broadening the urban redevelopment (renewal) program (1954)	...	...
National Commission on Urban Problems (NCUP)	1967	NCUP	To study building codes, housing codes, zoning, and local and federal tax policies; known as Douglas Commission	...	...
President's Committee on Urban Housing (PCUH)	1967	PCUH	To study housing problems; reflected in establishment of a ten-year national housing goal and an annual report on the goal (1968); known as Kaiser Committee	...	...
Urban Institute (UI)	1968	UI	To conduct research on urban problems, including housing; federally supported center, created in 1968	...	...

Abbreviations (other than those defined in body of table): ASCD, Assistant Secretary for Community Development (Department of Housing and Urban Development); DCMDA, Demonstration Cities and Metropolitan Development Act of 1966; DOD, Department of Defense; FHA, Federal Housing Administration; FmHA, Farmers Home Administration; HA, Housing Act (of indicated year); HHFA, Housing and Home Finance Agency; HUD, (Department of) Housing and Urban Development; HUDA, Housing and Urban Development Act (of indicated year); NHA, National Housing Act (1934); PL, Public Law; SRA, Servicemen's Readjustment Act of 1944 (known as GI Bill); USHA, United States Housing Act of 1937; VA, Veterans Administration.

Sources: *Basic Laws and Authorities on Housing and Urban Development, Revised through January 31, 1971*, House Committee on Banking and Currency, 92 Cong. 1 sess. (1971); *The Budget of the United States Government, 1973—Appendix* and relevant preceding issues; *United States Statutes at Large*, various years; U.S. Department of Housing and Urban Development, *1970 HUD Statistical Yearbook* and issues for 1966–69; Housing and Home Finance Agency, *Annual Report*, various years; *Progress Report on Federal Housing and Urban Development Programs*, Subcommittee on Housing and Urban Affairs of the Senate Committee on Banking and Currency, various issues. Data from the sources above were supplemented by information from various publications of government agencies and by unpublished data supplied by the agencies.

* Less than 500 units.
** Less than $0.5 million.
n.a. Not available.
a. In many cases the purposes, coverage, and maximum terms changed several times between the year the program was established and the early 1970s. In some instances the administering agency changed.

		Number of units assisted[c] (thousands)			Estimated volume of insurance, June 30, 1971		
Subsidy	Before 1960	1960– 1964	1965– 1970	Total	Total written (millions of dollars)	In force	
						Amount (millions of dollars)	Number of insurance contracts
...		...	...	...	...	...	...	...
...		...	...	...	...	...	...	...
...		...	...	...	...	...	...	...
...		...	...	...	...	...	...	...
...		...	...	...	...	...	...	...

b. As applicable, terms include (1) maximum amount insurable, per unit and per project, (2) maximum loan-to-value ratio, and (3) maximum term of the mortgage.

c. Data for programs administered by FmHA and DOD are for fiscal years. Other data are for calendar years. Numbers are rounded and may not add to totals.

d. Accelerated depreciation enables owners of rental property to defer taxes on current income and eventually to pay taxes on capital gains rather than ordinary income. This feature of the tax code is widely regarded as an implicit subsidy.

e. Estimate as of March 31, 1971.

f. Veterans Administration guarantees.

g. Direct loans which are fully disbursed.

h. Number of grants approved.

i. Total amount of grants disbursed.

j. Does not include direct loans.

k. Includes family and individual units.

l. Number of unit payments made in December 1970.

m. Number of beds.

n. Number of units authorized to be leased for fiscal year 1970.

o. Number of accommodations provided.

appendix B Special Elements
of Various
Federal Programs

This appendix includes detailed information on special elements of various programs described in the text.

Census Bureau Procedures for Estimating Housing Conditions, 1970

The Bureau of the Census did not measure housing quality in the 1970 census but is estimating the amount of dilapidated housing from census data. The bureau's estimate of the number of dilapidated units is based on the number lacking basic plumbing facilities plus an estimate of the number with complete plumbing facilities that would have been classified as dilapidated in 1960. This number was calculated by the following procedure for 1960. Each housing unit was put into one of 122 classes, depending on whether the unit was occupied or vacant, was in a one-family structure, and lacked central or built-in heating; whether vacant units were for rent or sale; whether the rent or home value was below the median for units lacking complete private plumbing; and whether the occupant was Negro, the number of persons per room exceeded 1.0, and the head of the household had completed less than five years of school. For each class the proportion of dilapidated units with complete private plumbing in 1960 was estimated; the number for 1970 is being estimated by applying these proportions to the 1970 census data.

The accuracy of the estimates depends crucially on the proportions, and at least some are implausible. To illustrate, for units lacking central or installed heat rented by Negroes, the proportion classified as dilapidated in 1960 is 0.095; if there were more than one person per room, the probability is 0.042; if the household head had less than five years of schooling, the probability is 0.106; if the unit was in a single-unit structure, the probability is 0.103. If all of these negative factors are present, however, the probability that the unit was classified as dilapidated is 0.000. In other words, such units would automatically be classified as standard.

Income and Other Limitations on Beneficiaries of Federal Housing Programs

Under most subsidized programs of housing assistance, families are eligible only if their incomes fall below specified limits. The limits for major programs are summarized in Table B-1.

The low rent public housing program uses one limit for entrance and another, generally 25 percent higher, for continued occupancy (see Table B-2). The limit for elderly families is lower than for nonaged; some localities have special limits for leased public housing (usually above those for conventional public housing) and for displaced families. The limits as well as regulations regarding income determination vary considerably since local housing authorities are given discretion in setting limits and in determining allowable deductions and exemptions.

Methods for determining family income depend on whether the family is applying for admission or for continued occupancy, on the size of the family, and on the locality or region of application. Several deductions and exemptions can be made from the annual income anticipated by all family members from all sources. Most localities allow service-connected disability and death benefits paid by the Veterans Administration (VA) to be exempted, and many exempt training allowances paid by the Office of Economic Opportunity. Some exempt the income of minors and certain adults, and some allow a fixed amount per minor to be deducted (usually $100, but as much as $300).

The maximum income limits for admission to section 221(d)(3) below-market-interest-rate (BMIR) projects are much higher than those for public housing in the same area (see Table B-3). The limits depend on the median income for families of that size in the area and the development costs of a prototype, two-story walkup project of moderate design in the locality; the maximum limit is set at the lower of the two, and 20 percent of gross family income only may be applied for housing expense. Usually the limits are determined by the construction costs. No deductions or exemptions are allowed in determining income for 221(d)(3) BMIR projects. Maximum income limits for selected cities during 1971 ranged from

Table B-1. Maximum Family Income and Assets, with Allowable Deductions and Exemptions, for Selected Federally Subsidized Housing Programs, 1970

Program	Maximum income	Allowable deductions and exemptions[a]	Maximum assets
Low rent public housing	See Table B-3	VA service-connected disability and death benefits, antipoverty payments, fixed amount per minor, income of minors; local variations in adjustments	Wide local variations
Federal Housing Administration (FHA) programs[b]			
Below-market-interest rate for low and moderate income families, under sec. 221-(d)(3) BMIR	Varies by family size and building costs and income in area	None	None
Below-market-interest rate for sales housing under sec. 221(h)	Same as for admission to low rent public housing	5% of total family income (for payroll deductions), $300 per minor, wages of minors	None
Rent supplements	Same as for admission to low rent public housing	$300 per minor, wages of minors[c]	$5,000 for elderly family, $2,000 for others
Interest credit for homeownership loans under sec. 235	135% of income limit for public housing (but, 20% of funds may assist persons with higher incomes that are less than	5% of total family income (for payroll deductions), $300 per minor, wages of minors	$5,000 for elderly family, $2,000 for others ($500 may be added for each dependent and an amount equal to applicant's

202

	90% of the local limit for sec. 221[d][3] BMIR)		share of the mortgage payment for one year)
Interest credit for rental projects under sec. 236	Same as for sec. 235	Same as for sec. 235	None
Farmers Home Administration (FmHA) programs[b]			
Interest credit for sec. 502 rural loans[d]	$7,000	None	$5,000
Loans for elderly and persons in rural areas under sec. 515			
Below-market-interest-rate loans	Varies by locality and by family size; may not exceed $6,000	None	None
Interest credits reducing effective interest rate to as little as 1%	Varies by locality and by family size; no maximum for elderly, $8,000 maximum for others	None	None

Sources: U.S. Department of Housing and Urban Development, "Annual Report on Maximum Income Limits and Rents in Low-Rent Housing as of December 31, 1970," HM, Section 222.0 (January 6, 1972; processed); HUD, "Regular Income Limits for Sections 235 and 236 Housing: United States List by States, Counties, Localities," HPMC-FHA 4400.30A (September 1, 1970; processed); *Independent Offices and Department of Housing and Urban Development Appropriations for 1971*, Hearings before a Subcommittee of the House Committee on Appropriations, 91 Cong. 2 sess. (1970), Pt. 3, p. 728; data supplied by the Federal Housing Administration and by the Farmers Home Administration.

a. For the low rent public housing and the FHA programs, all income from all sources, before taxes or withholding, of all members of the family living in the unit is used. For the FmHA programs, net farm and nonfarm business income and other dependable recurrent income from salaries, wages, social security, pension or welfare payments, and any interest received on state or municipal bonds by husband, wife, and any members of the family over 21 years old are used.

b. Section numbers refer to the National Housing Act.

c. No deductions or exemptions allowed before 1968.

d. No specific income or asset limitations apply for the regular sec. 502 loan program.

Table B-2. Median Income Limits for Admission and for Continued Occupancy, Low Rent Public Housing, Selected Years, 1950–70[a]

	Median income limit (dollars)				
Requirement	1950	1960	1965	1969	1970
For admission					
Average size family[b]	2,100	3,100	3,600	4,200	4,400
Displaced family[b, c]	n.a.	4,000	4,800	5,500	5,600
Elderly family					
Single person	n.a.	n.a.	2,600	3,000	3,200
Two persons	n.a.	n.a.	3,200	3,700	3,800
For continued occupancy					
Average size family[b]	n.a.	3,875	4,500	5,300	5,500

Sources: 1950, *Fourth Annual Report, Housing and Home Finance Agency, Calendar Year 1950*, p. 389; 1960–70, HUD, "Annual Report on Maximum Income Limits and Rents in Low-Rent Housing, as of December 31, 1970," Section 222.0, pp. 3, 5, 9, 11, 12.
n.a. Not available.
a. As of December 31 of year indicated.
b. Two adults and two minors.
c. Median limited to localities with special limits approved for displaced families.

Table B-3. Income Limits for Various Federally Subsidized Housing Programs, Selected Cities, 1970[a]

	Income limit (dollars)						
Program	Mont-gom-ery	Los Ange-les	Jersey City	De-troit	Phoe-nix	New York City	Okla-homa City
Public housing, admission[b]	4,000	5,000	5,900	5,500	4,200	6,337	4,200
Section 221(h)[c]	4,000	5,000	5,900	5,500	4,200	6,337	4,200
Rent supplement	4,000	5,000	5,900	5,500	4,200	6,337	4,200
Section 221(d)(3) BMIR[d]	6,722	10,111	10,222	10,500	8,889	12,000	7,778
Sections 235 and 236[e]							
Regular	5,400	6,750	7,965	7,425	5,670	8,555	5,670
Exception	6,050	9,100	9,200	9,450	8,000	10,800	7,000

Sources: HUD, "Regular Income Limits for Sections 235 and 236 Housing: United States List by States, Counties, Localities," HPMC-FHA 4400.30A (September 1, 1970; processed); HUD, "Exception Income Limits for Sections 235 and 236 Housing," FHA 4400.36A (December 1971; processed).
a. Limits are for an average size family (three to four members).
b. The income limit for continued occupancy is generally 25 percent higher than for admission.
c. Section 221(h) of the National Housing Act.
d. Section 221(d)(3) below-market-interest rate (BMIR) of the National Housing Act. Data are for 1971.
e. Sections 235 and 236 of the National Housing Act. Regular income limits are based on 135 percent of public housing admission limits. Up to 20 percent of assistance payments may be made on behalf of families whose incomes exceed 135 percent. These exception income limits are based on 90 percent of sec. 221(d)(3) BMIR limits.

a high in Fairbanks, Alaska, of $12,200 for an average family of three or four persons to a low of $3,350 in Ozark County, Missouri. In general, the range for such a family is between $6,000 and $9,000.

Income limits of other housing programs of the Federal Housing Administration are related to those for low rent public housing or the section 221(d)(3) BMIR program.

Basic FHA Credit Terms and Characteristics of FHA Transactions

Since 1934 the statutory and regulatory maximum credit terms on the basic FHA (section 203) mortgage insurance program have been continually liberalized. Actual average loan amounts, maturities, and loan-to-value ratios, shown in Table B-4, reflect these changes. Characteristics of transactions under the basic program are outlined in Table B-5 and under a number of multifamily programs in Table B-6.

Payoff Procedures under Housing Programs

The federal government assumes certain liabilities in the event of default or foreclosure on mortgages it insures or guarantees.

FHA-Insured Loans

For FHA-insured mortgages in serious default, the mortgagee may (1) convey the mortgage to FHA and receive either debentures or cash equal to the unpaid balance of the mortgage plus other incidental costs, or (2) foreclose the mortgage and sell the property or convey it to FHA in exchange for debentures or cash, in which case foreclosure costs may not be fully reimbursed. FHA does not provide protection against loss should the property be destroyed or damaged. The secretary of the treasury semiannually sets the interest rates payable on FHA debentures on the basis of the average yields on outstanding marketable U.S. obligations having a maturity of fifteen years or more.

Since 1961, mortgagees have been able to choose to receive payments in cash rather than debentures on section 220, 221, 233, 235(j), and 236 mortgages, and since 1964 on section 203(k) mortgages.

"Costs" to FHA include insurance claims, administrative expenses (including appraisal), and the costs of holding a mortgage or owning real

Table B-4. Loan Amounts, Maturities, Interest Rates, and Loan-to-Value Ratios for Holders of FHA's Section 203 Mortgages, Selected Years, 1935–70

Year	Loan amount (dollars)		Maturity (years)		Interest rate (percent)		Loan-to-value ratio (percent)	
	Maximum allowable	Actual average[a]	Maximum allowable	Actual average[a]	Regulatory maximum	Average yield	Maximum allowable	Actual average[a]
1935	16,000	4,013	20	n.a.	5.00	...	80	n.a.
1940	16,000	4,305	25	21.53	4.50	...	90	82.3
1945	16,000	4,709	25	n.a.	4.50	...	90	n.a.
1950	14,000[b]	7,233	25[c]	22.69	4.25[d]	4.17	90[e]	81.9
1955	20,000	10,048	30[c]	23.86	4.50	4.64	93[e]	83.2
1960	22,500	12,696	30	27.29	5.75	6.18	97	90.9
1965	30,000	14,599	35	29.22	5.25	5.46	97	92.7
1966	30,000	14,983	35	28.87	5.75[f]	6.29	97[g]	92.9
1967	30,000	15,606	35	28.76	6.00	6.55	97[g]	92.9
1968	30,000	15,938	35	28.70	6.75[h]	7.13	97[g]	92.9
1969	30,000[i]	16,510	35	28.99	7.50[j]	8.19	97[g]	92.6
1970	33,000	17,796	35	29.00	7.50[k]	9.05	97[g]	91.5

Sources: Housing and Home Finance Agency, *Second Annual Report, Calendar Year 1948*, p. 180, and *Eighth Annual Report, 1954*, pp. 124, 186, 191, 193; HUD, *1970 HUD Statistical Yearbook* (1971), Tables 163, 200, 202; *Economic Report of the President, January 1972*, p. 262; HUD, *Digest of Insurable Loans*, various issues; data supplied by the Federal Housing Administration.

n.a. Not available.
a. Weighted averages based on new and existing single-family units insured under section 203 of the National Housing Act.
b. $16,000 until July 1950.
c. There were some exceptions in 1950 and in 1955.
d. Rate was 4.5 percent until April 1950.
e. Ratio was lowered from 95 percent to 90 percent in July 1950, and from 95 percent to 93 percent in July 1955.
f. Rates during 1966 were set successively at 5.25, 5.5, 5.75, and 6 percent.
g. For veterans, 100 percent.
h. Effective May 1968.
i. Maximum loan amount was raised to $33,000 in December 1969.
j. Rate was increased to 7.5 percent in January 1969.
k. Rate was increased to 8 percent in December 1970.

Table B-5. Characteristics of Single-Family Home Transactions under
FHA Section 203 Program, Selected Years, 1950–70[a]

Characteristic	1950	1955	1960	1965	1968	1970
Average number of rooms	4.8	5.2	5.4	5.6	5.7	5.8
Average number of bedrooms	n.a.	2.7	2.9	3.0	3.0	3.2
Average sale price (dollars)	n.a.	12,219	13,859	15,381	16,792	18,903
Average mortgage amount (dollars)	7,233	10,076	12,699	14,612	15,954	17,651
Average monthly income of borrower (dollars)[b]	370	511	616	683	812	969
Average housing expense (dollars)[c]	78	100	127	144	171	215
Average expense as percent of income	21.1	19.5	20.7	21.1	21.1	22.2

Sources: HUD, *1968 HUD Statistical Yearbook* (1969), FHA Tables 4, 33; *1970 HUD Statistical Yearbook*, Tables 162, 194, 202.

n.a. Not available.

a. Figures are weighted averages based on new and existing single-family units insured under section 203 of the National Housing Act, and on FHA estimates of the income of the borrowers and monthly housing expenses.

b. Mortgagor's earning capacity (before taxes) likely to prevail during the first third of the mortgage term.

c. Includes mortgage payment, maintenance and repair, and heating and utilities for first year; does not include real estate taxes.

property as a result of defaults. FHA's income from insurance premiums, loan repayments, and proceeds from sales of conveyed mortgages has covered those costs (see Table B-7).

FHA's Mutual Mortgage Insurance Fund protects the basic mortgage insurance program (section 203). Mortgagors who do not default receive a rebate at termination of the mortgage, if their premiums exceed losses on all mortgages made in the same year. Since 1957, few groups have been eligible for payments; the average annual payment decreased from $131 in 1960 to $60 in 1969.

The General Insurance Fund pays no dividends; it is a conglomerate of many funds established separately. The Cooperative Management Housing Insurance Fund is a mutual, revolving fund; it has paid no dividends. The Special Risk Insurance Fund, for high risk programs, is eligible for congressional appropriations to meet expenses not covered by collections from insurance premiums and other regular income.

FmHA-Insured Loans

Under the Farmers Home Administration's insured loan programs, the mortgagor and the private investor have no direct relationship. FmHA

Table B-6. Characteristics of Units Insured under FHA Multifamily
Programs, Selected Years, 1955–70

Program and characteristic	1955	1960	1966	1968	1970
Section 207					
Average project size (units)	76.2	146.8	120.0	162.0ᵃ	148.5
Average number of rooms per unit	3.9	4.4	4.3	n.a.	n.a.
Average number of bedrooms per unit	n.a.	n.a.	1.6	1.3ᵃ	1.6
Median monthly rent per unit (dollars)	71.13	171.31	172.29	246.60ᵃ	227.24
Average mortgage amount per unit (dollars)	8,212	14,567	15,124	16,676ᵃ	16,334
Median mortgage amount as percent of FHA value	*80.0*	*89.6*	*89.2*	*86.9ᵃ*	*90.0*
Average value per unit (dollars)ᵇ	10,265	16,258	16,955	19,190ᵃ	18,149
Section 213 management					
Average project size (units)	113.7	131.2	175.7	80.1	n.a.
Average number of rooms per unit	5.0	4.9	4.6	n.a.	n.a.
Average number of bedrooms per unit	n.a.	n.a.	1.8	2.7	n.a.
Average mortgage amount per unit (dollars)	10,274	16,199	18,772	16,495	n.a.
Median mortgage amount as percent of replacement cost	*84.5*	*90.0*	*96.1*	*97.0*	n.a.
Average replacement cost per unit (dollars)ᶜ	12,159	17,999	19,534	17,005	n.a.
Section 220					
Average project size (units)	...	215.7	214.3	196.8	n.a.
Average number of rooms per unit	...	4.0	3.5	n.a.	n.a.
Average number of bedrooms per unit	...	n.a.	1.2	1.4	n.a.
Median monthly rent per unit (dollars)	...	158.13	169.15	238.51	n.a.
Average mortgage amount per unit (dollars)	...	14,596	16,107	19,345	n.a.
Median mortgage amount as percent of replacement cost	...	*88.6*	*88.4*	*88.0*	n.a.
Average replacement cost per unit (dollars)ᶜ	...	16,474	18,221	21,983	n.a.
Section 221 market rate					
Average project size (units)	...	179.5	125.0	98.3	97.8
Average number of rooms per unit	...	4.3	4.2	n.a.	n.a.
Average number of bedrooms per unit	...	n.a.	1.4	2.0	2.3
Median monthly rent per unit (dollars)	...	89.07	149.55	150.02	168.24
Average mortgage amount per unit (dollars)	...	8,847	13,300	11,786	11,938
Median mortgage amount as percent of replacement cost	...	*100.0*	*88.0*	*90.0*	*90.0*
Average replacement cost per unit (dollars)ᶜ	...	8,847	15,114	13,096	13,264

Sources: HUD, *Statistical Yearbook, 1966*, FHA Tables 43, 46, 47, 50; *1968 HUD Statistical Yearbook*, FHA Tables 51–58; *1970 HUD Statistical Yearbook*, Tables 241, 242, 244.

n.a. Not available.

a. Based on nine projects only.

makes loans from the Rural Housing Insurance Fund, a revolving fund established in 1965. The mortgagor's payments and insurance premium charges are deposited in the fund. Proceeds from FmHA's sale of the loan go to the fund. FmHA repays the loan and makes any required supplemental interest payments from the fund. If a mortgagor defaults, FmHA continues to make payments on the insured loan.

The decision to foreclose is left entirely to FmHA; traditionally, the agency has been very patient. FmHA also may grant moratoriums on mortgage payments for an unlimited period of time and may completely cancel interest charges during a moratorium period on some loans.

VA Loan Guarantees

The Veterans Administration becomes liable under its loan guarantee program when the mortgagee submits a claim because a borrower is delinquent. Generally, the mortgagee must foreclose and convey the property to VA; the amount of his claim is the difference between the value of the foreclosed property as determined by VA and the sum of the outstanding principal plus closing costs and past unpaid interest. Sometimes mortgagees assign the loan to VA (so that foreclosure is avoided) in return for the unpaid principal plus accrued interest. In both cases, claims are paid in cash.

Because VA traditionally charged few fees and collected no premiums, the costs of the program until 1964 were met entirely by the federal government—before 1961 as part of the lump sum appropriation for veterans' benefits, after that through the Loan Guaranty Revolving Fund. In 1964 Congress authorized the sale of participation certificates backed by pools of federal assets; VA received a fixed portion of the proceeds to carry out its loan program and pays the interest expenses on its portion of the participation pool. Since 1966, VA has required payment of one-time fees.

The guaranteed direct loan program has been administered through a revolving fund since 1951. Through 1963, VA depended on annual increases in its authorization to borrow from the Treasury in order to continue the program. Since then, direct loans have been included in the participation sales asset pool and VA has had ample funds to administer the program. Funds for the specially adapted housing grant program are appropriated by Congress.

---

b. Derived from (1) average mortgage amount per unit and (2) the mortgage amount as a percent of FHA value.

c. Derived from (1) average mortgage amount per unit and (2) the median mortgage amount as percent of replacement cost.

Table B-7. Coverage, Income, and Expenditures of FHA Insurance Funds, 1970

In millions of dollars

Fund	Year established	National Housing Act authority	Coverage Type of property	Income, fiscal year 1970	Expenses, fiscal year 1970	Income from fees, premiums, and investments cumulative through June 30, 1970	Operating expenses cumulative through June 30, 1970ᶜ
All funds				422.9	119.5	5,002.1	1,501.2
Mutual Mortgage Insurance Fund	1934	Sec. 203, except 203(k)	One- to four-family dwellings	317.0	70.1	3,464.7	1,037.6
General Insurance Fundᵇ	1965						
Title I Insurance Fund	1939	Sec. 2	Single and multifamily dwellings (property improvement only)	13.6	5.4	386.8	96.0
Title I Housing Insurance Fund	1950	Sec. 8	Single family dwellings	0.2	*	12.7	4.0
Housing Insurance Fund	1938	Secs. 207–10, 213, 231, 232	Multifamily dwellings, cooperatives, nursing and intermediate care facilities, including equipment	16.1	7.6	221.9	107.3
Section 203 Home Improvement Account	1961	Sec. 203(k)	One- to four-family dwellings primarily outside urban renewal areas (improvements only)	0.1	*	0.5	1.0
Section 220 Housing Insurance Fund	1954	Sec. 220	Single and multifamily dwellings in urban renewal areas	4.7	1.0	44.3	16.7
Section 220 Home Improvement Account	1961	Sec. 220	Single and multifamily dwellings in urban renewal areas (improvements only)	*	0.1	0.1	0.8
Section 221 Housing Insurance Fund	1954	Sec. 221	Single and multifamily dwellings	29.5	16.4	128.5	76.8
Servicemen's Mortgage Insurance Fund	1954	Sec. 222	Single family dwellings or individual units in condominiums	10.2	1.1	98.3	11.4
Experimental Housing Insurance Fund	1961	Sec. 233	Single or multifamily dwellings built with advanced or experimental technology	*	0.2	0.3	1.5
Apartment Unit Insurance Fund	1961	Sec. 234	Individual units in condominiums	0.8	0.8	2.0	2.7

Program	Year	Section	Coverage				
Section 240 Fee Simple Title to Land	1968	Sec. 240	Land on which is located one- to four-family dwellings under ground lease	*	0.1	*	0.1
Section 242 Mortgage Insurance Fund for Non-profit Hospitals	1968	Sec. 242	Hospitals	0.2	0.1	0.3	0.2
War Housing Insurance Fund	1941	Secs. 603, 608, 611	One- to four-family dwellings, rental and group housing, and projects of 25 or more single family dwellings	4.0	1.6	466.0	97.7
Housing Investment Insurance Fund	1948	Sec. 701	Rental dwellings in projects	ᶜ	ᶜ	0.3	0.1
Armed Services Housing Mortgage Insurance Fund	1949	Secs. 803, 809, 810	Single family dwellings and rental or sales multifamily projects for military personnel, and one- to four-family dwellings for civilian employees of military research and development installations	4.0	0.2	103.5	12.5
National Defense Housing Insurance Fund	1951	Secs. 903, 908	One- to two-family and multifamily dwellings in critical defense housing areas	0.7	0.4	33.3	15.0
Mortgage Insurance Fund for Land Development	1965	Sec. 1002	Land to be developed for subdivisions or new communities, including water and sewerage systems, streets, and related facilities	0.2	0.2	0.5	1.0
Group Practice Facilities Insurance Fund	1966	Sec. 1101	Facilities, including major movable equipment, for group practice of dentistry, medicine, or optometry	0.1	0.1	0.1	0.4
Cooperative Management Housing Insurance Fund	1965	Sec. 213	Cooperatives with 5 or more units	5.4	0.5	19.2	3.1
Special Risk Insurance Fund	1968	Secs. 223(e), 233(a)(2), 235, 236, 237	Single and multifamily dwellings, including cooperatives and experimental housing, and group practice facilities located in older declining urban areas	16.0	13.8	18.7	15.2

Sources: HUD, *1970 HUD Statistical Yearbook*, Tables 273, 274; U.S. Housing and Home Finance Agency, *Eighteenth Annual Report, 1964*, pp. 183–227; *United States Statutes at Large*, various issues; information supplied by the Federal Housing Administration. Figures may not add to totals because of rounding.

* Less than $50,000.

a. Components and total include expenses of $0.9 million for unfilled orders.

b. The General Insurance Fund was created in 1965 to consolidate FHA insurance funds, with the exceptions indicated in this table, and for use as a revolving fund for carrying out the provisions of the National Housing Act.

c. Repealed in 1965.

appendix C **Procedures
for Calculating
Program
Effects**

This appendix includes explanations of the procedures
used in calculating the effects of programs described in various parts of the
text.

Factors Influencing Fraction of Income Spent on Housing

Housing expenditures depend on income, family size, and age. Income
determines the capacity to buy housing services as well as other commodities. Family size influences the need to buy food and other commodities
more than it affects housing requirements. Young people are more likely
than old to be making mortgage payments and to be acquiring household
furnishings.

To test these hypotheses the equation

$$H_{ij} = aE_{ij}^b S_{ij}^c D_j^{d_j} e_{ij}$$

was fitted to data from the 1960–61 Survey of Consumer Expenditures.[1] In
the equation, H_{ij} is average total housing expenditure by the ith income
class and the jth age bracket, E_{ij} is average total household expenditure
(current consumption plus personal insurance), S_{ij} is average family size,
and D_j is a dummy variable for the age brackets (25–34, 35–44, 45–54,
55–64, 65–74, 75 and over). The parameters are a, b, c, and d_j; e_{ij} is an
error term. Household expenditures appear as an explanatory variable
rather than current measured income, because household expenditures are

1. U.S. Bureau of Labor Statistics, "Consumer Expenditures and Income: Total
United States, Urban and Rural, 1960–61," BLS Report 237-93—USDA Report CES-
15 (1965; processed), p. 16.

Table C-1. Coefficients Showing Relation of Housing Expenditures to Family Size, Age, and Income

Independent variable	Coefficient	t statistic
Average family size	−0.393	−3.83[a]
Age 25–34	0.141	2.56[b]
Age 35–44	0.112	1.97
Age 45–54	−0.003	−0.06
Age 55–64	−0.098	−1.89
Age 65–74	−0.107	−1.91
Age 75 and over	−0.095	−1.74
Average household expenditures	0.949	23.65[a]
Constant	4.20	16.42[a]
$\bar{R}^2$ = 0.968[a]		
Degrees of freedom = 59		

Source: Derived from equation described in the text.
a. Significantly different from zero at the 99 percent confidence level.
b. Significantly different from zero at the 90 percent confidence level.

a better guide to permanent income than is current measured income. The estimated equation results, using ordinary least squares, with housing expenditures as the dependent variable, are shown in Table C-1.

These results refute the frequent contention that low income households on the average spend disproportionately more on housing than do high income households. The coefficient of average household expenditures, 0.949, is not significantly different from 1.0, which would indicate that high and low income households on the average devote the same fraction of total outlays to housing after the influences of family size and age have been removed. Whether low income households get as much for their housing dollars is another and more important issue that can be settled only by comparison of rather elaborate measures of the quality of residential services with housing expenditures.

Indifference Curve Approach to Housing Subsidies

Many housing subsidies confront potential beneficiaries with an all-or-nothing choice. They may accept a certain quantity of housing services at a subsidized price or they may reject the subsidy. Low rent public housing presents potential occupants with such a choice.

The analysis of this kind of offer can be portrayed conveniently with indifference curves. In Figure C-1 the line AB represents the quantity of housing and other goods a household can buy if neither category of goods

Figure C-1. Indifference Curves for Alternative Approaches to Low Rent Public Housing Subsidies

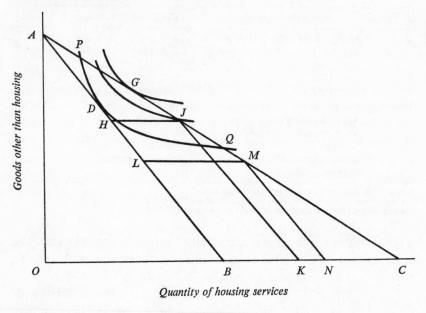

Quantity of housing services

is subsidized. The household would maximize welfare by purchasing the quantities of housing and of other goods shown at *D*. If housing is subsidized, say, 50 percent, and beneficiaries can purchase as much or as little housing as they wish at the reduced price, the budget line becomes *AC*, and the household maximizes welfare by buying the quantities of housing and of other goods shown at *G*. Alternatively, the government may give the household the choice between purchasing the quantity of housing services shown at *J* at the reduced price or of receiving no subsidy at all. The budget line then becomes the irregular line *AHJK* and the household maximizes welfare by accepting the all-or-nothing subsidy offer represented by *J*. If the government offered the household the choice between purchasing the quantity of housing services shown at *M* at the reduced price or of receiving no subsidy at all, the budget line would move from *AB* to *ALMN*. In this case, the household should refuse the proffered subsidy, as it is better off at *D* than at *M*. The household will accept any quantity of housing services offered, subject to a 50 percent subsidy, greater than the amount shown at *P* and less than the amount shown at *Q*.

FHA and VA Benefit Estimates

The income redistribution resulting from Federal Housing Administration (FHA) and Veterans Administration (VA) home mortgage insurance shown in Tables 5-3 and 5-4, Chapter 5, was calculated by the following procedures. The relative probability of default of loans by income bracket and the relative loss resulting from default were computed. Loan classes were defined by loan-to-value ratios, income of mortgagor, and whether the house was new or existing. The present discounted value of estimated premium income over ten years was taken as income and, assuming actuarial balance, set equal to default losses. (Income estimates do not include fees or prepayment charges imposed on mortgagors who pay in less than ten years.) The differences between premium income and estimated default losses were then computed.

FHA Loans

1. Default probability relatives, DPR_{ijk}, for FHA loans (see Table C-2) were computed for eighty loan classes, based on ten income brackets ($i = 1, \ldots, 10$), four loan-to-value classes ($j = 1, \ldots, 4$), and new and existing houses ($k = 1, 2$). Default probabilities were computed from the equation for new housing,

$$\ln D = -3.4328 - 1.4847 \ln [10(1 - L/V)] - 0.8240 \ln Y$$
$$(0.0601) \qquad\qquad\qquad (0.0732)$$

$$\bar{R}^2 = 0.4003 \qquad df = 1,160 \qquad S_e = 1.0712,$$

and the equation for existing housing,

$$\ln D = -3.9561 - 1.2668 \ln [10(1 - L/V)] - 0.6578 \ln Y$$
$$(0.0482) \qquad\qquad\qquad (0.0584)$$

$$\bar{R}^2 = 0.4024 \qquad df = 1,267 \qquad S_e = 0.9438,$$

where L/V is the ratio of loan to FHA's appraised value, Y is income, $\bar{R}^2$ indicates the coefficient of determination, df is degrees of freedom, and S_e is standard error of estimate. The numbers in parentheses are standard errors. D is defined as the total number of defaults registered annually

Table C-2. Indexes of Relative Default Probabilities for Single-Family Home Mortgages Insured by FHA, 1958–66[a]

Loan-to-value ratio of 0.96–0.97, income of less than $4,000, new structure = 100

Loan-to-value ratio of mortgage	Income bracket (dollars)									
	Less than 4,000	4,000– 4,999	5,000– 5,999	6,000– 6,999	7,000– 7,999	8,000– 8,999	9,000– 9,999	10,000– 11,999	12,000– 14,999	15,000 and over
	New structures									
0.76–0.89	39	36	33	31	30	28	27	26	24	22
0.90–0.92	54	60	46	44	41	40	38	36	34	31
0.93–0.95	71	65	60	57	54	51	49	47	44	40
0.96–0.97	100	91	85	80	76	73	70	66	62	57
	Existing structures									
0.76–0.89	26	25	23	22	21	20	20	19	18	17
0.90–0.92	35	33	31	29	28	27	26	25	24	22
0.93–0.95	44	41	38	37	35	34	33	31	30	28
0.96–0.97	59	55	52	49	47	46	44	42	40	37

Source: Derived from default rates in George M. von Furstenberg, "Risk Structures and the Distribution of Benefits within the FHA Home Mortgage Insurance Program," *Journal of Money, Credit and Banking*, Vol. 2 (August 1970), pp. 303–22.

a. Loans are those insured under sec. 203 of the National Housing Act.

during peak risk years (three or four years after origination) divided by the number of mortgages initially endorsed for any class.[4]

2. Loss relatives, LR_{ijk}, for FHA loans were computed from the fraction of the original face value of the mortgage lost on those mortgages where defaults occurred, L_j (0.275 on L/V of 0.96 to 0.97, 0.250 on L/V of 0.93 to 0.95, 0.225 on L/V of 0.90 to 0.92, and 0.19 on L/V below 0.90),[5] and the average mortgage amount by income bracket for new and existing housing, M_{ik}.[6] L_j and M_{ik} were multiplied by DPR_{ijk} to yield probability loss relatives, PLR_{ijk}.

3. The proportions of loans endorsed in 1966 within each income bracket that fell in each loan-to-value class, P_{ijk}, were used to compute for each income class a weighted probability loss relative, $WPLR_{ik}, = \sum_{j=1}^{4} P_{ijk}PLR_{ijk}$. Using the fraction of all insured mortgages falling within each income class, for both new and existing properties, P_{ik}, as weights, the average loss relative, $ALR, = \sum_i \sum_k WPLR_{ik}P_{ik}$.

4. The loss index for each class of mortgages, $LI_{ik}, = WPLR_{ik}/ALR$. A value of LI_{ik} greater (less) than 1.0 indicates that the expected loss per mortgage of the indicated class is greater (less) than the average expected loss per FHA mortgage.

5. The present discounted value of mortgage insurance premiums equal to 0.5 percent of outstanding balance, assuming an interest rate and a discount rate of 6 percent for a thirty-year fully amortized loan, was computed. Assuming prepayment without penalty after ten years, the present discounted value of premium payments, per dollar of original face value of the mortgage, is 3.402 cents.

6. Total premium income, $TPI, = TPI_{ik}$, where $TPI_{ik} = 3.402\ M_{ik}N_{ik}$, and where N_{ik} is the number of mortgages insured in each income bracket for new and existing property.

7. $\left[(LI_{ik}N_{ik})/\sum_i \sum_k (LI_{ik}N_{ik})\right]TPI = Z_{ik}$, the default loss that will be generated by mortgages in each income class for new and existing property, assuming actuarial balance.

---

4. George M. von Furstenberg, "Risk Structures and the Distribution of Benefits within the FHA Home Mortgage Insurance Program," *Journal of Money, Credit and Banking*, Vol. 2 (August 1970), p. 318, n. 31.

5. Ibid., p. 316, n. 29.

6. Calculated from U.S. Department of Housing and Urban Development, *Statistical Yearbook, 1966* (1968), pp. 87, 117, 125–28.

8. $Z_{ik} - TPI_{ik}$ is the net transfer, shown in Table 5-3, assuming actuarial balance.

VA Loans

The procedure followed for VA loans differed from that employed for FHA loans because data on loan-to-value ratio, L/V, were unavailable. Instead, loan-to-sales-price, L/P, data were used. Loans were classified into "no down payment" ($L/P = 1.0$) and "with down payment" ($L/P < 1.0$).

1. To convert VA data to the same conceptual basis as FHA's, the L/P for VA loans was multiplied by the P/V for FHA for each income bracket for new and existing houses.

2. Default probability relatives, DPR_{mnp}, for VA loans were computed for twenty-eight classes of mortgages, based on seven income brackets ($m = 1, \ldots, 7$), two L/V classes ($n = 1, 2$), and new and existing houses ($p = 1, 2$). Default probabilities were computed from the equations for FHA loans. For VA, some L/Vs of "no down payment" exceeded 0.97, which is outside the range of the equations. Furthermore, the logarithmic specification causes DPR to rise precipitously as $L/V \to 1.0$. Accordingly, where $L/V > 0.97$, DPR was computed using the derivative of the equations at $L/V = 0.97$.

3. Loss relatives, LR_{mnp}, were computed, as with FHA, assuming that the fraction of original face value lost was the same under VA as under FHA for equivalent L/V. Probability loss relatives, PLR_{mnp}, $= DPR_{mnp} \cdot L_n \cdot M_{mp}$, where L and M are defined as for FHA mortgages.

4. The percentage of loans within each income bracket falling in each L/V class, P_{mnp}, was used to compute for each income bracket a weighted probability loss relative, $WPLR_{mp}$, $= \sum_{n=1}^{2} P_{mnp} \cdot PLR_{mnp}$.

5. Using the fraction of all guaranteed home loans falling within each income bracket, new and existing, P_{mp}, the average loss relative, ALR, $= \sum_{m} \sum_{p} WPLR_{mp} \cdot P_{mp}$. A loss index, LI_{mp}, $= WPLR_{mp}/ALR$.

6. The ratio of ALR for VA to that for FHA indicates the relative riskiness, R, of VA. The number of VA guaranteed loans divided by the number of FHA insured mortgages equals the size weight, W. Under VA the default losses, D, $= TPI \cdot R \cdot W$.

7. The default loss for each income class is $\sum_{p=1}^{2} LI_{mp} \cdot D \cdot P_{mp}$.

Sampling Methods for Estimating Public Housing Subsidies

The estimates of public housing subsidies in Chapter 7 are based on a sample of replies to a Department of Housing and Urban Development (HUD) questionnaire given families reexamined during calendar year 1966 for continuous occupancy in public housing. The sample understates the fraction of public housing families headed by persons over sixty-five years old. Local housing authorities (LHAs) were classified in one of twelve categories, C_i, based on the size of developments managed by the LHA and the population of the city. The first nine categories were for developments with 1–25 units, 26–50 units, 51–75 units, 76–100 units, 101–200 units, 201–300 units, 301–500 units, 501–750 units, and 751–1,000 units; the other three categories, for developments with more than 1,000 units, were for cities with population of less than 100,000, between 100,000 and 500,000, and more than 500,000.

A sample of LHAs for each of the twelve categories was drawn randomly within each geographical region. Only those LHAs for which gap rents were available could be used, however, and this requirement is a source of undetermined bias. For each C_i, a weight, W_i, was calculated equal to the ratio of the number of units in all projects in all LHAs in the category to the number of units in all projects in the sampled LHAs in the category. The weights ranged from 2.5 to 293.7. Altogether the sample included 98,768 households for the year 1966 (at the end of the year, a total of 607,508 LHA units were occupied[7]).

The difference between the gap rent for an apartment of the same size the tenant occupies and the actual contract rent the tenant pays was multiplied by the appropriate W_i and tabulated. Gap rents were unavailable for some sizes of apartments in public housing; in that case, a gap rent was interpolated from available rent figures.

Estimating Costs of a Housing Assistance Plan

Estimates of the cost of the Housing Assistance Plan presented in Chapter 10 were computed for interview units reported in the 1967 Survey of Economic Opportunity.[8]

---

7. HUD, *Statistical Yearbook, 1966,* HAA Table 12, p. 264.
8. U.S. Bureau of the Census, Survey of Economic Opportunity, spring 1967, unpublished machine tabulations.

For each household, i, adjusted family income, AFI_i, was set equal to the sum of total family income from all sources, Y_i, and one-fifth of net worth NW_i:

(1) $$AFI_i = Y_i + 0.2\,NW_i.$$

Each family lived in one of sixteen places identified in the Survey of Economic Opportunity for which the Bureau of Labor Statistics (BLS) reported separate estimates of housing costs in 1967.[9] The estimate of annual housing costs for a family of four, C_j, in the BLS lower cost budget, in twelve metropolitan areas was: Baltimore \$1,361, Chicago \$1,449, Cleveland \$1,348, Detroit \$1,229, Houston \$1,167, Los Angeles \$1,427, New York \$1,238, Philadelphia \$1,188, Pittsburgh \$1,197, St. Louis \$1,323, San Francisco \$1,519, and Washington, D.C. \$1,479; the estimate for other metropolitan areas was: northeast census region \$1,120, north central census region \$1,362, south census region \$1,076, and west census region \$1,312.

The cost of housing in place j for a family with n members, C_{jn}, was set equal to the cost of housing for a four-member family, C_j, multiplied by a factor for families with n members, F_n,

(2) $$C_{jn} = C_j \cdot F_n.$$

The value of F_n for an unrelated individual is 0.48; for a two-person family 0.67; for a three-person family 0.86; for a four-person family 1.00; for a five-person family 1.14; for a six-person family 1.27; and for a seven-or-more-person family 1.38.[10] The subsidy for each household, S_i, was set equal to the difference between housing costs for a household of the appropriate size, C_{jn}, in that region and one-fourth of adjusted family income:

(3) $$S_i = C_{jn} - 0.25\,AFI_i.$$

The subsidy for any place was the sum of such individual subsidies. To allow for the possible impact of an increase in housing costs caused by the Housing Assistance Plan, equation (3) was modified by raising housing costs 10 percent,

(4) $$S_i = 1.1\,C_{jn} - 0.25\,AFI_i.$$

9. U.S. Bureau of Labor Statistics, *Three Standards of Living for an Urban Family of Four Persons, Spring 1967*, Bulletin 1570-5 (1969), pp. 16–25.

10. Derived from John D. Heinberg, "Income Assistance Programs in Housing: Conceptual Issues and Benefit Patterns," Working Paper 112-18 (Washington: Urban Institute, 1970; processed), p. 23.

appendix D **Analytical Data on Housing Programs**

Table D-1. Federal Individual Income Tax Collections as a Percent of Total Income of Homeowners and Nonhomeowners, by Income Bracket, Age, and Type of Deduction, 1966[a]

Taxpayer	Under 3,000	3,000– 5,000	5,000– 7,000	7,000– 10,000	10,000– 15,000	15,000– 25,000	25,000– 50,000	50,000– 100,000	Over 100,000	All brackets
					Income bracket (dollars)					
Homeowner	2.9	5.4	7.4	8.5	10.3	12.7	17.5	24.8	29.0	12.4
Under 65 years old	3.3	6.0	7.6	8.5	10.3	12.7	17.5	25.1	28.8	12.1
Itemized deductions	6.8	5.0	6.0	7.6	9.8	12.5	17.3	25.0	28.8	12.5
Standard deduction	3.0	6.7	8.9	10.2	12.1	14.8	20.6	28.0	27.6	11.0
65 and over	0.8	3.0	5.9	7.8	10.1	12.2	17.1	23.6	29.6	14.6
Itemized deductions	1.1	2.8	5.4	7.0	9.7	11.9	17.0	23.7	29.7	15.7
Standard deduction	0.7	3.7	8.0	10.5	11.7	13.1	17.6	20.5	23.8	9.4
Nonhomeowner	4.2	7.8	9.3	10.5	12.5	15.5	18.5	25.4	28.6	10.1
Under 65 years old	4.7	8.0	9.4	10.5	12.5	15.6	18.4	26.6	27.8	10.2
Itemized deductions	5.0	7.0	8.7	9.3	11.6	15.0	18.9	26.4	28.2	11.0
Standard deduction	4.7	8.2	9.9	11.1	13.1	16.1	16.3	30.8	16.3	9.8
65 and over	1.0	5.0	8.2	9.6	11.7	14.9	18.5	23.2	29.8	9.5
Itemized deductions	1.6	4.5	7.6	8.4	11.9	14.3	18.2	23.0	29.8	12.1
Standard deduction	0.9	5.3	9.0	10.5	11.3	16.0	21.2	30.2	27.4	6.8
All under 65 years old	4.3	7.3	8.3	9.1	10.7	13.1	17.6	25.2	28.7	11.6
All 65 and over	0.9	3.8	6.8	8.3	10.6	12.9	17.4	23.6	29.6	13.1
All returns	3.8	6.9	8.2	9.1	10.7	13.1	17.6	24.9	29.0	11.7

Source: Estimated from Brookings tax file, a sample of 90,000 federal individual income tax returns filed for the year 1966.
a. Total income equals adjusted gross income plus excluded dividends, excluded sick pay, and imputed rent. Capital gains and losses are included in income in full in the year realized, but no losses carried forward from previous years are deducted. Total income does not include unrealized capital gains, tax exempt interest, or the excess of percentage over cost depletion on income from natural resources.

Table D-2. Increase in 1966 Federal Individual Income Tax Collections If Mortgage Interest and Property Tax Deductions Were Disallowed, by Income Bracket and Age[a]

Item	Income bracket (dollars)									Total tax savings (millions of dollars)
	Under 3,000	3,000–5,000	5,000–7,000	7,000–10,000	10,000–15,000	15,000–25,000	25,000–50,000	50,000–100,000	Over 100,000	
All returns										
Increase in tax per family, in dollars	1	8	19	45	85	166	292	517	1,082	...
Increase in tax as percent of income	0.1	0.2	0.3	0.5	0.7	0.9	0.9	0.8	0.5	...
Increase in total tax, in millions of dollars	19	91	188	597	892	595	305	139	79	2,904
Homeowners										
Increase in tax per family, in dollars	3	21	32	64	106	196	329	562	1,144	...
Increase in tax as percent of income	0.2	0.5	0.5	0.8	0.9	1.1	1.0	0.9	0.5	...
Increase in total tax, in millions of dollars	19	91	188	597	892	595	305	139	79	2,904
Under 65 years old, with itemized deductions										
Increase in tax per family, in dollars	32	52	68	99	139	225	368	581	1,087	...
Increase in tax as percent of income	2.4	1.3	1.1	1.2	1.1	1.2	1.1	0.9	0.5	...
Increase in total tax, in millions of dollars	15	69	162	570	866	569	272	111	51	2,685
65 and older, with itemized deductions										
Increase in tax per family, in dollars	17	35	59	77	97	162	270	600	1,360	...
Increase in tax as percent of income	0.8	0.9	1.0	0.9	0.8	0.9	0.8	0.9	0.6	...
Increase in total tax, in millions of dollars	4	21	26	27	26	25	33	28	28	219

Source: Estimated from Brookings tax file. Figures are rounded and may not add to totals.

a. Total income equals adjusted gross income plus excluded dividends, excluded sick pay, and imputed rent. Capital gains and losses are included in income in full in the year realized, but no losses carried forward from previous years are deducted. Total income does not include unrealized capital gains, tax exempt interest, or the excess of percentage over cost depletion on income from natural resources.

Table D-3. Increase in 1966 Federal Individual Income Tax Collections If Imputed Net Rent on Owner Occupied Houses Were Taxed, by Income Bracket, Age, and Type of Deduction[a]

Item	Under 3,000	3,000–5,000	5,000–7,000	7,000–10,000	10,000–15,000	15,000–25,000	25,000–50,000	50,000–100,000	Over 100,000	Total tax savings (millions of dollars)
All returns										
Increase in tax per family, in dollars	11	20	36	58	103	180	433	654	1,217	...
Increase in tax as percent of income	0.8	0.5	0.6	0.7	0.9	1.0	1.3	1.0	0.5	...
Increase in total tax, in millions of dollars	228	228	352	769	1,079	643	453	176	89	4,017
Homeowners										
Increase in tax per family, in dollars	36	54	60	83	128	212	488	712	1,286	...
Increase in tax as percent of income	2.4	1.4	1.0	1.0	1.1	1.2	1.4	1.1	0.6	...
Increase in total tax, in millions of dollars	228	228	352	769	1,079	643	453	176	89	4,017
Under 65 years old										
Increase in tax per family, in dollars	38	56	61	82	128	213	481	678	1,211	...
Increase in tax as percent of income	2.6	1.4	1.0	1.0	1.1	1.2	1.4	1.0	0.6	...
Increase in total tax, in millions of dollars	208	189	321	728	1,032	604	384	135	58	3,659
Itemized deductions										
Increase in tax per family, in dollars	42	49	57	80	126	210	482	679	1,219	...
Increase in tax as percent of income	3.2	1.2	0.9	0.9	1.0	1.1	1.4	1.0	0.6	...
Increase in total tax, in millions of dollars	19	66	136	460	787	530	357	130	57	2,543
Standard deduction										
Increase in tax per family, in dollars	38	60	64	87	136	239	462	644	919	...
Increase in tax as percent of income	2.5	1.5	1.1	1.0	1.1	1.3	1.3	1.0	0.5	...

Increase in total tax, in millions of dollars	188	123	185	268	245	73	27	5	1	1,115
65 and older										
Increase in tax per family, in dollars	23	47	57	88	133	201	529	851	1,459	...
Increase in tax as percent of income	1.3	1.2	1.0	1.1	1.1	1.1	1.6	1.3	0.6	...
Increase in total tax, in millions of dollars	20	40	32	41	46	40	69	41	31	358
Itemized deductions										
Increase in tax per family, in dollars	26	40	57	88	132	195	525	856	1,466	...
Increase in tax as percent of income	1.2	1.0	1.0	1.1	1.1	1.0	1.5	1.3	0.6	...
Increase in total tax, in millions of dollars	6	25	25	31	35	30	64	40	30	287
Standard deduction										
Increase in tax per family, in dollars	22	62	57	87	136	223	589	697	1,055	...
Increase in tax as percent of income	1.3	1.6	0.9	1.0	1.1	1.2	1.8	1.0	0.6	...
Increase in total tax, in millions of dollars	14	15	6	9	11	9	5	1	b	71

Source: Estimated from Brookings tax file. Figures are rounded and may not add to totals.

a. Total income equals adjusted gross income plus excluded dividends, excluded sick pay, and imputed rent. Capital gains and losses are included in income in full in the year realized but no losses carried forward from previous years are deducted. Total income does not include unrealized capital gains, tax exempt interest, or the excess of percentage over cost depletion on income from natural resources.

b. Less than $500,000.

Table D-4. Difference in Federal Individual Income Tax Rates of Homeowners and Nonhomeowners under 1966 Law and If Imputed Net Rent on Owner Occupied Houses Were Taxed and Mortgage Interest and Property Tax Deductions Were Disallowed, by Age and Type of Deduction[a]

In percent[b]

Item	Income bracket (dollars)								
	Under 3,000	3,000–5,000	5,000–7,000	7,000–10,000	10,000–15,000	15,000–25,000	25,000–50,000	50,000–100,000	Over 100,000
All returns									
1966 law	1.4	2.4	1.9	2.0	2.2	2.8	1.0	0.6	-0.5
Assumed rules	-1.3	0.4	0.4	0.3	0.2	0.5	-1.5	-1.3	-1.6
All under 65 years old									
1966 law	1.5	2.0	1.9	2.0	2.2	2.9	0.9	1.4	-0.9
Assumed rules	-1.3	0.1	0.3	0.3	0.3	0.6	-1.6	-0.5	-2.0
Itemized deductions									
1966 law	-1.8	2.1	2.7	1.7	1.8	2.5	1.6	1.4	-0.6
Assumed rules	-8.0	-0.5	0.6	-0.4	-0.4	0.1	-0.9	-0.5	-1.7
Standard deduction									
1966 law	1.8	1.5	1.0	0.9	1.0	1.4	-4.3	2.8	-11.3
Assumed rules	-0.8	0.0	-0.1	-0.1	-0.1	0.0	-5.6	1.8	-11.8
All 65 and older									
1966 law	0.2	1.9	2.3	1.8	1.5	2.8	1.5	-0.4	0.1
Assumed rules	-1.5	0.0	0.5	0.0	-0.2	1.0	-0.8	-2.5	-1.0
Itemized deductions									
1966 law	0.5	1.8	2.2	1.4	2.2	2.4	1.2	-0.7	0.1
Assumed rules	-2.1	-0.3	0.2	-0.6	0.3	0.5	-1.1	-2.9	-1.1
Standard deduction									
1966 law	0.1	1.5	1.0	0.0	-0.4	2.9	3.6	9.7	3.7
Assumed rules	-1.1	-0.1	0.1	-1.0	-1.5	1.7	1.8	8.7	3.1

Source: Estimated from Brookings tax file.

a. Total income equals adjusted gross income plus excluded dividends, excluded sick pay, and imputed rent. Capital gains and losses are included in income in full in the year realized but no losses carried forward from previous years are deducted. Total income does not include unrealized capital gains, tax exempt interest, or the excess of percentage over cost depletion on income from natural resources.

b. Minus sign indicates that tax rate for homeowners is greater than that for nonhomeowners.

Table D-5. Loan-to-Value Ratios on Single-Family Homes Insured by FHA, 1969[a]

Value of house (dollars)[b]	Distribution of insured mortgages (percent)	Loan as percent of house value			
		Maximum allowable loan[c]		Actual loan	
		For non-veteran	For veteran	Mean value	Median value
Less than 10,000	5.4	97.0	100.0	94.7	96.3
10,000–11,999	7.6	97.0	100.0	95.4	96.4
12,000–13,999	11.7	97.0	100.0	95.5	96.4
14,000–15,999	14.7	97.0	100.0	95.4	96.4
16,000–17,999	15.1	96.2	98.8	94.3	95.4
18,000–19,999	14.1	95.5	97.9	93.4	94.9
20,000–21,999	10.0	95.0	97.1	92.1	93.5
22,000–24,999	10.9	94.5	96.4	90.6	91.5
25,000–29,999	7.6	92.9	94.8	88.9	90.4
30,000 and over	2.6	85.6	88.0	85.6	87.2

Sources: U.S. Department of Housing and Urban Development, *1969 HUD Statistical Yearbook* (1970), pp. 28, 67, 71, 72; "Digest of Insurable Loans and Summaries of Other Federal Housing Administration Programs," FHA G4700.1 (March 1970; processed).
a. Loans insured under sec. 203 of the National Housing Act.
b. FHA estimate.
c. Computed at midpoint of value range except in top bracket at $35,000 and in next highest at $28,000.

Table D-6. Distribution of Holders of FHA Insured Loans on Single-Family Homes, by Income Bracket, 1970[a]

In percent

Income bracket (dollars)	Holders of FHA insured loans			All U.S. families
	All	New homes	Existing homes	
0–5,999	2.0	0.4	2.4	25.1
6,000–6,999	3.7	1.6	4.2	6.0
7,000–7,999	6.5	3.8	7.1	6.3
8,000–8,999	8.0	6.2	8.4	6.9
9,000–9,999	9.9	8.8	10.2	6.7
10,000–11,999	19.3	19.0	19.4	12.7
12,000–14,999	26.0	28.3	25.5	14.1
15,000 and over	24.5	31.9	22.8	22.3
Median income (dollars)	...	12,912	11,815	9,867

Sources: *1970 HUD Statistical Yearbook*, pp. 149, 208, 209; U.S. Bureau of the Census, *Current Population Reports*, Series P-60, No. 80, "Income in 1970 of Families and Persons in the United States" (1971), p. 33.
a. Loans insured under sec. 203 of the National Housing Act.

Table D-7. Rent-to-Income Ratios of Low Rent Public Housing Tenants Reexamined for Continued Occupancy, 1961, 1966, and 1970

In percent

Rent as percent of income	Public housing tenants								
	1961			1966			1970[a]		
	All	Under 65 years old	65 and older	All	Under 65 years old	65 and older	All	Under 65 years old	65 and older
Less than 16	7.4	9.2	0.5	11.8	15.8	2.3	14.6	20.0	5.0
16–19.99	42.2	51.2	4.8	34.8	45.7	8.6	28.0	36.0	14.0
20–21.99	20.0	18.7	25.6	16.9	15.9	19.2	15.4	15.0	16.0
22–29.99	15.9	11.5	34.1	18.8	12.9	32.9	24.3	16.0	39.0
30 and over	14.4	9.5	35.0	17.8	9.7	37.0	17.7	13.0	26.0
Percent of all tenants[b]	100.0	80.6	19.4	100.0	70.5	29.5	100.0	63.7	36.3

Sources: HUD, Housing Assistance Administration, Statistics Branch, "Families in Low-Rent Projects: Families Reexamined During Calendar Year 1966 for Continued Occupancy," RHS-225.1 (April 1968), Tables I, L, pp. 19, 22, and "Families Reexamined for Continued Occupancy, Twelve Months Ending September 30, 1970" (September 1971; processed), p. 35. Percentages are rounded and may not add to totals.

a. For twelve months ending Sept. 30, 1970.

b. Figures underestimate elderly as a proportion of all public housing tenants because tenants under 65 must be reexamined every year, while the elderly may be reexamined once every two years at the discretion of the local housing authority. This practice was adopted in 1965.

Table D-8. Progress of Below-Market-Interest-Rate Program, Fiscal Years 1962–72[a]

Year	Loan authority (thousands of dollars)	Number of units Reserved	Started	Completed	Cumulative total completed
1962	130		656	176	176
1963	250	106,400[b]	4,581	925	1,101
1964	570		11,325	5,813	6,914
1965	462		14,414	8,361	15,275
1966	425	23,454	13,510	14,427	29,702
1967	325	19,300	13,216	12,324	42,026
1968	300	28,490	43,650	14,970	56,996
1969	350	30,877	44,668	34,018	91,014
1970	−30[c]	−4,222	28,337	43,672	134,686
1971[d]	—	...	17,400[c]	35,000[c]	169,686[c]
1972[d]	—	...	2,500[c]	24,000[c]	193,686[c]

Sources: HUD, machine tabulations (June 19, 1970); *HUD-Space-Science Appropriations for 1972*, Hearings before a Subcommittee of the House Committee on Appropriations, 92 Cong. 1 sess. (1971), Pt. 2, p. 171.
a. Loans insured under sec. 221(d)(3) of the National Housing Act.
b. Not separately available for 1962–65.
c. Official estimates.
d. Reduced to provide special assistance for homeownership mortgages (insured under sec. 235[j]) for lower income families.

Table D-9. Progress of Program Providing Rent Supplement Housing, Fiscal Years 1966–73

Year	Loan authority (millions of dollars) Requested	Appropriated	Number of units for rent supplement tenants Market rate housing program[a] Reserved	Started	Completed	All programs Reserved	Under payment[b]
1966	...	12	1,137	969	233	8,852	0
1967	35	20	1,696	613	385	24,848	930
1968	40	10	17,769	11,823	1,162	8,622	2,731
1969	65	30	17,529	16,632	11,239	18,905	12,299
1970	100	50	16,970	22,142	16,005	40,413	30,804
1971	75	...	11,103	16,444	20,141	30,408	57,786
1972	60	...	32,300[c]	20,400[c]	18,500[c]	60,200[c]	100,900[c]
1973	48	...	18,000[c]	32,100[c]	7,600[c]	38,000[c]	178,300[c]

Sources: Loan authority, 1966, *Basic Laws and Authorities on Housing and Urban Development, Revised Through January 31, 1970*, House Committee on Banking and Currency, 91 Cong. 2 sess. (1970), p. 266, n. 1; 1967–73, *Budget of the United States Government—Appendix*, issues for 1967–73, pp. 542, 547, 541, 520, 500, 495, 486, respectively. Other data, 1966–69, HUD, machine tabulations (Oct. 23, 1970); 1970–73, *Budget of the United States Government—Appendix*, issues for 1972 and 1973, pp. 496 and 486, respectively.
a. Loans insured under sec. 221 market rate of the National Housing Act.
b. End of year.
c. Official estimate.

Table D-10. Progress of Homeownership Assistance and Rental Assistance Programs, Fiscal Years 1969–73

| | Loan authority (millions of dollars) | | Number of units | | | |
Year	Requested	Appropriated	Reserved	Started	Completed	Under payment[a]
			Homeownership assistance[b]			
1969	...	25	27,698	2,715	1,933	5,454
1970	125	125	143,241	65,271	32,841	65,654
1971	130	130	142,154	137,575	119,251	204,832
1972	175	...	198,600[c]	183,400[c]	156,900[c]	379,300[c]
1973	170	...	198,600[c]	177,400[c]	187,700[c]	588,000[c]
			Rental assistance[d]			
1969	...	25	21,637	997	0	...
1970	120	120	131,744	51,392	8,212	5,437
1971	135	135	158,892	118,197	46,007	32,322
1972	175	...	239,200[c]	187,800[c]	123,100[c]	156,700[c]
1973	150	...	174,200[c]	249,000[c]	200,900[c]	331,200[c]

Sources: *Independent Offices and Department of Housing and Urban Development Appropriations for 1971*, Hearings before a Subcommittee of the House Committee on Appropriations, 91 Cong. 2 sess. (1970), pp. 697, 702; *Budget of the United States Government—Appendix*, 1972 and 1973, pp. 496–97 and 486–87, respectively; Federal Housing Administration, worksheets.

a. End of year.
b. Loans insured under sec. 235 of the National Housing Act.
c. Official estimate.
d. Loans insured under sec. 236 of the National Housing Act.

Table D-11. Appropriations for Farmers Home Administration Programs, Fiscal Years 1965–72

In millions of dollars

Type of program	1965	1966	1967	1968	1969	1970	1971[a]	1972[b]
Farming								
Loans								
Farm ownership	182.6	233.2	260.0	205.0	277.1	261.5	215.0	210.0
Farm operation	300.0	275.0	300.0	275.0	275.0	275.0	275.0	275.0
Emergency	78.4	100.5	94.6	108.2	114.7	89.4	67.0	67.0
Other	26.2	39.5	40.8	37.4	21.0	8.2	21.5	18.7
Total	587.2	648.2	695.4	625.6	687.8	634.1	578.5	570.7
Grants	0	20.0	26.0	31.4	29.1	46.0	44.0	42.0
Total farming loans and grants	587.2	668.2	721.4	657.0	716.9	680.1	622.5	612.7
Community services								
Water, sewer, irrigation, recreation, and miscellaneous other loans	77.4	151.8	226.6	208.0	203.0	164.1	183.7	201.0
Housing								
Rural housing construction loans	131.0	258.6	430.1	473.7	486.2	761.7[b]	1,436.2[b]	1,571.2[b]
Rural rental housing loans	2.0	4.3	5.5	13.2	17.3	28.4	37.0	35.0
Farm labor housing loans	...[c]	3.5	3.8	4.5	3.5	1.5	10.0	10.0
Farm labor housing grants	1.9[d]	2.2	2.7	2.7	5.0	2.1	3.7	3.8
Mutual self-help housing grants	...	...	...	...	...	...	2.4	2.4
Total housing loans and grants	134.9	268.6	442.1	494.1	512.0	793.7	1,489.3	1,622.4
All programs	799.5	1,088.6	1,390.1	1,359.1	1,431.9	1,637.9	2,295.5	2,436.1

Sources: *Agricultural Appropriations for Fiscal Year 1967*, Hearings before the Subcommittee of the Senate Committee on Appropriations, 89 Cong. 2 sess. (1966), Pt. 2, pp. 1113–27; *Department of Agriculture and Related Agencies Appropriations for Fiscal Year 1968*, Hearings before the Senate Subcommittee of the Committee on Appropriations, 90 Cong. 1 sess. (1967), Pt. 1, p. 883, and hearings with the same title for 1969, 1970, and 1971, Pt. 1, pp. 971–72, 350–51, and 1027–28, respectively; *Agriculture—Environmental and Consumer Protection Appropriations for 1972*, Hearings before a Subcommittee of the House Committee on Appropriations, 92 Cong. 1 sess. (1971), Pt. 1, pp. 295–96.

a. Official estimates.
b. Includes site loans.
c. Less than $50,000.
d. Rural housing grants; there were no labor housing grants in 1965.

231

Table D-12. Farm and Nonfarm Population and Median Family Income, Selected Years, 1940–70

| | Population | | | | | | |
| | Number (thousands) | | | Distribution (percent) | | Median family income (dollars) | |
Year	Total	Farm[a]	Nonfarm	Farm[a]	Nonfarm	Farm	Nonfarm
1940	132,165	30,547	101,618	23.1	76.9	n.a.	n.a.
1950	151,326	23,048	128,278	15.2	84.8	1,970	3,514[b]
1960	179,323	15,635	163,688	8.7	91.3	3,337	6,832[b]
1967	196,894	10,875	186,019	5.5	94.5	5,805	9,500
1970	203,212	9,712	193,500	4.8	95.2	6,773	10,006

Sources: Bureau of the Census, *Statistical Abstract of the United States, 1971*, p. 572; *Census of Population: 1970, Number of Inhabitants*, Final Report PC(1)-A1, *United States Summary* (1971), p. 1-42; and *Current Population Reports:* P-27, No. 42, "Farm Population of the United States: 1970" (1971), p. 1; P-60, No. 9, "Income of Families and Persons in the United States: 1950" (1952), p. 23; P-60, No. 36, "Average Income of Families Up Slightly in 1960" (1961), p. 2; P-60, No. 64, "Supplementary Report on Income in 1967 of Families and Persons in the United States" (1969), p. 28; and P-60, No. 80, "Income in 1970 of Families and Persons in the United States" (1971), p. 30.

n.a. Not available.

a. Excludes Alaska in 1940 and 1950 and Hawaii in 1940, 1950, and 1960.

b. Weighted average of median income for urban and rural nonfarm families.

Index

233

Housing and Home Finance Agency, 134
Housing policy, U.S.: below-market-
interest-rate program, 128–34, 137, 141,
165; criticism, 137–40, 166; defined, 4;
filtering strategy, 160–63, 164–67; goal,
38–43; homeownership assistance program, 127–44, 153, 160–61, 165–66; and
household formation, 38–39; Housing
Assistance Plan, 167–69, 171–73; and income class, 163, 164–65; as income distribution, 8–9, 11, 20–21, 44, 52, 61; institutional change, 51–52; justification
for, 3, 11–12, 38; "minimal standards"
position, 160–61; and private industry,
140–42; rent supplements, 133–36, 141,
143; rental assistance program, 137, 143,
153–54, 166; strategy choices, 159–62;
and vacancy rate, 20, 40–41. *See also*
Federal Home Loan Banks; Federal
Home Loan Mortgage Corporation;
Federal National Mortgage Association; Government National Mortgage
Association; Loan guarantees (VA);
Mortgage insurance (FHA)
Housing and Urban Development Act of
1968: and demographic trends, 39–40;
and FNMA, 94, 106; and GNMA, 94;
goal, 1–2, 20; and private industry, 2,
38–39. *See also* Housing policy, U.S.
Housing and Urban Development Act of
1969: 116*n*; and public housing, 111
Housing projections, 19–20, 38–42
Houthakker, H. S., 62*n*
HUD. *See* U.S. Department of Housing
and Urban Development
Huxtable, Ada Louise, 42*n*

Income class: and below-market-interest-
rate program, 129, 131, 133; and default
rates, 86, 88; FHA mortgage insurance,
78, 85–86, 89, 140; FHLBB middle income assistance, 104; and filtering, 161–
63; FmHA loans, 149–51, 154–55, 157–
58, 165; GNMA special assistance program, 97; and homeowner tax benefits,
56–57, 60–61, 70–71, 163; and homeownership assistance program, 136–44;
and housing classifications, 23–24, 30–
32, 41; and housing expenditures, 35–38;
and HUD low-middle income subsidy,
104; interest rate charges, 75; and loan
guarantees, 88–89; National Housing
Act of *1934* for lower, 78; in public
housing, 114–18, 123, 124, 164; and rent
supplements, 2, 133–35, 141–43; and
rental assistance, 165; in rural areas,
150. *See also* Income distribution

Income distribution: arguments for, 8–9,
11; and housing costs, 20–21; housing
policy effect, 20–21, 44–52; loan guarantees effect, 81–85, 88–89; "minimal
standard" strategy, 161; mortgage insurance effect, 81–89; public housing,
121–23, 124–26; and rent control, 20–21;
tax subsidy effect, 70
Income maintenance programs, 3
Income tax, 8, 44; alternatives, 54, 70–
73; below-market-interest-rate program,
133; corporation, 68–69; depreciation,
163; federal credit institutions, 94; housing benefit, 53–59, 61–62, 65–66, 84–85,
140–41, 164–65; and income class, 56–
57; public housing exemption, 112;
rental property, 66, 68, 70, 140–41; and
renters, 53–54, 56–57, 72–73
Interest rate: below-market-interest-rate
program, 79, 128–29; and default probability, 15; and federal credit institutions
effect, 107; FHA mortgage insurance,
19, 79, 156–57; and FHLBB rate setting,
100–01; FmHA loans, 151–52, 155–57;
and income class, 75; reform proposals,
105
Internal Revenue Code, 52, 54, 70

Jaffe, Dwight M., 96*n*, 103*n*
Jarutis, Eleanor L., 112*n*
Johnson, Lyndon B., 1–2, 38, 133

Kain, John F., 5*n*, 6*n*, 34*n*, 35*n*
Kane, Edward J., 101*n*
King, Thomas, 34*n*
Korean war, 109
Kristof, Frank S., 41
Kuh, Edwin, 167*n*

Labor, 7, 47–49
Laidler, David, 61
Laurenti, Luigi, 35*n*
Leaman, Sam H., 167*n*, 171*n*
Leasing, 119
Lee, Tong Hun, 62*n*
Lending institutions, 76; discrimination, 8;
and federal credit institutions, 51–52,
164; and FHA effect, 78; and loss risk
factor, 15–16, 81–84; and mortgage in-
terest deduction, 72; regulation of, 8
Lewis, Wilfred, Jr., 152*n*
Licensing, 15, 18
Lilley, William III, 90*n*, 138*n*
Loan guarantees (VA), 51; criticism, 90;
vs. FHA mortgage insurance, 88–89;
and FNMA, 92; and income class, 88–
89; and income distribution effect, 81–
85, 88–89; investor risk, 106; loan-to-